The University of Georgia

FIRST-YEAR COMPOSITION GUIDE

2016 EDITION

FOUNTAINHEAD PRESS

Book design by Susan Moore
Cover Design by Carol Hill

Copyright © 2016 Department of English at the University of Georgia
Copyright © 2016 Fountainhead Press, Signs: A Grammar Handbook

Books may be purchased for educational purposes.

For information, please call or write:

1-800-586-0330
Fountainhead Press
Southlake, TX 76092

Web site: www.fountainheadpress.com
Email: customerservice@fountainheadpress.com
Ninth Edition
ISBN: 978-1-68036-228-2
Printed in the United States of America

Table of Contents
Part 1: First-year Composition Guide

1 **Introduction to First-year Composition   1**

    Administration   2

    Why Write? FYC and Academic Discourse   2

2 **Description of First-year Composition Courses   4**

    English 1101: First-year Composition I   5

    English 1102: First-year Composition II   6

    English 1103: Multicultural First-year Composition II   8

    Alternative Approaches to First-year Composition   10

3 **Policies and Procedures   12**

    Placement   13

    Absences   14

    Grade Appeals   14

    Incompletes   15

    General Grading Weights   15

    Plus/Minus Grading   16

4 **Using Emma in the First-year Composition Program   17**

    What is Emma?   18

    FYC Digital Learning Labs   27

5 **Evaluation of Essays in the First-year Composition Program   28**

    What Do Teachers Want?   29

    What Grades on Compositions Mean   31

    FYC Grading Rubric   32

    Using the First-year Composition Rubric's Vocabulary   33

6 **Electronic Portfolios in the First-year Composition Program   48**

    The First-year Composition Electronic Portfolio   49

    Elements of the Portfolio   49

    How Are FYC Portfolios Evaluated?   52

7 **Academic Honesty and Plagiarism   58**

    UGA Academic Honesty Policy   59

    Plagiarism   59

    Workshop: How Not to Plagiarize   60

8 **Resources   62**

    Tutoring and Help with Writing   63

    Counseling and Psychiatric Services (CAPS)   65

9 What Comes Next? 66

    Writing Certificate Program   67

    Writing Intensive Program (WIP)   67

    The Major and Minor in English   68

    Advanced Courses in Writing   68

10 Donald E. Barnett Awards 72

    English 1101: Sujith Vadlamudi, "Miss Anachronism "   73

    English 1102: Farrah Agha, "Sexism in 'The Free Radio'"   85

11 Michael G. Moran Electronic Portfolio Awards 90

    English 1101: John Henline   90

    English 1102: Akilah Alexander   130

    English 1102: Andrea Morrison   150

Part 2: Signs: A Grammar Handbook

SECTION I   WORD LEVEL: BASIC GRAMMAR

1 Articles • 3

    (1a) Indefinite articles ✦ 3

    (1b) Definite articles ✦ 4

    EXERCISE 1 ✦ 5

2 Nouns • 7

    (2a) Singular or plural nouns ✦ 7

    (2b) Common or proper nouns ✦ 8

    (2c) Count or non-count nouns ✦ 8

    (2d) Concrete or abstract nouns ✦ 9

    (2e) Possessive nouns ✦ 9

    EXERCISE 1 ✦ 10

    (2f) Collective nouns ✦ 11

    EXERCISE 2 ✦ 11

3 Pronouns • 13

    (3a) Personal pronouns ✦ 13

        Table: Personal pronouns ✦ 14

    (3b) Possessive pronouns ✦ 14

        Table: Possessive pronouns ✦ 15

    EXERCISE 1 ✦ 16

(3c) Reflexive and intensive pronouns ✦ 16

        Table: Reflexive and intensive pronouns ✦ 16

   EXERCISE 2 ✦ 17

(3d) Relative pronouns ✦ 18

        Table: Relative pronouns ✦ 18

   EXERCISE 3 ✦ 19

(3e) Interrogative pronouns ✦ 20

(3f) Demonstrative pronouns ✦ 20

(3g) Indefinite pronouns ✦ 21

        List: Indefinite pronouns ✦ 21

(3h) Reciprocal pronouns ✦ 21

4 Pronoun/Antecedent Agreement • 23

(4a) Check if a noun is singular or plural ✦ 23

(4b) Check if a noun is definite or indefinite ✦ 23

(4c) Check if a noun is generic ✦ 24

(4d) Check for compound antecedents ✦ 24

(4e) Check for pronouns with correlative conjunctions ✦ 24

   EXERCISE 1 ✦ 25

5 Subjects • 27

(5a) Pronouns and nouns as subjects ✦ 27

(5b) Noun phrases and noun clauses as subjects ✦ 27

(5c) Other parts of speech as subjects ✦ 28

(5d) Delayed subjects ✦ 28

   EXERCISE 1 ✦ 29

6 Verbs • 31

(6a) Main verbs ✦ 31

   1.   Linking verbs ✦ 31

        List: Common linking verbs ✦ 31

   EXERCISE 1 ✦ 32

   2.   Intransitive verbs ✦ 32

   3.   Transitive verbs ✦ 33

   EXERCISE 2 ✦ 33

(6b) Auxiliary verbs and modals ✦ 34

        List: Auxiliary verbs and modals ✦ 34

(6c) Verbals ◆ 34

   1.   Gerunds ◆ 35

   2.   Infinitives ◆ 35

   3.   Participles ◆ 35

   EXERCISE 3 ◆ 36

(6d) Regular and irregular verbs ◆ 36

       Table: Common irregular verbs ◆ 38

(6e) Number and person of a verb ◆ 41

       Table: Conjugation of the regular verb *to sign* and
           the irregular verb *to fly* ◆ 42

(6f) Tense of a verb ◆ 42

   EXERCISE 4 ◆ 43

(6g) Aspect of a verb ◆ 43

   1.   Progressive ◆ 43

   2.   Perfect ◆ 44

   EXERCISE 5 ◆ 45

(6h) Voice of a verb ◆ 46

   1.   Active voice ◆ 46

   2.   Passive voice ◆ 46

   EXERCISE 6 ◆ 48

7 Subject/Verb Agreement • 49

(7a) Check for simple subjects or head nouns ◆ 49

(7b) Check for prepositional phrases ◆ 49

(7c) Check for parenthetical statements or interjections ◆ 50

(7d) Check for indefinite pronouns as subjects ◆ 50

(7e) Check for compound subjects ◆ 51

   EXERCISE 1 ◆ 52

8 Modifiers: Adjectives • 53

(8a) Forms ◆ 53

       Table: Irregular adjectives ◆ 54

(8b) Types ◆ 54

   EXERCISE 1 ◆ 55

(8c) Functions ◆ 56

9 Modifiers: Adverbs • 57

(9a) Forms • 57

Table: Irregular adverbs • 58

(9b) Types • 58

EXERCISE 1 • 58

(9c) Functions • 59

List: Common adverbial conjunctions • 60

10 Modifiers: Prepositions • 61

(10a) Forms • 61

(10b) Types • 62

EXERCISE 1 • 62

(10c) Functions • 63

List: List of prepositions • 65

SECTION II   WORD LEVEL: BASIC USAGE AND STYLE

11 Appropriate Word Choice • 69

(11a) Check for exactness and clarity • 69

1. Be precise • 69

2. Use specific, concrete words • 69

   Table: Using specific, concrete words • 70

3. Delete empty words and phrases • 71

   List: Weasel words • 71

4. Replace wordy prepositional phrases with more concise adverbs • 72

   Table: Using adverbs for conciseness • 72

5. Describe exactly who, what, when, where, why, and how • 73

6. Use figurative language when appropriate • 73

EXERCISE 1 • 74

(11b) Check for completeness • 75

(11c) Check for tired, stale, or unnatural language • 76

List: Some clichés to avoid • 76

(11d) Check for appropriate levels of formality • 78

Table: Pretentious words • 80

(11e) Check for sexist and offensive language • 81

   1.   Use appropriate words for gender • 81

       Table: Recommended terms for job titles • 82

   2.   Use appropriate words for age • 82

       Table: Recommended terms for age • 82

   3.   Use appropriate words for ethnicity or race • 82

       Table: Acceptable terms for ethnicity or race • 83

   4.   Use appropriate words for disability or illness • 83

       Table: Recommended terms for disability or illness • 83

   5.   Use appropriate words for geographical areas • 84

       Table: Recommended terms for geographical areas • 84

      EXERCISE 2 • 84

12 Commonly Confused or Misspelled Words • 85

(12a) Check for words that are always separate • 86

(12b) Check for words that can be written together or apart • 86

       Table: Different spacing, different meaning • 87

(12c) Check for words that are pronounced the same or similarly • 87

       Table: Most commonly misspelled homophones • 88

       Table: Other commonly confused words • 88

      EXERCISE 1 • 98

13 Using the Dictionary • 99

      EXERCISE 1 • 102

14 Using and Overusing the Thesaurus • 103

      EXERCISE 1 • 105

SECTION III REVIEW OF BASIC PUNCTUATION AND MECHANICS: AN EDITING GUIDE

15 The Comma • 109

(15a) Set off introductory words, phrases, and clauses • 109

   1.   Set off introductory words and phrases • 109

   2.   Set off introductory clauses • 110

      EXERCISE 1 • 111

(15b) Combine independent clauses in compound
 sentences ◆ 111

   EXERCISE 2 ◆ 112

(15c) Separate items in a series ◆ 113

(15d) Set off non-essential elements ◆ 113

   1. Relative clauses ◆ 113

   2. Participial phrases ◆ 114

   3. Appositives ◆ 115

   EXERCISE 3 ◆ 115

(15e) Separate coordinate adjectives ◆ 116

(15f) Set off interrupters ◆ 117

   1. Transitions ◆ 117

       List: Adverbial conjunctions ◆ 117

   2. Interjections ◆ 118

   3. Direct address ◆ 118

   EXERCISE 4 ◆ 118

   4. Tag questions ◆ 119

(15g) Set off quotations or dialogue ◆ 119

(15h) Set off geographic locations ◆ 119

(15i) Set off dates ◆ 120

(15j) Set off titles ◆ 120

(15k) Set off numbers ◆ 121

(15l) Prevent confusion ◆ 121

16 The Semicolon • 123

(16a) Connect independent clauses ◆ 123

(16b) Use with adverbial conjunctions or transitional
 phrases to connect clauses ◆ 123

       List: Transitional phrases ◆ 124

(16c) Separate groups that contain commas ◆ 124

   EXERCISE 1 ◆ 125

17 The Colon • 127

(17a) Connect independent clauses ◆ 127

(17b) Add emphasis ◆ 128

(17c) Introduce a series or list ◆ 128

(17d) Introduce a quotation or saying ✦ 128

(17e) Use for salutations in formal letters ✦ 128

(17f) Connect numbers ✦ 129

    1.   Connect ratios ✦ 129

    2.   Connect chapters and verses of holy texts ✦ 129

    3.   Connect hours, minutes, and seconds ✦ 129

(17g) Connect titles and subtitles ✦ 129

(17h) Separate geographical location and publisher name in bibliographic entries ✦ 129

    EXERCISE 1 ✦ 130

18 The Period, Exclamation Point, and Question Mark • 131

(18a) Use a period to end a sentence or separate initials or abbreviations ✦ 131

    1.   End a sentence ✦ 132

    2.   Separate initials or abbreviations ✦ 132

(18b) Emphasize with an exclamation point ✦ 133

(18c) End a direct question, show uncertainty, or embed a short question with a question mark ✦ 133

    1.   End a direct question ✦ 133

    2.   Show uncertainty ✦ 133

    3.   Embed a short question within a sentence ✦ 134

    EXERCISE 1 ✦ 134

19 The Apostrophe • 135

(19a) Mark omissions when parts of words are removed ✦ 135

    1.   Mark contractions when parts of words are removed ✦ 135

    2.   Mark numbers when parts of numbers are removed ✦ 135

    3.   Mark words used to represent oral language ✦ 135

(19b) Form plurals ✦ 136

(19c) Form possessives ✦ 137

    1.   Form singular possessives ✦ 137

A. Singular nouns ◆ 137

B. Personal pronouns ◆ 138

C. Indefinite pronouns ◆ 138

2. Mark plural possessives ◆ 138

3. Form possessive compound nouns ◆ 138

(19d) Form compounds ◆ 139

EXERCISE 1 ◆ 140

20 Quotation Marks • 141

(20a) Signal titles of short works ◆ 141

(20b) Set off a direct quotation ◆ 142

(20c) Set off dialogue in prose ◆ 142

(20d) Share a few lines of poetry ◆ 143

(20e) Share personal thoughts ◆ 143

(20f) Signal something being discussed , defined, or used in an unusual or ironic manner ◆ 143

EXERCISE 1 ◆ 145

21 The Hyphen • 147

(21a) Join words to make compound adjectives ◆ 147

(21b) Connect prefixes and suffixes to root words ◆ 147

1. Join certain prefixes (all-, ex-, half-, and self-) to a root word ◆ 147

2. Link a single letter to a noun or participle ◆ 148

(21c) Join words to make compound numbers ◆ 148

(21d) Join numbers ◆ 149

(21e) Prevent confusion ◆ 149

EXERCISE 1 ◆ 149

22 The Dash • 151

(22a) Highlight introductory material ◆ 151

(22b) Set off parenthetical, explanatory, or contrasted material ◆ 151

(22c) Add emphasis ◆ 152

EXERCISE 1 ◆ 152

23 Parentheses • 153

(23a) Enclose explanatory, minor, or secondary information • 153

(23b) Enclose in-text citations • 153

(23c) Enclose numbers or letters in outlines • 154

24 Brackets • 155

(24a) Use square brackets to signal corrections or errors • 155

    1. Signal editorial correction • 155

    2. Signal editorial error • 155

(24b) Use angle brackets to signal Web addresses • 156

25 The Slash • 157

(25a) Quote lines of poetry • 157

(25b) Show a choice • 157

26 Ellipses • 159

(26a) Signal omissions • 159

(26b) Signal a pause or hesitation • 160

27 Capitalization • 161

(27a) Indicate the first word • 161

    1. Indicate the first word in a sentence • 161

    2. Indicate the first word in a quotation • 161

    3. Indicate the first word inside parentheses • 161

    4. Indicate the first word in a sentence following a colon • 162

(27b) Indicate proper nouns and proper adjectives • 162

    1. Indicate proper nouns • 162

    2. Indicate proper adjectives • 163

(27c) Indicate titles and subtitles • 163

(27d) Indicate acronyms • 164

    EXERCISE 1 • 165

28 Italics • 167

(28a) Highlight titles • 167

    1. Highlight titles of longer works • 167

    2. Highlight legal cases • 168

    3. Identify naval and air ships • 168

(28b) Highlight special letters, words, phrases, or clauses • 168

1. Highlight non-English words • 168
2. Highlight referenced or discussed letters, words, phrases, and clauses • 169
   EXERCISE 1 • 170

SECTION IV SENTENCE LEVEL: BASIC GRAMMAR

29 The Simple Sentence • 173

(29a) The simple sentence • 173

(29b) Check for common errors with the simple sentence • 175

1. Check for overuse of simple sentences • 175
2. Check for fragments • 175
3. Check for parallelism • 176
   EXERCISE 1 • 176

30 The Compound Sentence • 177

(30a) The compound sentence • 177

(30b) Use appropriate punctuation for the compound sentence • 178

1. Punctuating a compound sentence—Option 1: Using a comma + conjunction • 178
   List: F A N B O Y S • 178
2. Punctuating a compound sentence—Option 2: Using a semicolon • 179
3. Punctuating a compound sentence—Option 3: Using a semicolon + adverbial conjunction • 179
4. Punctuating a compound sentence—Option 4: Using a colon • 181

(30c) Common sentence errors with the compound sentence • 182

1. Use a variety of punctuation, conjunctions, and adverbial conjunctions • 182
2. Check for comma splices • 182
3. Check for run-on or fused sentences • 183
   EXERCISE 1 • 184
   EXERCISE 2 • 185

31 The Complex Sentence • 187

(31a) The complex sentence ✦ 187

       List: Common subordinators ✦ 188

       List: Relative pronouns ✦ 188

(31b) Dependent clauses ✦ 188

(31c) Noun (or nominal) clauses ✦ 188

   1. Nominal relative clauses ✦ 189

   2. Appositive noun clauses ✦ 189

   EXERCISE 1 ✦ 190

(31d) Adjective (or adjectival) clauses ✦ 190

   1. Comparative clauses ✦ 190

   2. Relative clauses ✦ 191

   EXERCISE 2 ✦ 192

(31e) Adverb (or adverbial) clauses ✦ 193

       List: Common subordinators ✦ 193

   EXERCISE 3 ✦ 194

(31f) Common sentence errors with the complex sentence ✦ 195

   1. Check for fragments ✦ 195

   EXERCISE 4 ✦ 196

   2. Check for unnecessary commas ✦ 196

   3. Check for restrictive or non-restrictive punctuation ✦ 197

   4. Check for adverbial clause punctuation ✦ 197

32 The Compound-Complex Sentence • 199

(32a) The compound-complex sentence ✦ 199

   EXERCISE 1 ✦ 200

(32b) Common sentence errors with the compound-complex sentence ✦ 201

   1. Check for run-on or fused sentences ✦ 201

   2. Check for comma splices ✦ 201

   3. Check for fragments ✦ 201

Section V Sentence Level: Basic Usage and Style

33 Sentence Focus • 205

(33a) Use transitions • 205

   List: Transitions • 206

(33b) Emphasize key ideas • 206

 1. Use sentence order for emphasis • 206

 2. Use end-focus for emphasis • 207

 3. Use front-focus for emphasis • 207

 4. Reorder negative adverbials for emphasis • 207

 5. Use parenthetic expressions • 207

  EXERCISE 1 • 208

(33c) Be clear • 208

 1. Avoid tangents • 208

 2. Rephrase ambiguous expressions • 209

 3. Make sentence elements parallel • 209

(33d) Show confidence • 210

  EXERCISE 2 • 210

34 Sentence Functions • 211

(34a) Use declarative sentences to give information • 211

(34b) Use imperative sentences to give commands • 211

(34c) Use interrogative sentences to ask questions • 212

(34d) Use exclamatory sentences to show surprise • 213

  EXERCISE 1 • 214

35 Sentence Order • 215

(35a) Vary basic sentence order • 215

 1. Subject + intransitive verb • 215

 2. Subject + transitive verb + direct object • 216

 3. Subject + transitive verb + indirect object + direct object • 216

 4. Subject + transitive verb + direct object + object complement • 217

 5. Subject + transitive verb + direct object + adverbial complement • 217

  EXERCISE 1 • 218

6. Subject + linking verb + subject complement ◆ 218

7. Subject + linking verb + adverbial complement ◆ 219

(35b) Vary sentence openings ◆ 219

1. Add introductory words, phrases, and clauses ◆ 219

EXERCISE 2 ◆ 220

2. Avoid *subject-itis* ◆ 221

(35c) Fix misplaced modifiers ◆ 222

1. Check for misleading or misplaced modifiers ◆ 222

2. Check for dangling modifiers ◆ 224

EXERCISE 3 ◆ 224

(35d) Check direct v. indirect speech ◆ 225

(35e) Check for empty phrases and clauses ◆ 225

1. Check for empty *it* ◆ 225

2. Check for empty *there* ◆ 225

36 Sentence Length • 227

(36a) Check for choppy sentences ◆ 227

(36b) Check for excessive coordination ◆ 228

(36c) Check for excessive subordination and modification ◆ 229

EXERCISE 1 ◆ 229

(36d) Add descriptive words and phrases ◆ 230

1. Add descriptive nouns and noun phrases ◆ 230

2. Add descriptive verbs ◆ 231

3. Add descriptive adjectives ◆ 231

A. Adjectives as pre-modifiers ◆ 231

B. Adjectives as post-modifiers ◆ 231

C. Adjectives as complements ◆ 232

4. Add descriptive adverbs ◆ 232

5. Add descriptive prepositional phrases ◆ 233

EXERCISE 2 ◆ 233

Section VI Documentation

37 MLA Documentation • 237

(37a) Using MLA in-text citations ◆ 238

(37b) Using long or block quotations ◆ 241

(37c) Adding or omitting words in a quotation ◆ 242

(37d) Citing online sources ◆ 243

(37e) General formatting guidelines for the MLA Works Cited ◆ 244

(37f) Formats for print sources ◆ 246

(37g) Formats for online sources ◆ 250

(37h) Formats for other commonly used sources ◆ 253

(37i) Sample Works Cited using MLA ◆ 257

    EXERCISE 1 ◆ 258

    EXERCISE 2 ◆ 259

(37j) Sample Annotated Essay - MLA ◆ 261

38 APA Documentation • 269

(38a) Using APA in-text citations ◆ 270

(38b) Using long or block quotations ◆ 273

(38c) Adding or omitting words in a quotation ◆ 274

(38d) Citing online sources ◆ 275

(38e) General formatting guidelines for the APA References list ◆ 276

(38f) Formats for print sources ◆ 277

(38g) Formats for online sources ◆ 283

(38h) Formats for other commonly used sources ◆ 285

(38i) Sample References list using APA ◆ 287

    EXERCISE 1 ◆ 288

    EXERCISE 2 ◆ 289

(38j) Sample Annotated Essay - MLA ◆ 291

INDEX • 299

Part 1

First-year Composition Guide

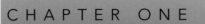

CHAPTER ONE

Introduction to First-year Composition

FIRST-YEAR COMPOSITION PROGRAM

Office: 128 Park Hall
Telephone: (706) 542-2128

Administration:

Dr. Christy Desmet, Director
Dr. Deborah Church Miller, Associate Director
Dr. Sara Steger, Assistant Director, Computer Support
Mr. Robby Nadler, Assistant Director, UGA Writing Center
Mrs. Kensie Poor, Administrative Associate II

Why Write? FYC and Academic Discourse

Writing is more than simply recording our thoughts, observations, and conclusions. Often it is a way of discovering what we think or feel. If it were merely the transcribing of what is in our minds, writing would never cause us any problems. Yet how many times have you sat down to write, thinking you knew what you wanted to express, only to find that your thoughts were jumbled or half-formed? Or you may have begun a writing assignment with nothing to say, but found, as you wrote, that you had a range of opinions and information about your subject. In both cases, you discovered what you actually knew or thought only in the act of writing.

Scholars and researchers have long known that writing is itself "a way of knowing." The act of writing improves comprehension of academic material and fixes that material in our memories. Even more important, writing can play a crucial role in the process of learning itself. Writing helps us to make connections among different pieces of information and between information and ideas; it also provides us with a visible record of those connections and (for instance, in the case of multiple drafts) shows us how our ideas change over time. In other words, writing allows us to produce not just information, but knowledge.

The kind of writing focused on in First-year Composition (FYC) is called academic discourse. At the University of Georgia, you will be asked to do many different kinds of writing for your classes. As you move into your academic major toward graduation, you will become increasingly involved in writing tasks that draw on specific genres and conventions for your academic

2

field. Psychologists, for instance, engage in different kinds of research and writing than do literary critics. First-year Composition cannot prepare you directly for all these advanced experiences in writing; what we do instead is to give you a grounding in academic discourse, which lays a foundation for later thinking and writing experiences by practicing kinds of writing that seek to inform and persuade a range of audiences. In FYC courses, you will do research on various topics and, together with your teacher and fellow students, work through writing and discussion to use that information to produce knowledge. You will also test the persuasiveness of your knowledge for a variety of audiences, including your teacher, peers, and others.

Two other important goals of FYC are the arts of revision and collaborative critique. For each writing assignment, FYC classes engage in drafting and revision, and for each they engage as well in peer review. You get the opportunity to demonstrate your proficiency in these two crucial areas in the Composing/Revision and Peer Review exhibits in the Electronic Portfolio that you submit as your final requirement in the course. (The Electronic Portfolio is discussed in detail later in this book.) Your skill in these areas will stand you in good stead as you leave your current teacher and classmates, moving through the core curriculum and your chosen major at the University of Georgia. Finally, our program emphasizes writing in the new electronic environments that are important not only to academics and the world of business, but also to individuals in their private lives. You will experience a variety of technologies in FYC, including the program's own electronic writing environment, Emma, which we use both for work during the semester and for constructing final FYC Electronic Portfolios.

The Instructors and Administration of UGA's First-year Composition Program sincerely hope that you enjoy your experiences with writing this year and that you leave our program with the skills and work habits necessary to succeed in writing tasks throughout the curriculum and in the world of work. More broadly, we hope that you leave us feeling confident of your critical thinking, your composing and revision skills, and your ability to comment intelligently on your own and others' writing. Finally, we hope that you will continue to enjoy and practice writing during your years at the University of Georgia. For that reason, we will give you information later about further opportunities for reading and writing at UGA.

CHAPTER TWO

Description of First-year Composition Courses

All FYC courses share core goals, or learning outcomes, which are detailed below and are also reflected in the program Grading Rubric and capstone Electronic Portfolio assignment (both of which are discussed in greater detail later in this *Guide*).

English 1101: First-year Composition I

English 1101 focuses on informational, analytical, and argumentative writing (the principal genres of academic discourse that students will encounter in many courses across the curriculum) and on research skills and critical thinking. While there are different varieties of English 1101 classes and instructors design their own syllabi, you can get a general sense of what an English 1101 course looks like by consulting the ENGL 1101 Sample Syllabi posted on the First-year Composition Program's website, available online through the English Department Home Page at: http://www.english.uga.edu/.

Prerequisites

Students must either place into English 1101 or pass out of the Academic Enhancement Program.

Goals

In English 1101 students will learn to:
- compose papers in and out of class using processes that include discovering ideas and evidence, organizing that material, and revising, editing, and polishing the finished paper;
- think critically so that they can recognize the difference between opinion and evidence and so that they can support a complex, challenging thesis;
- address papers to a range of audiences;
- understand the collaborative and social aspects of the writing process and demonstrate an ability to critique the writing of themselves and others;
- develop a sense of voice appropriate to the subject, the writer's purpose, the context, and the reader's expectations;
- understand how genres shape reading and writing and produce writing in several genres;
- follow the conventions of standard edited English and MLA documentation;

- use electronic environments for drafting, reviewing, revising, editing, and sharing texts;
- understand and exploit the differences in the rhetorical strategies and in the affordances available for both print and electronic composing processes and texts.

Requirements

Students will compose a minimum of three written projects (1,000-1,500 words or longer) that count for at least 50% of students' final grades. In addition to writing papers and doing other work, all students will create a final electronic portfolio that counts as 30% of their final grade. The ePortfolio is discussed at greater length below.

Course Texts

Required: *First-year Composition Guide*, 2016 ed. (Fountainhead Press)
Primary Text(s) may be selected by Course Instructor
Or instructors may choose from one of the following standard selections:
Palmquist. *Joining the Conversation,* 2nd Ed.
Rosenwasser and Stephen. *Writing Analytically,* 7th Ed.
Braziller and Kleinfeld. *Bedford Book of Genres, a Guide.*
Any standard college dictionary, such as:
American Heritage Dictionary
Random House College Dictionary
Webster's New Collegiate Dictionary
Webster's New World Dictionary

English 1102: First-year Composition II
Prerequisites

To enroll in English 1102, students must have either exempted English 1101 or passed it with a "D" or better. To graduate, however, students must have earned a grade of "C" in English 1101 and have a combined average grade of "C" in English 1101 and 1102/1103. Students therefore are strongly advised not to enroll in English 1102/1103 until they have received a "C" in English 1101.

According to the University policy on plus-minus grading, a grade of "C-" will not satisfy the requirement for a "C" in ENGL 1101; a combined average of "C-" or 1.7 in English 1101 and 1102 will not satisfy the requirement for a combined average of "C" in the two courses. For more information on plus-

minus grading, see: http://www.bulletin.uga.edu/PlusMinusGradingFAQ.
html. FAQ #9 is particularly relevant to the requirements of First-year
Composition.

Goals

English 1102 shares the core goals, or learning outcomes, of English 1101
but includes as well other goals specific to the course. The content also
varies: while English 1101 focuses on different varieties of non-fiction writing,
English 1102 focuses on informational, analytical, and argumentative writing
through literary texts in various genres; as in English 1101 and English
1103, research and critical thinking skills are also emphasized. While there
are different varieties of English 1102 classes and instructors design their
own syllabi, you can get a general sense of what an English 1102 course
looks like by consulting the ENGL 1102 Sample Syllabi posted on the First-
year Composition Program's website, available online through the English
Department Home Page at: http://www.english.uga.edu/.

In English 1102 students will learn to:
- read fiction, drama, and poetry and write analytically about them;
- understand literary principles and use basic terms important to
  critical writing and reading;
- complete written projects in and out of class using processes that
  include discovering ideas and evidence, organizing that material, and
  revising, editing, and polishing the finished paper;
- think critically so that they can recognize the difference between
  opinion and evidence and so that they can support a complex,
  challenging thesis, and more specifically, document writing using
  textual evidence;
- address written work to a range of audiences;
- understand the collaborative and social aspects of the writing
  process and demonstrate an ability to critique the writing of
  themselves and others;
- develop a sense of voice appropriate to the subject, the writer's
  purpose, the context, and the reader's expectations;
- understand how genres shape reading and writing and produce
  writing in several genres;
- follow the conventions of standard edited English and MLA
  documentation;
- use electronic environments for drafting, reviewing, revising, editing,
  and sharing texts;

- understand and exploit the differences in the rhetorical strategies and in the affordances available for both print and electronic composing processes and texts.

Requirements

Students will compose a minimum of three written projects (1,000-1,500 words or longer) that count for at least 50% of the student's final grade. In addition to writing papers and doing other work, all students will create a final electronic portfolio that counts as 30% of their final grade. The ePortfolio is discussed at greater length below.

Course Texts

Required: *First-year Composition Guide*, 2016 ed. (Fountainhead Press)
Primary Text(s) may be chosen by Course Instructor
Or instructors may choose from one or more of the following standard selections:

Schilb and Clifford. *Making Literature Matter,* 6th Ed.
Rosenwasser and Stephen. *Writing Analytically,* 7th Ed.

Any standard college dictionary, such as:

American Heritage Dictionary
Random House College Dictionary
Webster's New Collegiate Dictionary
Webster's New World Dictionary

English 1103: Multicultural First-year Composition II

English 1103 focuses on developing effective critical writing, reading, and research skills using core texts that explore the multicultural dimensions of American literature and culture, with an emphasis on African American, Latino/a American, Asian-American, and/or Native American literary traditions. This course offers three hours of credit toward the First-year Composition requirement and satisfies the Franklin College Multicultural Literacy requirement. While English 1103 instructors design their own syllabi, you can get a general sense of what an English 1103 course looks like by consulting the ENGL 1103 Sample Syllabi posted on the First-year Composition Program's website, available online through the English Department Home Page at: http://www.english.uga.edu/.

Goals

In English 1103 students will learn to:

- read fiction, drama, and poetry—with an emphasis on African American, Latino/a American, Asian-American, and/or Native American literary traditions—and write analytically about them;
- situate literature in the historical and cultural context of production and reception;
- understand literary principles and use basic terms important to critical writing and reading;
- compose written work in and out of class using processes that include discovering ideas and evidence, organizing that material, and revising, editing, and polishing the finished project;
- think critically so that they can recognize the difference between opinion and evidence and so that they can support a complex, challenging thesis, and more specifically, document writing using textual evidence;
- address compositions to a range of audiences;
- understand the collaborative and social aspects of the writing process and demonstrate an ability to critique the writing of themselves and others;
- develop a sense of voice appropriate to the subject, the writer's purpose, the context, and the reader's expectations;
- understand how genres shape reading and writing and produce writing in several genres;
- follow the conventions of standard edited English and MLA documentation;
- use electronic environments for drafting, reviewing, revising, editing, and sharing texts;
- understand and exploit the differences in the rhetorical strategies and in the affordances available for both print and electronic composing processes and texts.

Requirements

Students will create a minimum of three written projects (1,000-1,500 words or longer) that count for at least 50% of their final grade. In addition to writing papers and doing other work, all students will create a final electronic portfolio that counts as 30% of their final grade. The ePortfolio is discussed at greater length below.

Course Texts

Required: *First-year Composition Guide*, 2016 ed. (Fountainhead Press) Primary Text(s) may be chosen by Course Instructor

Or instructors may choose from one or more of the following standard selections:

Schmidt and Crockett. *Portable Legacies,* 2nd Ed.
Schilb and Clifford. *Making Literature Matter,* 6th Ed.
Rosenwasser and Stephen. *Writing Analytically,* 7th Ed.

Any standard college dictionary, such as:

American Heritage Dictionary
Random House College Dictionary
Webster's New Collegiate Dictionary
Webster's New World Dictionary

Alternative Approaches to First-year Composition

The First-year Composition Program is involved in a number of innovative programs on campus and offers several alternative versions of its core courses. Each of these courses has the same prerequisites, goals, and requirements as the more traditional versions.

Honors Courses for First-year Composition II

Honors students have the option of substituting for English 1102 either English 1050H (Composition and Literature) or English 1060H (Composition and Multicultural Literature). These courses have the same general goals as other First-year Composition courses at the University of Georgia, but each class is designed individually by the instructor, often around a special topic.

English Composition for ESOL Students

Special sections of English 1101 and 1102/1103 are reserved for students who have a native language other than American English and who can benefit from an English for Speakers of Other Languages (ESOL) emphasis in these classes. Students enroll only with the permission of the department (POD), but the classes are not marked differently on their transcripts. The ESOL sections, like classes for native speakers, focus on writing academic argument in English 1101 and writing about literature in English 1102/1103. In addition to offering three hours of credit toward the First-year Composition requirement, English 1103 ESOL will also fulfill the Franklin College Multicultural Literacy requirement.

First-year Composition classes for ESOL offer non-native speakers opportunities for vocabulary development, for grammar practice, and for orientation to American styles of writing and organization. Residents of the United States whose first language is not American English, as well as international students, may qualify for these classes. To determine your eligibility and to obtain a POD to register for the ESOL classes, contact the First-year Composition Program Office (706-542-2128) or Kensie Poor, kpoor@uga.edu.

First-year Composition Online

In the regular, eight-week "Thru Term" of summer school, the First-year Composition Program offers English 1102E, a fully online, asynchronous course. Students in 1102E meet all the standard FYC ENGL1102 requirements while completing a series of units (or "modules"). Students work as a cohort between specified dates, but do not meet as a group during particular class times, either online or face-to-face. The course includes a remotely proctored final essay exam that requires a nominal additional charge (currently around $30). Assignments fall due on most weekdays throughout the summer session.

Special Topics

Experienced instructors may design a special topics version of FYC that is approved in advance by the First-year Composition Committee. These courses often focus on topics related to the instructor's research or scholarly interests, and the sections are marked by a special note in ATHENA.

UGA Learning Communities

The FYC Program has played a major role in the development of UGA's Learning Communities. As part of each Learning Community, students take a First-year Composition class that is linked to the theme of the Learning Community and sometimes to the content of their other courses in the Community. A description of the UGA Learning Communities and a current list of Learning Communities being offered may be found online at: http://learningcommunities.uga.edu/.

Reacting to the Past

The FYC Program frequently offers sections of composition that incorporate the innovative pedagogy of UGA's Reacting to the Past curriculum. You can find out more about Reacting to the Past at the University of Georgia at: http://www.reacting.uga.edu/.

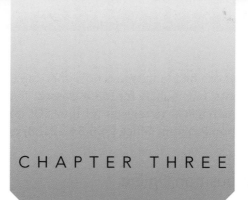

CHAPTER THREE

Policies and Procedures

Placement

Most university students will take six hours of FYC (English 1101 and 1102/1103) during their first year at UGA. However, some students will receive credit for these hours based on the following tests. Complete information about Placement is available on the Registrar's website, under the heading "Credit from Testing."

1. **The Advanced Placement Test:** Students who earn a score of 3 or 4 on the National Advanced Placement Test in Literature and Composition or Language and Composition receive three hours of credit for English 1101; those who earn a score of 5 receive six hours of credit for English 1101 and 1102. All AP equivalencies are available on the Registrar's website.

2. **The International Baccalaureate (IB) Test:** Students who earn a score of 4, 5, or 6 on the International Baccalaureate Test at the Higher Level (HL) in English receive three hours of credit for English 1101; those who earn a score of 7 on the International Baccalaureate Test at the Higher Level (HL) receive six hours of credit for English 1101 and 1102. Students who earn a score of 5, 6, or 7 on the Standard Level (SL) test receive three hours of credit for English 1101. All IB equivalencies are available on the Registrar's website: http://www.reg.uga.edu/creditFromTesting/internationalBaccalaureate/uga_ib_credit_equivalencies.

3. **Cambridge International A Level and Cambridge AICE Diploma:** "Admitted students are encouraged to contact UGA departments for placement and credit until credits are published. The University of Georgia is currently reviewing credit equivalencies for Cambridge International A Level and Cambridge AICE examinations." Please check the Registrar's website for updates as more information becomes available. http://www.reg.uga.edu/creditFromTesting/CambridgeInternationalALevelandCambridgeAICEDiploma.

4. **The English Departmental Placement Test**: Students not placed by a national placement test such as AP will fall into two groups. Students with an SATV score of 590 and above or an ACT score of 26 or above place automatically in ENGL 1101 and may register for that class without any further testing; if these students choose to do so, they may take the English Departmental Placement Test voluntarily with an eye to earning three credit hours for English 1101.

    Students with an SATV score of 580 or below who have not been placed by a national placement test are **required** to take the English Departmental Placement Test before registering for any First-year

Composition class. Specific information about the Departmental English Placement Test can be found at the Testing Services Website: http://testing.uga.edu/english.php/.

The Departmental English Placement Test consists of two parts, mechanics and rhetoric. A score of 22 (part 1) and 20 (part 2) will place students in English 1102 and gives them three hours of credit for English 1101. Students whose test scores indicate that they might have trouble in English 1101 will write an essay to determine whether they will be advised to take English 1101 or an Academic Enhancement class, such as UNIV1115.

Students should take the test at a First-year Orientation Session. Those who miss the test at Orientation may take it later at University Testing Services in Clark Howell Hall. However, the test is not open to students who have taken or are currently enrolled in First-year Composition here or elsewhere. For more information, please call (706) 542-3183 or visit the website: http://testing.uga.edu.

Absences

Because writing skills develop slowly over time and because in-class activities are crucial to the final Portfolio, students' regular attendance is essential in First-year Composition.

Consequently during fall and spring semesters, on the fifth absence (MWF classes) or the fourth absence (TTh classes), no matter what the reason, students can expect to be administratively withdrawn with a W before the withdrawal deadline and administratively withdrawn with an F after the withdrawal deadline.

For the Summer Thru Term, on the fourth absence, no matter what the reason, students can expect to be administratively withdrawn with a W before the withdrawal deadline and with an F after the withdrawal deadline.

Grade Appeals

It is the instructor's responsibility to judge work and assign grades. Consequently, students with questions about final grades should first discuss those questions with their instructors. If the problem cannot be resolved in discussion, students may prepare a grade appeal in writing according to the guidelines established by the Franklin College Faculty Senate Bylaws, Article V. The bylaws are available at: https://www.franklin.uga.edu/content/faculty-senate-laws. Search for "Grade Appeals."

In First-year Composition appeals, the Director of First-year Composition replaces the Department Head of English in the appeals procedure, in accordance with the English Department bylaws. See Section II, "Appeals at the Department Level." Once a ruling on the grade appeal has been made, if either the student or instructor wants to take the appeal further, the appeal will be conducted according to the guidelines set out in Section III, "Appeals at the College Level."

Before appealing a grade, students should be aware of the following conditions established by the Franklin College Bylaws:

1. A student may appeal a grade if, and only if, he or she is able to demonstrate that the grade was based on factors other than a fair assessment of the student's academic performance in the course.
2. The standards by which grades are assigned, the number and relative weight of assignments on which grades are based, and decisions to allow students to make up or retake missed examinations or assignments, are *not* grounds for appeal.

Incompletes

The University assigns certain grades that are not computed in the grade point average. The Incomplete ("I") is one of these. It indicates that students have completed almost all of the course work satisfactorily but are unable to meet the full requirements of the course for reasons beyond their control.

When assigning Incompletes, instructors will explain in writing what students must do to finish the course and to calculate a grade, providing a copy of these instructions to both the student and to the FYC office. Students who receive Incompletes may have no longer than three semesters to complete all of their remaining work satisfactorily. Instructors can require that students complete work in a shorter period of time. If an "I" is not removed after three terms (including Summer Thru Term), it changes to an "F." Incompletes are assigned sparingly and at the discretion of the instructor when a small amount of essential work remains. FYC Instructors must first obtain permission from the Director of the First-year Composition Program to assign a grade of "I." An "I" is never assigned prior to mid-semester or for the purpose of allowing students to repeat courses.

General Grading Weights

The meaning of grades is defined generally in the undergraduate version of the *University of Georgia Bulletin:* http://www.bulletin.uga.edu/.

The meaning of grades according to the First-year Composition Program and the Program Grading Rubric is defined as follows:

C	Competent / Credible / Complete	(70-79)
B	Skillful / Persuasive	(80-89)
A	Distinctive	(90-100)
D	Ineffective	(60-69)
F	Extremely Ineffective	(<60)
W	Withdrew	

See the discussion of the FYC Grading Rubric below for more information about grading procedures.

Plus/Minus Grading

Plus and minus grades are assigned only to a student's final average for the course. For the final course grade in First-year Composition, the numerical range for each plus/minus grade is as follows:

A	4.0	(92–100)
A–	3.7	(90–91)
B+	3.3	(88–89)
B	3.0	(82–87)
B–	2.7	(80–81)
C+	2.3	(78–79)
C	2.0	(70–77)
C–	1.7	(68–69)
D	1.0	(60–67)
F	0.0	(<60)

CHAPTER FOUR

Using Emma in the
First-year Composition Program

What is Emma?

Emma is a web application designed specifically for writing and revising in academic communities. Students and instructors use Emma throughout the composing process, from brainstorming and drafting through peer review, revision, grading, and commenting. Emma organizes tools useful for multi-modal composition within a digital environment. The Emma environment, by providing both public and private spaces where students can collect their work and receive feedback from their peers and instructor, fosters an academic learning community.

Creating an account

Emma uses UGA's MyID. To create an account, open a web browser to the Emma homepage (http://www.emma.uga.edu) and click the "Sign in" button. Enter your MyID and password. Once you have logged in, please fill out the profile page. Enter your name carefully, as you will not be able to edit it later. You may update your photo and biography at any time.

Please update your Profile

Photo URL

http://www.english.uga.edu/~rbalthai/balthazor_ron_hdt.jpg

Tell us a little about youself.

Ron Balthazor, Ph.D. is an academic professional at the University of Georgia. He teaches composition and Environmental Literature and is the lead developer of the project, a web application for writing.

His scholarship has appeared in Portal, The Journal of General Education, Readerly/Writerly Texts, Literary and Linguistic Computing, and ATQ. His continuing interests include Environmental Literature and Eco-criticism, Thoreau, E.O. Wilson, PHP, Symfony, and gardening. He writes a blog that offers his reflections on life in the garden: gardenhouseporch.blogspot.com

Words: 78

Your Institution

University of Georgia

Update

4

Enrolling in a course

Once you have completed your profile, please enroll in a course. Click the Enroll button and carefully enter your instructor's last name. A list of courses will come up; select your section by clicking the Enroll button (Tip: Note carefully the time of your section—many instructors teach several FYC sections). Until your instructor approves your request, your course will be listed as Pending.

Courses Pending	
Demo	Remove
Ron Balthazor , 10:00 am	
Please check back soon.	Check now

Once approved, the course will display under Courses Enrolled: click the name of the course to enter it.

Courses Enrolled
Demo
Ron Balthazor , 10:00 am
Click course name to enter.

The Class Workspace in Emma

Most pages in Emma will have a navigation bar across the top for the major tools in the application and a side navigation bar on the left for working within the selected tool. The first page is the Course Home Page, which includes information about the course: the upcoming events in the calendar, an announcement space, and access to the roll and your classmates' profiles.

On the top navigation bar, you will see the major tools in Emma. Each will be described below.

Resources

Your instructor will post your syllabus, assignments, readings and other resources here. Note the menu on the left: you will be able to select various categories of files.

Emma	ENGL 1102 ▾ Resources Projects Calendar ▾ Journal ▾ Notes ▾

Resources	**ENGL 1102: Essay Assignments** Search in list

Help: Emma
Help: WH

Title	‖ Folder
ENGL 1102: Syllabus and Course Information	html Drama Essay Assignment	Shared ENGL 1102: Essay Assignments
ENGL 1102: Essay Assignments	html Poetry Project Assignment	Shared ENGL 1102: Essay Assignments
ENGL 1102: Resources for Readings	html Short Story Essay Assignment	Shared ENGL 1102: Essay Assignments
ENGL 1102: Writing Workshop Materials
ENGL 1102: Portfolio Resources
ENGL 1102: Peer Reviews and Postwrites

Projects

The Projects space, which is the document-collection space, is where you will do much of your work in Emma. Every document in Emma belongs to a project, and within that project, students add labels to organize their files and drafts. For example, for a Poetry Project, you might have files labeled as Draft 1, Draft 2, Peer Review, and Final. You can find your files and the files of your classmates using the various menus on the left as well as the toolbar just above the file list.

Emma	Current Dev ▾ Resources Projects Calendar ▾ Journal ▾ Forum Notes ▾ Portfolio	Ron Balthazor ▾

Projects	My Files Shared Files Search in list	4 files found Files open in a new tab.

Create ✏

	Title	‖ Author	‖ Folder	‖ Labels	‖ Modified	‖
Files	pdf Review	Portfolio me	Paper 1		02/06/15, 3:32 pm	
Reviews	html Example 2	Feedback Portfolio me	Paper 1	Draft2	02/06/15, 3:32 pm	
Paper 1	html Example 3	Feedback me	Paper 1		02/04/15, 1:44 pm	
Paper 2	html New Document	Feedback me	Paper 1	Draft1	08/26/14, 3:47 pm	
Paper 3	Settings Create Review Upload Review Files that have feedback can not be deleted.					

Portfolio Prep
All Projects

▪ Draft1
▪ Draft2
▪ Final

The First-year Composition Program encourages Process Writing, a practice that emphasizes the stages of composition as much as the final documents. Emma allows you to store and label each stage easily. If you mis-label a document, you can change the label by clicking on the Settings below each file listing.

On the left navigation, you will find the Create button (as you will in many of the tools in Emma). Clicking Create gives you a drop-down menu for choosing whether you want to create an Emma document, upload a document or other file, or create a link to other websites or documents.

Similarly, Emma makes it easy to offer Peer Review. Find the document of the peer you would like to review (by selecting Shared Files and then the name of the author on the tool-bar), open the document, and then click Create Review.

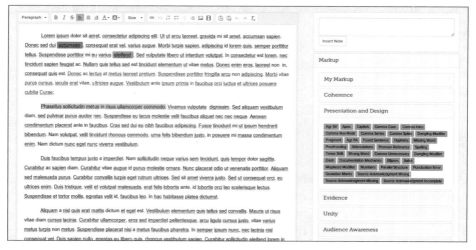

The Peer Review will be connected to the original file and labeled as a Peer Review Document.

To find Reviews by you or for you, click Reviews on the left menu and then select the options you need on the toolbar.

Documents created in Emma can take advantage of the application's built-in tools, which include an array of editing and formatting tools, note insertion, and built-in markup highlighting.

When your instructors read and evaluate your documents, they can include markup links to information and exercises to help you resolve grammatical, mechanical, or rhetorical issues.

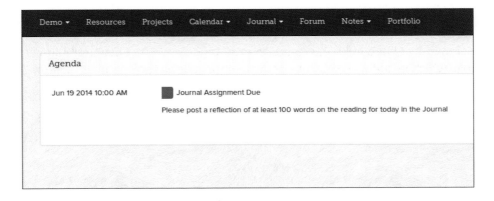

Calendar

Your instructor may post assignments and deadlines in the class Calendar. There are several views, including a month display and an agenda listing that shows events for the whole term. Upcoming events are also displayed on the Course Homepage.

Journal

Emma includes several tools for low-stakes writing. The Journal, as the name suggests, is a simple place for informal writing that is seen only by you and your instructor. Click the Create button to get started. Your instructor may offer feedback on your journals; these comments will display beneath your posting.

Forum

The Forum offers a shared writing space for conversations. Students can post comments and replies to each other within a discussion topic.

Tell me what you think

by Ron Balthazor, Jun 18 2014

Comment   Edit

about this reading.

Ron Balthazor says: Jun 18 2014   Reply   Edit

Very interesting.

Ron Balthazor says: Jun 18 2014   Edit

I agree.

Notes

In the Notes space, you can collect ideas for essays, save research, or take notes in class.

Another Note

Very interesting.

New Note

Lorem ipsum dolor sit amet, consectetur adipiscing elit. Ut ut arcu laoreet, gravida mi sit amet, accumsan sapien. Donec sed dui accumsan, consequat erat vel, varius augue. Morbi turpis sapien, adipiscing id lorem quis, semper porttitor tellus. Suspendisse porttitor mi eu varius eleifend. Sed vulputate libero ut interdum volutpat. In consectetur est lorem, nec tincidunt sapien feugiat ac. Nullam quis tellus sed est tincidunt elementum ut vitae metus. Donec enim eros, laoreet non vulputate in, consequat quis est. Donec ac lectus at metus laoreet pretium. Suspendisse porttitor fringilla arcu non adipiscing. Morbi vitae purus cursus, iaculis erat vitae, ultricies augue. Vestibulum ante ipsum primis in faucibus orci luctus et ultrices posuere cubilia Curae;

Portfolio

For your final Electronic Portfolio, you will collect and construct exhibits of your work and reflect upon the composition process and other activities in your classroom learning community. To add any previously created and shared Emma file to your portfolio, just click the Add button. (Tip: Emma files **must** be Shared before they can be added to your portfolio).

FYC Standard
The standard portfolio for UGA FYC

Intro to you: the author's "Homepage"   Add +
Post here a short introduction to yourself

[txt] Portfolio doc   Change Remove

Cover letter and Introduction to the Portfolio   Add +
Post here an introduction and reflection on your portfolio and its contents.

Original Paper or Project 1   Add +
Post one graded paper or project from this class here for later revision

First Revised Paper or Project   Add +
Post a revised version of "Original Paper or Project 1" here

Original Paper or Project 2   Add +
Post one graded paper or project from this class here for later revision

Revised Paper or Project 2   Add +
Post a revised version of "Original Paper or Project 2" here

Exhibit of Revision Process   Add +
Post a document here that traces your revision process for a section of an essay

[html] Review me too   Change Remove

Exhibit of Peer Review Process   Add +
Post a document here that demonstrates the way you review a classmate's work in this class

Wild Card   Add +
Post something here that develops your "ethos"! Any format is fine as long as you include some of your own text.

[jpg] AugPick.jpg   Change Remove

Technical Information

Because Emma has been designed as a multi-modal composition platform, it accepts many types of files, including those containing multimedia elements, such as images, videos, and hyperlinks. There is a 10MB size limit for files uploaded to Emma. Depending upon the file format and the browser you are using, these files may be accessed within the browser in Emma, or you may need to download them.

Files in proprietary formats—such as .doc, .wpd, or .docx—can only be downloaded and accessed using the proprietary software with which they were created; therefore, your instructor may or may not accept assignments in these formats during the course of the semester. **For the final ePortfolio, all final drafts should be created using Emma documents (eDocs) or should**

be converted to PDF. Microsoft Word documents (.doc or .docx format) will not be accepted in the ePortfolio. (n.b., Firefox, Chrome, and Safari are "Emma-friendly"; Internet Explorer is incompatible with Emma.)

Students should *always* back up their Emma documents with files saved elsewhere in their preferred document format (OpenOffice, Word, etc). Students and Instructors also should remain aware that the file conversion of documents to Emma document HTML files may result in formatting changes, so check final submissions carefully. Students can get help with personal word processing solutions in the main, trouble-shooting Emma Lab, Park 118.

FYC Digital Learning Labs

The First-year Composition Digital Learning Labs are located on the first floor of the new wing in Park Hall. We have two teaching labs:

- Park 117 has movable tables and mediascape screens, but no computers. A limited number of laptops will be available for checkout for use in the 117 during the class period. Students must bring their UGA id card to Park 118 to check out a laptop.

- Park 119 has 24 computers and a projector.

Your instructor will let you know if you are scheduled to meet in the teaching labs.

Park 118 of the FYC Digital Learning Labs is open to First-Year Composition students and instructors every weekday 8:00-5:00. This lab has computers and a scanner that students can use to work on assignments related to their FYC classes. Students can visit Park 118 on a walk-in basis to meet with a member of our support team for technical assistance with Emma or other FYC technologies. Students can also make an appointment to meet with a Writing Center Consultant in Park 118 for assistance with their compositions. All members of our support team are experienced teachers who use Emma and other relevant FYC technologies in their own classrooms, so they are a tremendous resource for students taking FYC courses.

CHAPTER FIVE

Evaluation of Essays in the First-year Composition Program

What Do Teachers Want?

Because all writing, no matter how personal, attempts to communicate with some audience, writing is a social art. And all writers—whether students writing to develop their skills, amateurs writing to satisfy personal ambition, or professionals writing to support themselves—need to get some reaction to their writing. One form of reaction students get is from **peer review**. By critiquing one another's papers constructively in workshops, student writers gain immediate insight into the effectiveness of their argumentation and prose. Peer review is an important part of the assessment of students' work, for it allows students to get feedback from a range of real readers; the process of responding to other students' essays helps students to become good critics of their own and of others' writing. This skill is important to much college work and is often cited by employers as being crucially important to the world of work. Because peer review is an important skill cultivated in First-year Composition, the capstone Electronic Portfolio includes a demonstration/discussion of the writer's Peer Review process. Students also receive comments and other feedback on some drafts and on graded essays from their First-year Composition teachers; this feedback, along with peer review commentary, is important to the job of revising graded essays for inclusion in the ePortfolio.

Another form of reaction students get to their writing is from their teachers. How teachers grade a written project should interest all students. First, they should understand that no exact correlation exists between the number of marks, or even comments, on a paper and the grade that paper receives. A composition does not begin as a "100" and then lose points as the teacher finds mistakes. Although errors can seriously damage the overall effectiveness of a piece of writing, to write well students must do more than merely rid their work of grammatical and mechanical errors. Effective communication depends primarily on rhetorical concerns; in other words, how effectively does the writing assignment being evaluated meet the needs of a particular audience and accomplish a particular purpose?

To ensure consistency and good communication across the Program, all FYC classes use a common FYC Grading Rubric, designed by a volunteer committee of teacher here in our English Department, which explains in detail our criteria for different grades. There are four basic categories:

- **Competent/Credible/Complete,** which describes compositions that are satisfactory and passing and therefore fall into the "C" range

- **Skillful/Persuasive,** which describes compositions that are well above average—clearly superior to competent work—and fall into the "B" range

- **Distinctive,** which describes compositions that stand out from even very competent work in a singular or important way and therefore fall into the "A" range

- **Ineffective,** which describes work that, for different reasons, does not meet the basic criteria for competency.

Teachers and peers will offer comments and feedback to help you improve your work during successive stages of the drafting process. But when your instructor grades the final draft of your project, she or he will decide, first of all, which of the four categories the composition falls into, using the particular criteria listed under each category for guidance. If your project has Unity, Evidence and Development, and follows basic rules for Presentation and Design, it has earned a C. If in addition, your project also has Coherence and Audience Awareness, you have entered the "B" range, and so forth. Once the instructor has commented on your work and determined the general category into which your work falls, he or she will then decide holistically what place in the given point spectrum your grade falls. For instance, if the project has Unity, Evidence, Presentation/Design, and is beginning to develop good Coherence, the instructor may determine that it falls toward the lower end of the Skillful/Persuasive spectrum (80-89 points): in such a case, your composition might earn an 82 or 83. If your project has, in addition to the qualities detailed above, a strong personal voice that clearly demonstrates Audience Awareness through its ability to communicate with "real people," it might earn an 87 or 88.

Of course, there is no exact mathematical formula for determining grades. For instance, it is always possible that a project that contains a few grammatical errors (Presentation/Design) or changes or loses direction at one or more points (Unity) excels so clearly in more advanced criteria—say, a sense of voice showing a clear Audience Awareness or an especially complex and original or imaginative argument—that the instructor decides it really should earn a B. In general, though, students should expect to satisfy all of the criteria for the Competent/Credible/Complete category in order to receive a passing grade.

The FYC Grading Rubric gives both students and teachers a **common vocabulary** for talking about writing quality and a set of important criteria for evaluating projects and/or compositions that are submitted for a grade during the semester and also those revised works submitted in the capstone electronic portfolio. Some instructors use a special template in Emma that links comments to criteria of the FYC Grading Rubric (which helps students to understand their grades). Students can also use the Rubric to assess the progress of their own work as they move through the drafting process. Finally, as the Rubric indicates, teachers may include special requirements that affect students' final grades, adding or subtracting points based on those

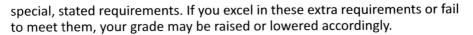
special, stated requirements. If you excel in these extra requirements or fail to meet them, your grade may be raised or lowered accordingly.

What Grades on Compositions Mean

In more specific numerical terms, the meaning of grades is defined by the undergraduate version of the University of Georgia Bulletin: http://www.bulletin.uga.edu. The meaning of grades according to the First-year Composition Program is defined as follows:

C	Competent / Credible / Complete	(70-79)
B	Skillful / Persuasive	(80-89)
A	Distinctive	(90-100)
D	Ineffective	(60-69)
F	Extremely Ineffective	(<60)
W	Withdrew	
I	Incomplete	

Plus / Minus Grading

Plus and minus grades are assigned only to a student's final average for the course. For the final course grade, the numerical range for each plus/minus grade is as follows:

A	4.0	(92-100)
A-	3.7	(90-91)
B+	3.3	(88-89)
B	3.0	(82-87)
B-	2.7	(80-81)
C+	2.3	(78-79)
C	2.0	(70-77)
C-	1.7	(68-69)
D	1.0	(60-67)
F	0.0	(<60)

FYC Grading Rubric

Here is the actual rubric that your teacher will use when evaluating your essays and often will encourage you to use when critiquing your peers' essays and making judgments about your own work.

Student's Name_____ Teacher _____

Project #____ Special Assignment Requirements: _____

"Enter a pertinent quote here." (Teachers can self-select)

Conference_____

Writing Center_____

_____ **Competent/Credible/Complete**

If you meet these first three standards, you are writing competently and you will earn a grade of "C." (70-79)

  1. **Unity**
     - Contains a center of gravity, a unifying and controlling purpose, a thesis or claim, which is maintained throughout the composition.
     - Organizes writing around a thesis or according to the organizational requirements of the particular assignment (e.g., summary, narrative, argument, analysis, description, etc.)
  2. **Evidence/Development**
     - Develops logical and relevant supporting detail and/or evidence.
     - Includes more specific, concrete evidence (or details) than opinion or abstract, general commentary.
  3. **Presentation and Design**
     - Follows guidelines for Standard English grammar, punctuation, usage, and documentation.
     - Meets your teacher's (or the MLA's) and the First-year Composition program's requirements for length and/or format.

_____ **Skillful/Persuasive**

If you meet all of the competency standards above and, in addition, achieve coherence and exhibit audience awareness, you are writing skillfully and you will earn a grade of "B." (80-89)

  4. **Coherence**
     - Uses words and sentences, rhythm and phrasing, variations and transitions, concreteness and specificity to *reveal and emphasize the relationship* between evidence and thesis.
     - Explains how, why, or in what way the evidence/detail provided supports the claim/ point /thesis/topic ideas.
     - Incorporates evidence from outside sources smoothly, appropriately, and responsibly.
  5. **Audience Awareness**
     - Demonstrates a sense that the writer knows what s/he's doing and is addressing real people.
     - Reflects a respect for values that influence ethos (e.g., common ground, trustworthiness, careful research).

_____ **Distinctive**

If you meet all of the competency standards, achieve coherence and exhibit audience awareness, and, in addition, demonstrate a mastery of one or more features of superior writing, you are writing distinctively and you will earn a grade of "A." (90-100)

  6. **Distinction**
     - Your writing stands out because of one or more of the following characteristics: complexity, originality, seamless coherence, extraordinary control, sophistication in thought, recognizable voice, compelling purpose, imagination, insight, thoroughness, and/or depth.

Essay Grade _____ +/- Points for special assignment requirements _____ =

Final Grade

_____ **Ineffective**

If your work does not meet competency standards, either because you have minor problems in all three competence areas (1-3 above) or major problems in one or two competence areas, you will earn a grade of "D" (60-69) or "F" (<60), and you should schedule a conference with your teacher.

University of Georgia First-year Composition Grading Rubric 2016-2017   update: June 27, 2016

Using the First-year Composition Grading Rubric's Vocabulary

We use the FYC Grading Rubric throughout our First-year Composition program because it helps teachers, tutors, students, and sometimes advisors, parents, and administrators to understand what our program values and looks for in student writing. Many teachers use an electronic version of this Rubric and mark compositions with coded electronic tags and inserted comments, while other teachers clip or staple a paper copy of the Rubric, along with their handwritten notes, directly to student work. Whether paper or electronic—whichever form of the Rubric they use—teachers depend on the standard Rubric's language to guide their evaluation of student compositions, while students must depend to some degree on the Rubric's language to understand their teachers' comments. Finally, the Rubric's common vocabulary helps students comment on one another's work and to make judgments about their own projects. The Rubric helps to keep all parties on the same page!

In order to help students (and teachers) use the Rubric most effectively, here we discuss some of the key terms:

Competent/Credible/Complete

In order to receive a passing and satisfactory grade of "C," students' work needs to meet the three principal criteria of Unity, Evidence/Development, and Presentation and Design.

1. Unity = Staying on topic and providing structure

> ✓ "Contains a center of gravity, a unifying and controlling purpose, a thesis or claim, which is maintained throughout the composition."

First-year compositions can be organized in many different ways. Compositions may have an implicit or explicit thesis, or they may simply have a unifying purpose or theme. In any unified composition, however, every sentence and every word will contribute in some way towards the exposition and development of the "main" idea.

Notice, too, that at the level of Competency "unity" does not require a particularly complex, clever, or imaginative thesis, nor does unity require strong coherence. Typically, a thesis can be described as having two parts: a topic plus a comment about that topic. For example, if my thesis were "cats are annoying," then the topic would be "cats" and the comment would be "are annoying." In a composition with such a thesis, unity only requires that every sentence be related to either the topic ("cats") and/or the comment on that topic ("are annoying"). Teachers and peer reviewers sometimes need to read between the lines to notice an underlying or implied unity. For instance, sometimes a writer includes an apparently unrelated detail, such as "Cats often have long, fluffy fur." The writer may need to add just a word or two (perhaps adding a word or two about annoying shedding, allergies, or long cat hair on couches!) to firmly demonstrate the detail's underlying unity with the topic "annoying."

 "Organizes writing around a thesis or according to the organizational requirements of the particular assignment (e.g., summary, narrative, argument, analysis, description, etc.)."

Simply put, to "organize writing around a thesis" or other central point means that the composition reveals, under examination, an overall organizational plan or strategy. To evaluate organization, a reader might ask questions such as these: Could this work be outlined? Does each paragraph play a role in developing the thesis? Does the work have a definite beginning, middle, and end? An organized composition might use logical, spatial, chronological, or even associational order—but the strategy will be employed to suit the topic and the purpose of the writing project.

2. Evidence/Development = Providing support (examples, details, or specifics)

 "Develops appropriate, logical, and relevant supporting detail and/or evidence."

This criterion asks you to note whether the writer uses examples and/or other evidence to support his/her argument, position, or idea and whether that evidence is fairly used, accurate, and relevant.

Depending on the type of writing assignment, good evidence may include anecdotes, images, descriptions, dialogue, quotations (from primary and/or secondary sources), graphs, and/or charts; typically, evidence will include quotations from a variety of sources—often including the texts read in class. In this case, you are evaluating the **quality** of evidence provided and sources used. To evaluate the quality of evidence, a reader might ask questions such as these: Did the writer use examples accurately and not take them out of context? Were selected quotations clearly related to the writer's argument? Was the source of the evidence credible? For a descriptive or narrative assignment, readers might ask if a particular scene is described with accurate, concrete, and specific details.

 "Includes more specific, concrete evidence (quotations, interviews, charts, statistics, details, description, observation, and dialogue) than opinion or abstract, general commentary."

This criterion asks you to gauge **quantity** of evidence. To evaluate the quantity of evidence, you might ask questions such as these: Has the writer made many general claims about a topic without supplying specific supporting evidence? What is the ratio of sentences providing opinions compared to sentences providing support (giving examples, quotations, and details)? Typically, readers hope to find a good deal more evidence than opinion. On the other hand, you might ask: Does the writer string together a long series of quotations and facts into lists or lengthy quoted passages? Is there *too much* unincorporated and unexplained evidence?

3. Presentation and Design = Correctness and formatting issues

 "Follows guidelines for standard English grammar, punctuation, usage, and documentation."

To meet this criterion, here is a general rule of thumb: To pass at the level of Competency, a paper should contain two or fewer major errors plus four or fewer minor errors per 250-words (250 words is about a page). If there are no major errors, a composition should have eight or fewer minor errors per 250-words. All the major errors have to do with either sentence boundary recognition or Standard English grammar issues. For our purposes, the major errors are:

- Comma Splice
- Fragment
- Fused Sentence
- Subject/Verb Agreement
- Pronoun/Antecedent Agreement

All other errors are considered minor errors. If a student's paper has more errors than the standard described above, the paper is not meeting competency guidelines for a final draft.

Remember, however, that this standard is just a guideline. Simply lacking a large number of errors does not necessarily make a project "Competent" or passing. As we point out in the Introduction to this section: "A composition does not begin as a '100' and then lose points as the teacher finds mistakes."

"Meets your teacher's (or the MLA's) and the First-year Composition Program's requirements for length and/or format."

The standard format and documentation requirements for First-year Composition follow those for MLA formatting. Teachers, however, may have special requirements, which might include the use of specialized or alternative style sheets (such as CBE, CSE, APA, or Chicago), images, graphs, video, particular fonts, minimum word counts, bibliographies, appendices, notes, abstracts, etc.

EXAMPLES:

Here are two brief examples from the 2015 Barnett Award winners that effectively demonstrate the qualities needed in a Competent/Credible/ Complete composition. Each essay shows how **evidence** can be used effectively to support different purposes. In addition, both excerpts reveal careful attention to **presentation and design** (the samples are error free and follow standard documentation and formatting requirements). Finally, even in these brief excerpts, each writer's overall purpose and topic is clear, meeting the standard for **unity**.

In the first example (below), we see ENGL1101 writer, Sujith Vadlamudi, develop a **clear and complex central thesis**, contributing to a unified academic argument (UNITY). In addition, Vadlamudi develops substantial EVIDENCE in the body of his essay as he deftly integrates **paraphrase, summary, and direct quotations** from many sources to support his thesis. In the example below, Vadlamudi introduces his thesis (in bold) while extending and complicating it, but first he provides some initial evidence—an engaging anecdote that serves also to pique reader interest. In the next paragraph, the essay's eighth, Vadlamudi employs both paraphrases and direct quotes to support his topic claim. Finally, Vadlamudi fulfills the third area of competence, PRESENTATION AND DESIGN, by providing accurate, thorough documentation and formatting and editing his paper to MLA standards. (Examples of evidence are highlighted in red; the thesis and topics are in purple.)

Paragraph 1 Vadlamudi

The morning after she was crowned Miss America in 1951, in a meeting with Miss America's board of directors, Yolande Betbeze was shocked to learn she was expected to attend a variety of public events in her bathing suit. One engagement in particular perturbed her: appearing in a Milwaukee department store wearing nothing but a bathing suit and heels. Betbeze outright refused to be paraded in such a state (Sinclair). She believed that such antics were unbecoming of the winner of a scholarship competition. Unfortunately, she didn't realize that she hadn't won a scholarship competition; she had won a beauty pageant. Of the countless forms of female objectification present in popular culture, one of the most high profile and controversial examples is the Miss America Pageant. The Pageant explicitly reinforces the idea that a woman's form is significantly more important than her function, as it's little more than a yearly ritual of ceremoniously judging a woman's body. Despite the many changes

---

implemented throughout the years, every aspect of the Miss America competition is deeply rooted in the belief that a woman's value is primarily based on her appearance and–implicitly–on how desirable she is to men.

Paragraph 8 Vadlamudi

Slaughter's scholarship would prove to be her most significant and impactful contribution to Miss America. If the pageant's website is any indication, its addition was one of the most important moments in Miss America's long history. The telecasts of pageants today are littered with references to their scholarship fund, as is the Pageant's website. If not for the abundance of women showing more skin than they covered, Miss America could be mistaken for a run of the mill scholarship competition. The incessant talk of scholarships, unfortunately, is just that–talk. The Miss America foundation claims to offer over 45 million dollars in scholarships to young women (MissAmerica.org). In reality though, the pageant spends no more than 500,000 dollars on scholarships (Oliver). John Oliver, as part of an investigation on his HBO program Last Week Tonight, uncovered the reason for the discrepancy after poring through all the public tax records of every national, state, and local Miss America pageant he could get his hands on. He reported, in an obvious state of disbelief, that the most generous analysis of financial records indicated that Miss America grossly misrepresented the amount awarded to pageant winners and contestants. The pageant calculates every possible scholarship a participant can accept in theory, even though, in actuality, a contestant can only accept one of the scholarships offered to them. Thus, the pageant can claim with much braggadocio to "make available" 45 million dollars to young women while, in reality, only awarding less than one percent of that (*Last Week Tonight with John Oliver*).

Excerpted from: "Miss Anachronism"
ENGL1101—2015 Barnett Essay Awards
Student: Sujith Vadlamudi
Teacher: Al Dixon

Unlike the television show and websites quoted in Vadlamudi's research paper above, 2014 ENGL1101 writer Scott Davis, in his researched composition "Fine, whatever . . . " deploys direct observation, images, expert testimony, and a range of sources to provide Evidence validating his argument that the use of emoticons and emoji in Computer Mediated Composition (CMC) effectively contribute to the human ability to communicate shades of meaning and are, in a way, simply an extension or evolution of traditional punctuation. Below is paragraph four of his composition in which he quotes and paraphrases expert sources and draws on common experiences to provide evidence for the continuing evolution of punctuation now occurring in digital spaces.

Paragraph 4

In text messaging the characteristics of brevity, speed, and simplicity are the name of the game, and with this purpose much punctuation is often dropped, leading to many punctuation marks acquiring new meanings. The primary and most important example is the period. The line break has replaced the period as a separator of speech, and the period has slowly shifted to accept a new meaning (Crair 2). Additionally, "The unpunctuated, un-ended sentence is incredibly addicting," says Choire Sicha, editor of the Awl. "I feel liberated to make statements without that emphasis, and like I'm continuing the conversation, even when I'm definitely not" (qtd.in Crair 2). In text messaging and even in IM messages, the default way to end your phrase is to just end it, no period involved. I mean, why would we use a period when everything we are typing is usually one sentence and is just meant to represent conversation? Thus, since the appearance of a period is rare in the texting world, it adds new meaning when it *is* used because the reader tries to figure out why it was used. The period is not used as a punctuation mark anymore but rather as a tone differential, subliminal message, or indication of the end of the conversation (not just the sentence) (Crair 3). That tone differential has come to have a negative connotation, usually either to indicate that the writer is upset, angry, or another similar emotion. Ben Crair explains that "people use the period not simply to conclude a sentence, but to announce 'I am not happy about the sentence I just concluded'" (1). It is truly an amazing innovation, in that a punctuation mark that was used to express separation and pause in speaking and literature has now adapted to indicate tone (Crair 3).

Davis's composition also presents an excellent sample of distinctive "Presentation and Design" because his incorporation of images goes "above and beyond" correct mechanics and grammar, providing not only pathetic appeal, but in addition, presenting logical evidence for and clarification of his claims. Below is a screenshot of Davis's page three, showing his distinctive use of images.

‹ Messages   **Katy**   Details

Hey, don't forget about work tomorrow 6:30 0:)

ER, 6:15 at least

Breakfast available on request

Tuesday 8:19 PM

Sounds good - breakfast would be great :)

Yesterday 8:08 AM

Your ham and cheese egg burrito is hot and ready

characteristics of normal human conversation, such as audio tone and visual cues, had been lost (Sherwood 1). In fact, statistically, 93% of human communication occurs visually through body language, and through tone of voice (Harmon 70). This is where the emoticon comes in. Judith Meyer says, "Nowadays, we often use writing as a form of quick communication in text messages and chats. These don't leave the time to carefully consider how we can avoid misunderstandings of our tone, so emoticons are a very useful tool" (et al 2). With the help of the emoticon, we are able to clarify emotional context with what would have been otherwise ambiguous emotional standing within a message, as well as make text messaging more human. Take, for example, the text message displayed above on the left, from a friend of mine to me.

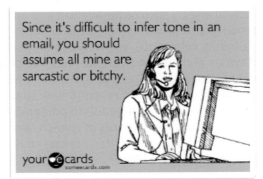

Since it's difficult to infer tone in an email, you should assume all mine are sarcastic or bitchy.

your ⊙ cards
someecards.com

She started the conversation with, "Hey, don't forget about work tomorrow 6:30 0:)", reminding me to give her a ride to work. However, if she had said the same phrase without the smiley face featuring a halo, the message could have come across as selfish, nagging, and possibly even condescending. With the addition of a simple smiley face, especially an angelic reference of

Excerpted from "Fine, Whatever. . . "
ENGL 1101—2014 Barnett Essay Awards
Student: Scott Davis
Teacher: Al Dixon

Skillful/Persuasive

In order to reach the level of a "Skillful/Persuasive" paper, an argument must have two additional qualities: Coherence and Audience Awareness.

4. Coherence = The "Flow"

 "Uses words and sentences, rhythm and phrasing, variations and transitions, concreteness and specificity to reveal and emphasize the relationship between evidence and thesis."

In general, while students can achieve unity by creating a strong thesis and staying on topic, they create coherence by focusing their reader's attention on **the relationship between** thesis and evidence (or theme and detail). Creating Coherence is about **controlling emphasis.**

Students may use diction to emphasize the thesis-to-evidence connection by choosing words carefully, by repeating key words and phrases, by avoiding the repetition of unimportant words and phrases, and by using transitional phrases accurately. Writers can also use syntax—that is, sentence structure—to direct emphasis by varying sentence structures, by employing syntactical effects such as parallelism and antithesis, or simply by changing sentence length or reversing normal Subject-Verb-Object sentence patterns. In evaluating coherence, you may ask these questions: Has the writer used syntax and diction to create links and bridge gaps between his or her thoughts? Does the writer use transitional phrases and words frequently and accurately to help the reader follow the writer's thinking from sentence to sentence and from paragraph to paragraph? Does the writer's use of repetition, parallelism, figures of speech, and rhythm help to emphasize main points, or does the writer's choice of diction and syntax distract the reader from the main ideas?

 "Explains how, why, or in what way the evidence/detail supports a point/claim/thesis/topic ideas."

Writers need to include explanations. In fact, writers usually need to explain why each detail or item of support has been included in an essay. It is a rare bit of evidence that is so clear that it speaks for itself. Coherence develops as writers explain how each part of their arguments' evidence provides support for their theses.

 "Incorporates evidence from outside sources smoothly, appropriately, and responsibly."

The writer will consistently incorporate quotations and references to other outside sources into her own sentences. Coherent writers move often between paraphrasing, summarizing, and brief selected quotations from different sources. Few, if any, quotations will be left "hanging"—that is, standing alone in separate sentences; instead, they will be embedded in the writer's own sentences, usually with explanatory remarks linking the quotations to the topic or thesis. Lengthy quotations, serial quotations, or long summaries rarely occur in a "Skillful" writer's composition. The excerpt below offers good examples of smoothly inserted quotations and responsible citation practices.

EXAMPLE:

In the example below, 2015 ENGL1101 Moran ePortfolio writer John Henline develops a subtle thesis that explores the relationship between his own finances as a University of Georgia student and Pierre Bourdieu's theory of capital as expressed in his article "The Forms of Capital." In this excerpt, Henline moves skillfully among expert opinions and his own reading of Bourdieu—summarizing, paraphrasing, and quoting, yet never losing sight of his own position and purpose. Notice how Henline uses explanatory sentences, key words, linking phrases, repetition, parallel structures, and transitional phrases to create **coherence**, keeping the reader focused on his own argument—that Bourdieu's theories about the relationship between economic and social/cultural practices can be successfully applied to an individual's (specifically Henline's!) "social and cultural investments." (Examples of increased coherence are highlighted in **Green.**)

Paragraph 1

Personal Finance of Cultural and Social Capital

Pierre Bourdieu's 1986 article "The Forms of Capital" lays out a detailed analysis of the ways in which economic ideas of capital and investment translate to social and cultural situations. In his article, Bourdieu concludes that social and cultural capital are linked in their very nature to economic capital, and that many of the same rules that govern Capitalism as an economic system also govern the flow of social and cultural capital from society to an individual (and, from one individual to another). Accordingly, many standard practices of personal finance can be applied to the management of social and cultural capital. Using Bourdieu's theories of investment of labor-time in social and cultural settings, an individual is capable of securing for themselves a successful start in society while maintaining a diversified, forward-thinking portfolio of social and cultural investments.

Paragraph 2

Bourdieu's analysis in "The Forms of Capital" finds that individuals have at their disposal numerous forms of capital separate from, and in addition to, economic capital. Two distinct forms of capital emerge alongside traditional economic capital in Bourdieu's theory:

> [C]ultural capital, which is convertible . . . into economic capital and may be institutionalized in the forms of educational qualifications; and . . . social capital, made up of social obligations ('connections'), which is convertible . . . into economic capital and may be institutionalized in the forms of a title of nobility (Bourdieu 98).

Cultural capital includes the capacity to imbibe, retain, use, and transfer cultural and institutional knowledge on an individual basis, whereas social capital refers to the sense of self in society, connections people make with others, and the ideals they carry with them when forming into groups. These two non-traditional forms of capital carry many of the same rules and best practices from the capitalistic economy, namely the investment of time and labor, the accumulation of wealth, transferring of wealth in exchange for goods or services, the conversion of capital from one form to another, competition among consumers and manufacturers, supply and demand, free markets, business ethics, and capital gains from investments. These forms of capital are inherently linked to economic capital, and "the most material types of capital-those which are economic in the restricted sense-can present themselves in the immaterial form of cultural capital or social capital and vice versa." (97) Essentially, social and cultural capital can be treated identically to economic capital in many ways, and can be earned through the conversion of economic capital and/or investment labor-time. "The Forms of Capital" goes so far as to offer some best-practice approaches to certain social and cultural settings, specifically the weighing of time and energy against expected future gains, speculation of the market in making financial decisions, and the importance of connections in investment planning. This parallel led me to consider the possibility of applying all forms of financial planning and economic guidance to the capital of society and culture.

Paragraph 3

In thinking about this problem, I found myself relating my personal situation as a student at the University of Georgia, as well as the financial management experience I have accumulated over the course of my life, to the concept of social and cultural investment. A college student such as myself must effectively manage all aspects of his academic, social, cultural, and financial needs, and most don't have the luxury of relying upon a financial planner or life coach along the way. According to Bourdieu, "ability or talent is itself the product of an investment of time and cultural capital"

(98) and, "[c]apital is accumulated labor." (96) In order to gain new talents, experiences, knowledge, or abilities, a person must invest time and/or labor into the process. Bourdieu's "accumulated labor" is referencing time and energy, so one might say capital itself is the direct result of a time and energy investment. A diversified investment portfolio is needed to succeed in this way, or more to the point, a person must take from one form of capital (usually, economic capital) to pay for gains in another form. Capital, in the various forms, can flow from one such market to another to fulfill this need; however, the conversion itself also requires an investment of accumulated labor:

> Profits in one area are necessarily paid for by costs in another (so that a concept like wastage has no meaning in a general science of the economy of practices). The universal equivalent . . . is nothing other than labor-time (in the widest sense); and the conservation of social energy through all its conversions is verified if . . . one takes into account both the labor-time accumulated in the form of capital and the labor-time needed to transform it from one type into another (106).

In terms of social capital, college students have almost limitless opportunities for investment of their accumulated labor. It is clear that Bourdieu recognizes the importance of social affluence as well, stating that it "provides each of its members with the backing of the collectivity-owned capital, a 'credential' which entitles them to credit, in the various senses of the word"(103). Individuals spend this social 'credit' throughout their lives, from the first semester of school to their retirement from the workforce and beyond. It stands to reason that social capital, and the accumulation of it at an early age, is paramount to a successful existence (not merely a successful career). He explains in very direct terms that this "network of relationships is the product of investment strategies, individual or collective, consciously or unconsciously aimed at establishing or reproducing social relationships that are directly usable in the short or long term." (103) When choosing avenues for the investment of their accumulated labor, college students are certainly free to choose social investments as the sole market for their accumulated labor, foregoing the accumulation of cultural capital and traditional economic capital in the process. However, this strategy will result in a one-dimensional portfolio, focusing only on one very high-risk investment. A heavy investment in social capital requires that the student's funds are taken from other investments such as academic advancement, cultural gains, and furthering their economic position. Finally, the return on the student's social investments will come much later than those from traditional economic investments (107). The student runs the risk of poor academic performance, finding himself unable to sustain his budget due to a lack of available accumulated labor-time. While this single-prong approach to college finances may result in a fun and exciting few years of university, it is not a viable

> long-term strategy for success, and the delayed return on social investments means a more balanced portfolio is required for overall success.

Excerpted from "Personal Finance of Cultural and Social Capital"
ENGL 1101, 2015 Moran ePortfolio Award
Student: John Henline
Teacher: Nathan Camp

5. Audience Awareness = Writing should speak to real readers

 "Demonstrates a sense that the writer knows what s/he's doing and is addressing real people."

Showing that a writer "knows what s/he's doing" means that the writer works to develop his or her credibility (ethos). He or she might mention and/or demonstrate particular knowledge or research concerning a topic, demonstrate comfort and familiarity with appropriate jargon or professional vocabularies, or simply use sound logic and clear reasoning in his or her discussion. Credibility can be, however, developed in many ways.

✓ "Reflects a respect for values that influence ethos (e.g., common ground, trustworthiness, careful research)."

Respect for an audience and values can be shown at every level. A reader evaluating writing for respect might ask these questions: Has the writer chosen an appropriate level of formality in his or her diction—avoiding the too formal for an audience of close friends, the too familiar with teachers or general audiences? Has the writer avoided unnecessary jargon or slang? Has the writer avoided sexist or racist language? Is the writer's choice of supporting examples and evidence appropriate, fairly used, relevant, and judiciously applied? Does the writer show a high level of integrity about facts and correctness at every level? Does the writer implicitly and explicitly show courtesy and good will towards readers whose opinions may differ? Does the writer acknowledge counter-arguments and other positions?

EXAMPLES:
Two very different excerpts demonstrate the qualities of "respect for values" and "a sense that the writer knows what h/she's doing."

In the first example, notice how this excerpt from Scott Davis's paper, "Fine, Whatever. . . ," combines an overtly colloquial voice—addressing the reader as "you," posing rhetorical questions, using first person pronouns, and explaining or providing examples—with effectively integrated expert evidence and personal observation. This combination creates a sense of both personality and authority. While Davis's voice is personal, it is also convincing and well-informed.

In the second example, Farrah Agha's traditional scholarly literary analysis, "Dealing with Damaged Relationships," Agha directs her analysis to a general, formal academic audience. Agha adopts the conventions and impersonal style of academic discourse. She avoids the first-person singular and more frequently adopts passive voice, carefully integrates quotations into her own sentences, adopts formal diction, and documents sources fully in the text and Works Cited, following the proper disciplinary (MLA) style.

(Examples of adaptations to show AUDIENCE AWARENESS are highlighted in orange.)

Selection 1: Scott Davis

In the digital age, expressing your emotion can be as easy as typing one or two punctuation characters, such as a colon and parentheses to make a smiley face :). You have probably seen this string of characters or other ones like it various times throughout texting, email, IM messaging, or other examples of CMC (computer-mediated communication), but where did it all come from? CMC is essentially any human communication that occurs by two or more electronic devices ("Computer-mediated communication"), which would inherently include texting. The character shown above, as well as :(:-) :-(:P :/ and many others, are examples of "letters" or "configurations" in the alphabet of emoticons. However, perhaps the "emoji," easily considered emoticon 2.0, is of more importance and weight in today's communications,

as it is more modern: ☺. Although you, the reader, may not be as familiar with these as you are with emoticons, you have still likely seen them by some form of CMC. While most people over the age of 25 likely think of emoticons and emojis as pointless and as adding little meaning to writing (Marsden 2), these characters have a big effect on today's CMC, especially emotionally. In fact, they were made explicitly for emotional expression, created to fill the emotional, tonal, and modal hole that had been created naturally in CMC. Additionally, long before the emoticon, ever since writing was established, we have had punctuation as a writing tool to help establish tone and emotion. In a world of short and brief text messages, punctuation and emojis/emoticons determine the tone of the text message more than the actual words do. This makes the textual interaction more human and allows us to communicate more naturally as well as personally by allowing us to add visual components of communication that were originally lost.

Excerpted from "Fine, Whatever . . ."
ENGL 1101
Student: Scott Davis
Teacher: Al Dixon

Selection 2: Farrah Agha

Paragraphs 1 and 2

Sexism in "The Free Radio"

Salman Rushdie's "The Free Radio" reflects the heavy gender bias of twenty-first century rural India. Rushdie's narrator recounts the tale of an animated rickshaw driver, Ramani, who is misled into agreeing to a vasectomy in exchange for a state-sponsored free radio; yet the radio never arrives, and Ramani seems to become slowly disillusioned with his reality. Ramani's path is purportedly chosen for him by the woman whom he eventually marries, a widow who desires no more children. Although ultimately both the widow and Ramani are, in many ways, powerless, suffering poverty and great hardship, it is the widow who is repeatedly blamed for Ramani's seemingly exponential misfortune. The widow is vilified due to her unconventional independence and initiative.

The narrator, an old man obviously colored by the sexism of his time, introduces the Widow as an almost unstoppable, destructive force. She appears almost inhuman, described as having "claws" or "hooks," and as lurking in the shadows, waiting for the opportune time to strike. When out with her five children, they are depicted as a pack, with the widow ahead, leading her brood. When the widow begins to pursue Ramani, this imagery is heightened, as older women courting younger men are often, quite sexist-ly, viewed as predators. Yet, this initial characterization is not truly due to the widow's actions, but rather to her perceived identity as a tainted woman.

Conclusion and Works Cited

The widow is condemned because of her status as a self-sufficient woman. Though she suffers greatly to ensure the survival of her family, she cannot overcome the stigma of her independence as a woman. While her story is specific to the political turmoil in India in the 1970s, the expectations and judgments placed on the widow as a woman are universally applicable. Regardless of how progressive a society claims to be, women are quite often expected to be only so independent and eventually to surrender their lives and settle down. However, each woman is free to shape her own future regardless of society's expectations. Just as the widow found herself fat and happy in Bombay, every woman is able, if truly willing, to have control over her own life.

Works Cited

Rushdie, Salman. "The Free Radio." *The Bedford Introduction to Literature.* Ed. Michael Meyer. Boston: Bedford/St. Martin's, 2008. 696-701. Print.

Excerpted from: "Sexism in 'The Free Radio'"
ENGL 1102
Student: Farrah Agha
Teacher: Carmen Comeaux

Distinctive

To earn the highly coveted grade of "A," a writer must go beyond basic criteria required for a competent composition, exceed the expectations for a skillful composition, and provide something else that gives the composition real "value added," sticks in the reader's memory, or catches her attention.

6. Distinction: A few words about distinction

"Your writing stands out because of one or more of the following characteristics: complexity, originality, seamless coherence, extraordinary control, sophistication in thought, recognizable voice, compelling purpose, imagination, insight, thoroughness, and/or depth."

No single quality reveals distinction; that's why we've listed so many possibilities. A paper should **meet standards in all five of the other criteria** before it is considered for "Distinction." This does not mean that students' papers must necessarily excel in all five criteria (although many will and most will excel in three or more criteria), but papers should be average or better in every category and should not be deficient in any category when being considered for Distinction.

The FYC Grading Rubric was designed by a volunteer team of instructors who carefully examined a range of compositions, deciding what qualities papers at different grade levels share in common. Based on their work, we now have a common vocabulary that students and teachers can use to understand how to succeed in First-year Composition.

CHAPTER SIX

Electronic Portfolios in the First-year Composition Program

The First-year Composition Electronic Portfolio

Every student who takes a First-year Composition course at the University of Georgia composes an electronic portfolio over the course of the semester. The ePortfolio gives students an opportunity to revise and polish their work—even after it has been evaluated for a grade during the semester—to showcase their work in a personalized context, to reflect on their writing and their writing processes, and, finally, to "publish" their work to a broader audience. The use of an electronic portfolio for all FYC classes means that students have an opportunity to raise their grades through steady work and revision; but it also means that students need to schedule adequate time to do their very best work in the portfolio, as it counts for 30% of their final grade.

Students develop portfolios throughout the semester using the First-year Composition Program's Emma writing environment—adding, updating, and revising elements under teachers' directions and using the support available in the FYC Digital Learning Labs, headquartered in Park Hall 117. Students will also find that using feedback from their classmates in peer review sessions, both in and out of class, will make portfolio development a much more rewarding process.

The details of using Emma to compose your ePortfolio will be described during Emma Orientation sessions and during classes. In addition, individual teachers will make specific assignments for various parts of the portfolio. In broad outline, however, the essential seven components of our ePortfolios are consistent in every FYC course and are described briefly below:

> **Note:** *You cannot re-use or recycle any exhibit from your English 1101 portfolio, including the Biography or Introductory Reflective Essay, for your English 1102/1103 portfolio. This would be Academic Dishonesty and handled under the Academic Honesty policy and procedures.*

Elements of the Portfolio

Front Page: Biography

The Biography is a short introduction to you, the author of the portfolio. Your class or teacher may specify particular information to include in your Biography, but, in general, the Biography should act as an author's headnote.

Images on your Biography page are optional, but readers like them, so you should try to include some image that is relevant. You can select a representative image (a windmill, a horse, or anything you can find on the Web—just remember to include a citation), or you can select an image of yourself. Think of it as a dust jacket image on the back of a book—how do you want to represent yourself? The goal of your Biography page should be to establish a credible ethos.

Note: The Biography MUST be constructed as an Emma *eDocument in order to display properly in your* Emma *portfolio. We strongly recommend creating it using eDocs. You must also check carefully to make sure that the Biography displays properly, as this will provide portfolio readers with their first impression of you as a writer.*

Introductory Reflective Essay (IRE)

The most important element in your ePortfolio, the Introductory Reflective Essay provides a reader with an introduction and guide to the rest of your work. A strong IRE ties together all the exhibits in your portfolio; it helps you describe and reflect on your writing processes, with your exhibits providing the supporting evidence. The IRE is also the first item evaluators will read after they open your Biography page. Your teacher may provide you with a specific prompt or may direct you to some specific portion of the FYC program sample prompt to help you get started. In your IRE, you might discuss how the various exhibits you have chosen for your portfolio reveal the way you have engaged with the goals of the course listed earlier in this *FYC Guide* and/or the FYC Grading Rubric's criteria. Some very successful portfolios have re-organized the author's work for the semester around a common theme that the writer sees in her or his own work. In fact, the goal of the IRE should be to cohere and organize the portfolio in a meaningful way; it is the most active portion of the portfolio. 750-1500 words is the average length for an IRE, although some of the Moran Award winners have written longer IRE's.

Two Revised Essays from the Course

You will include in your Electronic Portfolio two of the three graded papers you have written for the class, revised and polished and posted to the portfolio. They should be substantive and well-argued, carefully edited, error free, and completely, thoroughly, and correctly documented in MLA format.

Note about the Revised Essays: We recommend a thorough revision for the Revised Essays exhibits in your Portfolio—not just a quick proofreading for surface errors. Could more evidence be developed, a new perspective raised, for instance, a change in tone attempted, or a firmer line of reasoning followed?

When choosing essays to put in your Electronic Portfolio, think about how they will work together to help make the portfolio a unified whole. Some students choose the essays that received the highest grades, but this is only one criterion. You may want to choose the essays you like the best, the ones you can improve the most, or the ones that fit best with your chosen theme.

Exhibit of Composing/Revision Process

This exhibit demonstrates your composing and revision process. Typically, students construct this document by copying and pasting the same or similar sections of a selected essay into a single document. You can then add commentary explaining the significance of the different versions, pointing out and explaining the changes you made through successive drafts. The Revision Exhibit gives you a chance to demonstrate not so much your best products for the semester, but the skill set that you have built up over the course of the semester. The trick is to make it easy for a reader to follow the process; the explanation is just as important as, or perhaps more important than, your chosen examples. This exhibit gives you a chance to reflect on your progress throughout the semester and to perform a self-assessment.

Exhibit of Peer Review Process

One of the goals for all FYC courses states that students will "demonstrate an ability to critique the writing of themselves and others." For this exhibit, which speaks directly to that goal, you will select and post to your portfolio one of the peer reviews that you have written during the semester, including commentary to help the reader understand your peer review process. One option is to choose a review you completed for one of your classmate's papers. Try to choose one that you believe was helpful and focused; you might want to ask your classmates about which ones were helpful to them. You may also copy and paste together several brief examples of peer reviews you have completed and construct a new document with inserted commentary. Explanations about the assigned peer review are often helpful here, too. As in the previous case, the Peer Review Exhibit gives you a chance to demonstrate not so much your best products for the semester, but the skill set that you have built up over the course of the semester. As with the Composing/Revision Process Exhibit, the Peer Review Exhibit gives you a chance to reflect on your progress throughout the semester and to perform a self-assessment.

Wild Card

This exhibit is up to you. The only limitations are that your Wild Card 1) must be an electronic file or link that "fits" in your Emma portfolio; and 2) must include some of *your* writing, which may appear as captions, short descriptions, or introductory commentary. In the past, students have submitted journals, papers, photos with captions, short stories, poems, letters, song lyrics, scans of drawings with comments, news articles, podcasts, and music files. Some students create new exhibits especially to fit with their portfolio theme. In thinking about selecting or creating a Wild Card, consider how it fits into your overall portfolio rationale and how its inclusion will impact ethos and pathos.

Special Note on Presentation and Publication of your ePortfolio

Importance: The electronic portfolio, as the capstone project that showcases your achievements and learning, is very important; it counts for 30% of your final grade.

Digital Publication: The ePortfolio is not merely a loose collection of word-processed documents, but a **unified digital artifact** whose parts fit together in a rational and harmonious manner. It is therefore not enough to just put your final documents in the Portfolio Prep folder. You must construct the ePortfolio using the Portfolio Tool; this is the only way that your readers can access your work. If you do not complete the ePortfolio properly, you may receive a grade of zero for this important project. Help with the technical aspects of uploading student portfolios may be found under the "Help" module in Emma.

Presentation and Design: Just as the Grading Rubric considers Presentation and Document Design as important to the rhetorical success of your essays, so too does the ePortfolio. Your portfolio therefore must meet the highest standards for presentation and document design; failure to do so will seriously hurt your grade for the ePortfolio.

Readability and Access: Finally, this is an *electronic* (rather than a print) portfolio that will be read online by two different readers. It is your responsibility to make sure that:

- the front page of your ePort and all of the exhibits display properly without significant formatting issues;
- all exhibits are in one of the acceptable file formats (see below);
- it can be navigated easily and efficiently by your readers.

Open your portfolio on several different computers and click through all the exhibits to make sure that the portfolio is reader-friendly.

How Are FYC ePortfolios Evaluated?

At the end of the semester, every FYC student's Emma Portfolio is read by at least two FYC teachers: his or her own teacher and one other. The presence of a second reader gives writers another real reader for their work. If the scores assigned to any portfolio differ by ten or more points, a third FYC teacher also reads and scores that Portfolio. To arrive at a final portfolio score, the two closest scores awarded are averaged. The Portfolio grade counts as 30% of an FYC student's final course grade. (See your teacher's syllabus for more information.)

Technical Note: Acceptable File Formats for ePortfolio Exhibits

Because at least two teachers must be able to read successfully your ePortfolio online and not all teachers will have available the proprietary word processing package contained on your personal computer, the FYC Program accepts only the following file formats for ePortfolio Exhibits that are primarily text documents:

- PDF
- Emma eDocuments

Emma eDocuments: This accepted format is easy to use; eDocs have the added advantage of allowing you to do all your writing and editing in the web browser itself.

PDF documents: Students who include a large number of images in their documents or have special design and formatting needs often choose to upload the documents in their portfolios as PDF documents. This is the only format in which you can be absolutely sure that the document appears exactly the same in your word processor and the web display.

In order to evaluate them, teachers read portfolios holistically. This means that the readers "norm" themselves, getting a sense of what "constitutes" an A, B, C, etc. among the group of portfolios that they are reading, then judge each portfolio as a whole, assigning it a single grade. As teachers read through students' portfolios, they particularly gauge how well a student's Introductory Reflective Essay (IRE) describes the content found in the other exhibits and whether or not the student has been able to use writing to express his or her own encounter with goals and evaluative criteria of the course. In other words, expect FYC teachers to use the IRE as a guide for reading your other documents, in order to get a sense of how well they match the expectations you set up in your Introduction. Of course, teachers always look for evidence of care, originality, hard work, and excellent writing, but in the portfolio we are also interested in students' ability to write reflectively and accurately about their own writing.

In addition, teachers often use the following Rubric, based on the standard FYC rubric and using the same or similar terminology, to help them get started when they are beginning to evaluate portfolios each semester. They may also point you towards this rubric to help you evaluate your own or your classmates' portfolio during a workshop.

ELECTRONIC PORTFOLIO RUBRIC

BIOGRAPHY
- Is present and complete;
- Is carefully proofread and edited, with very few errors of a grammatical, mechanical, or typographic nature.
  [CCC] _____
- Shows clear and appropriate awareness of audience;
- Gives a coherent picture of the writer.
  [SP] _____

- Is distinctive for its:
  - imaginative quality;
  - extraordinary and effective care in craftsmanship and presentation;
  - prose style;
  - compelling authorial voice;
  - persuasive argumentation.
  [DIST]_____

INTRODUCTORY REFLECTIVE ESSAY
- Is present and complete;
- Makes a clear and complete statement about the writer's ethos, development, and/or skill set that is more than an autobiographical narrative or list of exhibits (unity-thesis);
- Offers a clear rationale for the choice of exhibits and their order (unity-organization);
- Explains the role of each exhibit in the overall portfolio and in proving the thesis (evidence);
- Is carefully proofread and edited, with very few errors of a grammatical, mechanical, or typographic nature.
  [CCC] _____
- Offers a strong, and vivid understanding of the writer and writing (audience awareness);
- Is particularly persuasive about how exhibits contribute to the whole portfolio (coherence).
  [SP] _____

- Is distinctive for its:
  - imaginative quality;
  - extraordinary and effective care in craftsmanship and presentation;
  - prose style;
  - compelling authorial voice;

- persuasive argumentation.
[DIST] _____

TWO REVISED MAJOR COMPOSITIONS
- Are present and complete;
- At a minimum, meet the FYC Rubric qualifications for CCC;
- Are carefully proofread and edited, with very few errors of a grammatical, mechanical, or typographic nature.
[CCC] _____
- At a minimum, meet the FYC Rubric qualifications for SP.
[SP] _____
- At a minimum, meet the FYC Rubric qualifications for a DIST or a "high" SP that shows extraordinary thoughtfulness and care.
[DIST] _____

EXHIBIT OF COMPOSING AND/OR REVISION PROCESS
- Present and complete;
- Offers a clear and complete statement about and/or example of the composing and/or revision process (unity);
- Supports that thesis with specific examples (evidence);
- Presents the examples in a logical manner (unity-organization);
- Is carefully written, edited, and proofread, with essentially no distracting errors of a grammatical, mechanical, or typographic nature.
[CCC] _____

- Offers strong and vivid examples of the writer and writing (audience awareness);
- Is particularly persuasive about how the examples support the thesis (coherence).
[SP] _____

- Is distinctive for its:
  - imaginative quality;
  - extraordinary and effective care in craftsmanship and presentation;
  - prose style;
  - compelling authorial voice;
  - persuasive argumentation.
[DIST] _____

EXHIBIT OF PEER REVIEW PROCESS

- Is present and complete;
- Offers a clear exhibit of a peer review (unity);
- Arranges one or more examples of peer review in a logical manner (unity-organization);
- Is carefully presented so that both the original and comments are easily seen. Errors in grammar or spelling don't interfere with conveying comments (presentation & design).
  [CCC] _____

- Shows a strong, and vivid understanding of the writer and commentary (audience awareness);
- Is persuasive because comments show a clear understanding and response to the work (coherence).
  [SP] _____

- Is distinctive for its:
    - imaginative quality;
    - extraordinary and effective care in craftsmanship and presentation;
    - prose style;
    - compelling authorial voice;
    - persuasive argumentation.
  [DIST] _____

WILD CARD

- Is present and complete;
- Fits into the portfolio as a whole in a logical way that is described in the introductory reflective essay;
- Is carefully written, edited, and proofread, with few errors of a grammatical, mechanical, or typographic nature that distract from the purpose of the exhibit.
  [CCC] _____

- Offers a strong and vivid understanding of the writer and writing (audience awareness).
  [SP] _____

- Is distinctive for its:
    - imaginative quality;
    - extraordinary and effective care in craftsmanship and presentation;
    - prose style;
    - compelling authorial voice;
    - persuasive argumentation.

  [DIST] _____

CHAPTER SEVEN

Academic Honesty and Plagiarism

UGA Academic Honesty Policy

The University of Georgia is committed to "A Culture of Honesty." The First-year Composition Program supports this commitment and strictly follows the university's policies and procedures for dealing with possible instances of academic dishonesty. Information about "A Culture of Honesty" and the "UGA Academic Honesty Policy" and procedures can be found at the web site of the Office of the Vice President for Instruction: http://www.uga.edu/honesty/.

All FYC students should become very familiar with this site!

Plagiarism

A particular form of academic dishonesty that First-year Composition students need to understand and guard against is plagiarism. *Plagiarism* is the use of another's words or interpretations without giving credit. Plagiarism occurs when writers fail to use quotation marks to indicate exact words from a source, when they fail to paraphrase a passage completely, when they provide faulty sources, or when they fail to cite the source of any quotation or paraphrase.

In recent years, cutting and pasting information from the World Wide Web has led students to commit plagiarism. This occurs particularly when they have forgotten where the information was copied from or lose the ability to tell the difference between their own words and those copied from an electronic source. Students should also take additional care to ensure that the Wild Card exhibit for the final electronic portfolio is their own work and correctly identifies any work by other authors included in that piece.

To avoid plagiarism, writers should always:

1. Put quotation marks around any words taken from sources. When writers use an open book for writing a paper or taking notes, or when writers take notes by cutting and pasting from an online source or website, they must be careful not to plagiarize unintentionally.

2. Paraphrase material completely; changing or rearranging a few words or the tense of a verb is not paraphrasing. Writers should read the passage to be used, close the source book or minimize the web browser, and then write in their own words what they have read. They should then compare the paraphrase to the source; if by chance key words from the original are included, these should be changed or enclosed in quotation marks.

3. Give accurate and complete citations for all material. In the handbook section in the second half of this *Guide,* you will find

information about MLA and APA documentation styles. Writers should refer to this source when creating compositions or should consult with their instructors as to what form is required in a particular course.

4. Avoid borrowing entire arguments or approaches to a subject from another writer. In general, college papers should argue an original idea and should not be paraphrases of another writer's work. All papers that students submit must be original work. The advantages to writers of a well-documented paper are obvious: documentation shows that writers know their subjects, and citations give ideas validity.

Workshop
How to Use Sources (and Not to Plagiarize)

The Provost of the University of Georgia has asked FYC to conduct a program-wide workshop on plagiarism in every ENGL 1101, 1102, and 1103 class in order to support the University of Georgia's efforts to educate students on this subject. The Workshop seeks to inform students about the nature of plagiarism and about ways to avoid plagiarism in their writing. It is designed in two parts, to be completed over two to three class periods, but instructors may wish to complete the entire workshop within one class period. Your teacher will give you specific instructions.

Part 1: Recognizing Plagiarism

1. Review the discussion of "**Academic Honesty and Plagiarism**" in this *First-year Composition Guide, University of Georgia.*

2. On the Web, follow the link to the University of Georgia site on Academic Honesty that is referenced in this section of *First-year Composition Guide.* Review carefully the policies and procedures outlined there.

3. Write a short entry of about 250 – 350 words in your Emma journal. In this entry, define plagiarism in your own words. Your teacher may ask you to consider the different kinds of plagiarism found in specific disciplines or genres. Follow your definition with two brief passages in which you plagiarize something. After each passage, explain exactly what and how you plagiarized.

4. In class: Discuss Homework results.

Part 2: Acknowledging Sources

1. Read about MLA (or APA) documentation styles in your *First-year Composition Guide, University of Georgia.*

2. Write an entry in your Emma journal as follows:

    a. Copy and paste a paragraph from today's *New York Times* (or another source your teacher chooses) into the top of your entry. Write a full MLA (or APA) citation for it;

    b. **summarize** the paragraph, including an "in-text" citation of your source;

    c. **paraphrase** a sentence or two from the paragraph and provide an in-text citation;

    d. choose a passage, a few words, or a phrase from the paragraph and **quote it within one of your own sentences**. Use an in-text citation to document your source;

    e. finally, write a brief paragraph describing and defining what it means to summarize, paraphrase, and quote. What are the distinctive features of each? In what situations might you choose to use one or another of these forms?

3. In class: View and discuss your passages and your findings. Be prepared to discuss the results and implications of these exercises. Be prepared to ask whatever questions you may have about how to avoid plagiarism in summaries and paraphrases and about integrating quotations with correct citations.

The goals of this Workshop are to support the UGA Academic Honesty Pledge—"I will be academically honest in all of my academic work and will not tolerate academic dishonesty of others"—and to help students use sources wisely in all of their written work.

Resources

Academic Honesty (A Culture of Honesty). Office of the Vice President for Instruction. http://www.uga.edu/honesty/.

First-year Composition at UGA Website. http://english.uga.edu/fyc/pages/1

"*MLA Handbook* Bibliographic Format for References." Research Central. http://www.libs.uga.edu/ref/mlastyle.html.

CHAPTER EIGHT

Resources

Students who are new to the University of Georgia are often unsure about what services are available to them and where to go for help of various kinds. This section offers you places to go for help with writing, research, and personal issues.

Tutoring and Help with Writing

The university offers writers in First-year Composition a wide range of services at different locations across campus.

The UGA Writing Center

The Department of English operates the UGA Writing Center in Park Hall 66 as a third-party resource for students looking for help with writing in a 100% confidential space. Undergraduate students, whether in an FYC course or not, are welcome to use its services anytime during their careers at the University of Georgia for up to thirty minutes per week. Serving students and majors across the campus, the Writing Center welcomes all types of writing including but not limited to essays, lab reports, application statements, and CVs/resumes. Common reasons for utilizing the Writing Center include help with content development, overall organization and flow, thesis creation, research, and citations. The Writing Center operates at four additional locations: a satellite center in the Science Library Room 201 (South Campus Writing Center); students with writing for science classes often seek assistance at this location from a Writing Intensive Program consultant with a background in science writing, a location in the Miller Learning Center for after-hours help, a location in the FYC Digital Composition Center in Park Hall 118 (FYC students are encouraged to seek assistance at this location for help with assignments or questions related to Emma and FYC Portfolios), and an online consultation service. For hours, policies, and scheduling for all five locations, see the Writing Center's scheduling website at: https://uga. mywconline.com. For general information see the Center's website: http:// writingcenter.english.uga.edu/.

Schedules for the Writing Center are posted by the start of the first week of each academic semester. The Writing Center accepts drop-in clients if no students are scheduled for the desired walk-in time, but scheduling an appointment is the most reliable way to meet with a Writing Center consultant.

Milledge Hall Academic Resource Center

Located in Milledge Hall, the Division of Academic Enhancement provides appointment-based, drop-in, and online tutoring for undergraduate and graduate students across campus and disciplines. Experienced English as a

Second Language specialists are available to work in person with multi-lingual students. In addition to Milledge Hall, Academic Enhancement tutoring services are available in the Miller Learning Center and in the South Campus Writing Center, located in the Science Library. For more information, go to the Academic Resource Center website.

The UGA Libraries

Homepage: http://www.libs.uga.edu

UGA has the largest library in the state with 4.6 million books, thousands of periodical subscriptions, hundreds of online databases, and many librarians to help you navigate through it all. Library buildings on campus include:

- **Main Library on North Campus:** humanities, social sciences, and business;
- **Science Library on South Campus:** science, technology, and agriculture;
- **Miller Learning Center:** electronic library resources;
- **Special Collections Library:** rare books, manuscripts, media archives, and many fascinating exhibits.

For college-level research projects and papers, your instructors will expect you to use *published scholarly* resources and *critically evaluate* any sources you take from the web. Fear not: in addition to its large book collection, the Libraries subscribe to many online databases that include articles and books suitable for college research.

Starting at the Libraries' homepage, follow the "Books" tab to **GIL-Find,** the online catalog of books, ebooks, and films. To find articles from magazines, scholarly journals, and newspapers, start with the default **Multi-Search** tab. Multi-Search lets you limit your results to only full-text articles, only scholarly articles, only newspapers, only ebooks, and other options.

More extensive databases are under the "Resources by Subject" or "Databases A-Z links":

- *For English 1101*, use Academic Search Complete for magazine and scholarly journal articles, LexisNexis Academic for newspaper articles and TV/radio transcripts, and CQ Researcher Plus for analyses of current issues.

- *For English 1102/1103*, use JSTOR or the MLA International Bibliography for literary criticism published in scholarly journals, and Literature Resource Center for biographies of authors.

All of our online resources can be used from anywhere with your MyID and password. Ask a librarian for help choosing keywords, creating a search strategy, and finding more focused databases and resources for your projects.

Need help? Use our "Chat with a Librarian" link on the library homepage or ask at the reference desk in any of the library buildings. The reference desk at the Main and Science libraries is located on the entry floors; the reference desk at the Miller Learning Center is located at the top of the stairs on the third floor. All students are welcome to sign up for one-on-one conferences with a librarian at http://www.libs.uga.edu/ref/instruction/conform.html.

Counseling and Psychiatric Services (CAPS)

CAPS is dedicated to student mental health and well-being. We support students in achieving both academic and personal life goals. CAPS offers:

- Short-term individual counseling
- Groups and workshops
- Consultation
- Psychiatric services
- Crisis intervention
- Referral assistance to other providers, both on campus and in the local community.

CAPS is located on the second floor of the University Health Center. We are open from 8:00 a.m. to 5:00 p.m., Monday through Friday. For more information about CAPS services, please call 706-542-2273 or see our website www.uhs.uga.edu/caps. For after-hours emergencies call 706-542-2200 (UGA police) and ask for the on-call clinician.

CHAPTER NINE

What Comes Next?

Research into the writing process shows that the use of writing as a part of the learning process and frequency of writing are both crucial to improving and maintaining the writing skills and critical thinking processes that students acquire in their First-year Composition classes. What is more, employers consistently report on the importance of basic communication skills, especially in writing, for the workplace. Research has also suggested a close connection between reading and writing proficiency, and UGA students have shown that they enjoy reading and discussing books outside their formal classes. For all of these reasons, the University of Georgia encourages you to seek out other opportunities for practice in reading and writing. We would like to conclude by telling you about future opportunities to practice your literacy skills, to use writing as a powerful learning tool, and to develop the writing skills that will be important for your professional careers.

Writing Certificate Program

The University of Georgia offers an interdisciplinary certificate program in writing. The purpose of the Writing Certificate Program (WCP) is to give undergraduate students from all colleges and majors at the University of Georgia an opportunity to develop and document their writing skills as they move from First-year Composition through the core curriculum and their academic majors en route to further education, professional training, or the workplace. Their writing skills will be developed in the context of their particular academic studies and interests and will be documented in a capstone electronic portfolio developed in a one-hour workshop course, **ENGL 4834: Electronic Writing Portfolio Workshop,** that presents and reflects on the students' writing projects and experiences throughout their undergraduate career. The writing done for the WCP will enhance students' understanding in their chosen field of study and will provide evidence to outside evaluators (such as admissions committees or employers) of the students' critical thinking, research, and communication skills, plus their understanding of genres and conventions of writing within their chosen discipline. For more information about the program, visit: http://write.uga.edu.

Writing Intensive Program (WIP)

The Writing Intensive Program at the University of Georgia provides students with opportunities to strengthen their writing throughout their undergraduate experience. The program offers writing-intensive courses in varying disciplines—from Art History to Biology to Music to Sociology, for example. A key goal of the program is to foster student writing *in the disciplines*, by helping students understand the conventions—or "ways of knowing"—of a particular field: how knowledge is constructed and communicated, and what rules of evidence and argumentation are practiced. To accomplish the goals of the program, each Writing Intensive Program

(WIP) course is supported by a specially trained "writing coach," who works with students to improve their writing and performance in the course by providing constructive and personal feedback. The advantages of this coaching—and WIP courses, in general—are many. A compelling majority of students enrolled in these courses consistently report that their experience with the Writing Intensive Program strengthened their writing skills; built their confidence in the writing process; encouraged a deeper engagement in course content, discussions, and assignments; taught them the writing conventions of their discipline; heightened their critical thinking skills; and prepared them for writing in other courses and future goals, such as graduate school or career-related work. **All WIP courses count toward requirements for the Writing Certificate Program**.

For more information about the program and its benefits, as well as for a list of current WIP courses, visit: http://**www.wip.uga.edu**.

The Major and Minor in English

The skills in writing and critical thinking that you have learned in First-year Composition will serve you well if you decide to major or minor in English. English majors learn to read, interpret, and analyze texts (novels, stories, plays, films, poems, essays, images, and other forms of cultural production) and to write with poise, brevity, and elegance. Majors can choose Areas of Emphasis for their Program of Study; areas of Emphasis include Creative Writing, American Literature, Multicultural American Literature, Rhetoric and Composition, Humanities Computing, Medieval Literature, Studies in the Novel, Poetics, Advanced Studies in English, Interdisciplinary Renaissance Studies, and English Language Studies. Majors and minors can go on to careers in almost anything: teaching, publishing, law, journalism, management, human resources, business communication, medicine, grant-writing, screen-writing, technical writing, and so on. Employers take an English major or minor as evidence of strong skills in writing, creativity, and critical thinking. You can find more information about the English major and minor at the program website: https://www.english.uga.edu/undergrad/pages/9.

Declared English majors may join the Student Advisory Council, "SAC," and help plan events such as graduation and our new undergraduate speaker series, "Life after Park Hall." Contact the Undergraduate English Office in Park 111 for more information.

Advanced Courses in Writing

The English Department offers several upper-division courses in writing that are open to students in other majors. The Academic Enhancement Program, housed in Milledge Hall, also offers an array of writing classes for native and non-native speakers.

UNIV 1105. Improving Grammar, Usage, and Style. 3 hours.
Athena Title: IMPROVING GRAMMAR.

> This course teaches students to master formal grammar rules and terminology, to achieve a clear, fluent writing style, and to recognize common problems of usage so that they can effectively write and edit papers for academic and professional audiences.
>
> **Note**: Students may enroll in this course simultaneously with ENGL 1101.

UNIV 1115. Introduction to Academic Writing. 3 hours (institutional credit).
Athena Title: Academic Writing.

> The objective of the course is to prepare students for the kinds of writing required in English 1101 and other University courses. To meet that objective, UNIV 1115 stresses strategies for generating ideas and improving writing fluency, conventions of academic usage and style, patterns for organizing thought and arranging written material, and critical thinking and analysis. In the classroom and in individualized instruction, students receive extensive practice drafting, editing, and revising expository and persuasive essays.
>
> **Note**: This course carries institutional credit and will not count toward graduation.

UNIV 1117. Basic Composition for Multilingual Writers. 3 hours (institutional credit).
Athena Title: MULTILINGUAL COMP.

> This course is designed for both undergraduate and graduate students whose first language is not English. Its objectives include mastering English grammar, idioms, and sentence structure; building an academic vocabulary; and composing short academic papers. The course emphasizes problems that non-native speakers typically experience with proofreading, revision, and writing for an American audience. Assignments may be tailored to students' majors.
>
> **Note**: This course carries institutional credit and will not count toward graduation.

ENGL 3590W. Technical Communication. 3 hours.
Athena Title: TECH AND PROF COMM.

> This course deals with writing in the professional domains, with an emphasis on research methods, clear and accurate presentation of ideas and data, and computer-mediated communication. If you want an introduction to the role of writing in the workplace, this course would be for you.

ENGL 3600W. Advanced Composition. 3 hours.
Athena Title: ADV COMPOSITION

> Advanced Composition focuses less on professional contexts than on writing as a process, with an emphasis on the conventions of discourse situations, invention, revision, editorial skills, and document design. This course is particularly useful for students who want to practice and improve their academic writing.

ENGL 3850S. Writing and Community. 3 hours.
Athena Title: WRITING AND COMMUNITY

> This course is a study of how writing functions in the formation and maintenance of communities and the role of written communication in addressing community needs and concerns. It will have a service-learning component in addition to being writing intensive, with students creating texts about community issues and for community partners.

ENGL 3860W. Science Writing for General Audiences. 3 hours.
Athena Title: SCIENCE WRITING GENERAL AUDIEN.

> Clearly conveying complex scientific information to the public is becoming increasingly important. This course is a writing-intensive introduction to reading and writing about scientific research in order to bring scientific information to the general public.

ENGL 4830W. Advanced Studies in Writing. 3 hours.
Athena Title: ADV STUDIES WRITING.

> Advanced study of writing as process and product, focusing on particular discourse situations or kinds of texts. Topics might typically be advanced technical communication, academic writing for literary scholars, or text and hypertext.

ENGL 4831W. The Critical Essay. 3 hours.
Athena Title: CRITICAL ESSAY.

> The primary goal of the course will be to initiate students into the academic dialogue practiced by scholars of English. Each student will join this scholarly conversation by producing a research-based, academic paper of 20 to 30 pages in length about some aspect of English Studies to be workshopped in stages throughout the drafting process.

ENGL 4832W. Writing for the World Wide Web. 3 hours.
Athena Title: WRITING FOR THE WEB.

> This class deals with both the theory and practice of digital rhetoric and composition. Here you will learn to use the basic tools to construct a wide variety of digital, multimodal texts for a range of audiences and purposes.

ENGL 4833W. Composition Theory and Pedagogy. 3 hours.
Athena Title: COMP PEDAGOGY

> This course introduces you to the history and theories of college composition teaching. With a strong practical emphasis, ENGL 4833 prepares students to work as college writing tutors or as classroom writing assistants.

ENGL 4836W. Writing about Health and Medicine. 3 hours.
Athena Title: WRITING ABOUT HEALTH AND MED.

> This writing-intensive English course introduces students to the narrative arts and trains them to identify, construct, and use narrative in fictional and non-fictional writing about health, wellness, medicine, and able-bodiedness.

ENGL 4837W. Digital Storytelling. 3 hours.
Athena Title: DIGITAL STORYTELLING.

> An introduction to the study and practice of narrative within digital environments. Students will work independently and collaboratively to analyze and create digital stories. At the end of the semester, students will participate in a Digital Story Showcase to share their work with a public audience.

CHAPTER TEN

Donald E. Barnett Awards for
2015–2016

Donald E. Barnett Awards for 2015–2016

Each year, the First-year Composition Program recognizes excellent writing in English 1101, 1102, and 1103 by presenting three Barnett Awards. Named in honor of Donald E. Barnett, who directed the Freshman English Program for many years, the awards consist of cash prizes and publication of the winning compositions in the *First-year Composition Guide* required of all students registered in our courses and on the FYC site at http://www.english.uga.edu/fyc/pages/10.

The following essay, nominated by Al Dixon, was written by English 1101 student, Sujith Vadlamudi, who won the 2015 Barnett essay award.

Miss Anachronism

The morning after she was crowned Miss America in 1951, in a meeting with Miss America's board of directors, Yolande Betbeze was shocked to learn she was expected to attend a variety of public events in her bathing suit. One engagement in particular perturbed her: appearing in a Milwaukee department store wearing nothing but a bathing suit and heels. Betbeze outright refused to be paraded in such a state (Sinclair). She believed that such antics were unbecoming of the winner of a scholarship competition. Unfortunately, she didn't realize that she hadn't won a scholarship competition; she had won a beauty pageant. Of the countless forms of female objectification present in popular culture, one of the most high profile and controversial examples is the Miss America Pageant. The Pageant explicitly reinforces the idea that a woman's form is significantly more important than her function, as it's little more than a yearly ritual of ceremoniously judging a woman's body. Despite the many changes implemented throughout the years, every aspect of the Miss

---

America competition is deeply rooted in the belief that a woman's value is primarily based on her appearance and—implicitly—on how desirable she is to men.

The Miss America Pageant was first held in Atlantic City in 1921, following the success of another beauty pageant held the previous year by a handful of businessmen seeking to capitalize on the appeal of young, attractive women (MissAmerica.org). At its genesis, the Pageant was fairly candid about its intentions. The organizers of the early Pageants believed that gathering a host of beautiful women together in one place would attract a great deal of attention—and money—from all over the country (PBS). They were right. Advertisements, promising nothing more than a bathing suit parade featuring the most beautiful women in the country, were widely circulated in anticipation of the inaugural event. The scantily clad bodies of young women was all Miss America offered and, for the hundred thousand people that flocked to the inaugural pageant, that was enough. Following the staggering turnout, the men behind the first Miss America competition were convinced they had a winning formula on their hands. So, for the next eight years, the subsequent pageants they organized attempted to replicate the pageant of 1921 as faithfully as possible. This meant that for the rest of the decade—the same decade that saw the enfranchisement of women—the sole focus of the competition that purported to elect a woman to represent all of the United States was physical appearance. Following the established precedent, the judges charged with evaluating a contestant's looks went about their task without the slightest discretion. They went as far as disparately rating individual body parts. Points were awarded for different appendages (five points for the construction of the head and the limbs, three points for the torso, two points for the legs, etc), mirroring a butcher shop that might charge different amounts for different cuts of meat (PBS). The way the pageant evaluated living, breathing people was so thorough and effective, it can't simply be called objectification; it was an explicit denial of personhood. The proceedings of the early pageants obviate the possible existence of any altruistic motivations for the creation and continuation of the Miss America Pageant. The financiers of the pageant had wanted nothing more than to use the bodies of young women to make a large amount of money. Even at the time, this blatant sexual objectification taking place in Atlantic City disgusted large swaths of people all over the country—albeit for a variety of different reasons. Conservative religious groups joined forces with liberal women's clubs and waged an all-out PR war. Unwilling to see Atlantic City's reputation tarnished, the city's Chamber of Commerce canceled the pageant (PBS). Had the story of Miss America ended there, the cancelation of future pageants would have been one of the many strides women made towards equality that decade. Unfortunately, that wasn't the case.

In less than four years, the Great Depression gutted the city's economy, and Atlantic City could no longer afford to turn away the large amounts of money the extremely well attended pageant was sure to generate. Thus, in 1933, Atlantic City's moneyed interests revived the pageant and scheduled a nominally new Miss America Pageant—which was, in reality, a facsimile of its previous iteration—to take place later that year (MissAmerica.org). Fully cognizant of all of the reasonable objections previously raised by concerned Americans all over the country, the organizers of the 1933 pageant did nothing to address a single complaint. Even though small, common-sense procedural changes could have shown that, at the very least, Miss America had the young contenders' best interest at heart. Consequently, everyone—including the contestants themselves—understood that the women's bodies were the reason for all the pomp, circumstance, and excitement Miss America provided. The 1933 pageant, the first one after Miss America's brief suspension, saw fifteen year-old Marion Setzer crowned. She later said of her victory, "To the judge's eyes, I was the typical American girl. Totally unsophisticated, very naïve, had a lot of enthusiasm, had a lot of talent that they didn't ask for, but I did have that. . . My figure then as they described it was a typical Mae West figure which was hourglass, thirty-four bust, a twenty-six waist, eighty-two buns" (PBS). Despite being an underclassman in high school at the time, Setzer was able to discern what the judges found important.

As Miss America endured through the years, surviving to this very day, it embraced a variety of changes in order to remain relevant. These changes certainly haven't resolved all of the issues presented by beauty pageants, in general, and Miss America, in particular, but they at least attempt to afford contestants some respect. The first round of meaningful changes to Miss America came in 1935, when a nude statue of that year's sixteen year-old winner was unveiled in her hometown (Pittsburgh Post-Gazette). Amid a media firestorm, the pageant turned to twenty nine year-old public relations specialist, Lenora Slaughter. Her guidance over the course of the next thirty years is largely responsible for making Miss America what it is today. As soon as she took the job, Slaughter instituted a strict set of rules designed to protect the Pageant from any further ignominy. She set a minimum age requirement of eighteen, added a talent portion to accompany the swimsuit competition, required contestants to be in the company of a chaperone at all times, instituted a curfew, banned contestants from visiting bars or taverns, and forbade any private interactions with men (PBS). In many ways the changes Slaughter wrought did have some beneficial effects: Her rules compelled judges to consider something more substantial than looks when selecting a winner. Furthermore, disallowing participants under the age of eighteen prevented the sexualizing of children on Miss America's stage. But, along with the changes that infused Miss America with common decency, Slaughter also enacted measures that, while reducing the degree of objectification to which the competitors were directly subjected, firmly reaffirmed a woman's inferior societal position. Rules restricting where and with whom pageant contestants spent their time robbed the women of their autonomy. Counterintuitively, the rules designed to limit the undue sexualizing faced by the participants of preceding pageants only perpetuated the notion that women had to be treated like fragile objects that need to be protected and watched over.

Slaughter's initial round of reforms had their shortcomings, but she was not one to rest on her laurels. Before long, despite having fully rehabilitated Miss America's public image, she implemented more changes in an attempt to make the competition even more rewarding to the women actually competing in it. While the policies she put into place before aimed to protect the contestants, the measures she would later implement were designed to *empower* women. In 1944, at the height of America's war time efforts, Lenora Slaughter accomplished something truly remarkable: she established, and found sponsors to fund, a scholarship prize for the pageant's winner. Slaughter's scholarship plan challenged the zeitgeist of the time. Despite an abundance of over 200 sponsors bankrolling the pageant, Slaughter was able to convince no more than five to fund the scholarship (MissAmerica.org).

After successfully incorporating a scholarship into the pageant, Slaughter spent the rest of the decade championing the rights of her gender within the competition. It was during her tenure at the helm that Miss America saw the incorporation of a talent portion, a "Personality and Intellect" category, and an "on stage question" segment. Slaughter even required contestants wear one-piece bathing suits that covered more of their body (PBS). Unfortunately, her efforts to innovate eventually succumbed to increasing opposition on several fronts. Even relatively inconsequential measures—like allowing the winner to be crowned in her evening gown instead of her bathing suit—were met with fierce opposition from the pageant's financiers. Slaughter resorted to making minute changes. For example, she replaced the term "bathing" with the term "swim," believing that a swimsuit sounded less demeaning than bathing suit (Riverol). Aside from minor procedural tweaks, 1947 proved to be the last time the pageant underwent any kind of substantial transformation.

After being rebuffed by Yolanda Betbeze in 1951, Miss America's biggest sponsor, Catalina Swimsuits—already weary of Slaughter's progressive changes—pulled their support for Miss America. Catalina even started two pageants of their own in order to challenge Miss America's hegemony (Deam). The undue pressure from Catalina ended with their sponsorship in 1952, but it did little to change the state of affairs at Miss America. Less than two years after Catalina's departure, the Miss America Competition rocketed into the stratosphere when the pageant was broadcast nationwide by ABC. Nearly half of America's television audience, more than 47 million people, tuned in, making Miss America the most viewed television program to date (PBS). The success of the television broadcast ensured that the basic structure and the format of pageant would stay the same.

Slaughter's scholarship would prove to be her most significant and impactful contribution to Miss America. If the pageant's website is any indication, its addition was one of the most important moments in Miss America's long history. The telecasts of pageants today are littered with references to their scholarship fund, as is the Pageant's website. If not for the abundance of women showing more skin than they covered, Miss America could be mistaken for a run of the mill scholarship competition. The incessant talk of scholarships, unfortunately, is just that—talk. The Miss America foundation claims to offer over 45 million dollars in scholarships to young women (MissAmerica.org). In reality though, the pageant spends no more than 500,000 dollars on scholarships (Oliver). John Oliver, as part of an investigation on his HBO program *Last Week*

Tonight, uncovered the reason for the discrepancy after poring through all the public tax records of every national, state, and local Miss America pageant he could get his hands on. He reported, in an obvious state of disbelief, that the most generous analysis of financial records indicated that Miss America grossly misrepresented the amount awarded to pageant winners and contestants. The pageant calculates every possible scholarship a participant can accept in theory, even though, in actuality, a contestant can only accept one of the scholarships offered to them. Thus, the pageant can claim with much braggadocio to "make available" 45 million dollars to young women while, in reality, only awarding less than one percent of that (*Last Week Tonight with John Oliver*).

Almost as disingenuous as the pageant's scholarship claims are the segments of the Pageant intended to perpetuate the notion that Miss America is primarily a scholarship competition. The façade is mainly supported by the question and answer portion of the show. Its mere existence would seem to indicate that Miss America was concerned with more than just outward appearance. Unfortunately, the question and answer portion—like every other part of the competition—is less about what the competitors say than how they say it. The questioning portion, in its earliest iteration, makes this painfully obvious, and subsequent alterations prove to be inadequate in overcoming the segments insidious roots. In 1947, when the on-stage interview was first given a prominent place along the swimsuit and talent segments, the questions posed to the women were brutally honest about the pageant's view of women and what they had to say. They were inane or outright hostile to women.

One contestant was asked what she thought was the best way to start a conversation with a young man. The woman answering the question dutifully responded that when starting a conversation with a young man, the focus should be on him and his interests. She suggested sports and, if he isn't receptive to that, she recommended staying "quiet for the rest of the evening." Another contestant was asked if women have "become too dominant" and were at risk of usurping men in society. She indignantly answered, "I believe that there are far too many women in the working world. I can see many cases where this is a necessary arrangement, but I do feel that a woman's place is in the home with her husband and with her children" (PBS). In recent years the questions were revamped and seemingly more relevant to issues in the real world. In 2014, for example, Miss Virginia was asked how, in light of recent beheadings, ISIS should be dealt with. Such a question has no simple answer and continues to puzzle policy makers, scholars, and heads of state all over the world today. Asking an eighteen year old such a complex question, just moments after she was paraded around the stage in a bikini, is truly laughable and clear evidence that her response is immaterial to the pageant. Unsurprisingly, despite a remarkably coherent and sensible response—so impressive, in fact, that John Oliver quipped that Miss Virginia did a better job of addressing the issue than President Obama had done in his previous week's address to the nation—Miss Virginia was not crowned the winner (*Last Week Tonight with Jon Oliver*). On the other hand, this year's pageant saw Miss Georgia crowned despite not making much sense while answering a much simpler question. News outlets and bloggers were quick to question how she could have won the pageant after making a fool of herself during the question and answer portion. The answer is obvious: Miss Georgia certainly sounded like a fool, but she looked great doing it.

Ultimately, the scope of the direct damage inflicted by the Miss America Pageant is relatively small. No more than fifty women can be tricked into participating in their dehumanizing exhibition. Unfortunately, the number of the pageant's immediate victims pales in comparison to the number of women it victimizes indirectly. The pageant establishes an ideal every time it crowns a young woman "Miss America." As a *New York Times* editorial proclaimed after the very first pageant in 1921, "Margaret Gorman represents the type of womanhood America needs," the *Times* declared, "strong, red-blooded, able to shoulder the responsibilities of homemaking and motherhood. It is in her type that the hope of the country rests." From the very beginning, the significance of Miss America wasn't lost on anyone. During World War II, all public events were discontinued—except the Miss America Pageant. Organizers successfully argued that Miss America was a vital part of the culture that would help the war effort if allowed to continue as normal (PBS). As Kathy Peiss, an American historian, noted in her book *Hope in a Jar: The Making of America's Beauty Culture*, beautiful women are a reminder of the women left behind; they were a reason to keep fighting. After the war, pageant winners weren't reminders to men but, rather, to other women. Miss America became the standard bearer for all women. She was the pinnacle that all women should mold themselves after. In the words of former Miss America CEO, Leonard Horn, "[t]he concept of Miss America as an ideal American woman was consistent with society's ideas of what an ideal young woman was. She was your everyday young girl who any man would be happy to call daughter, any man would be happy to call wife. Miss America was the American girl next door. She was an ideal that many women aspired to." By selecting the best looking woman even though she was not the most talented or the most articulate, the message to other women is clear: It's important to be talented, and being able to hold conversation is desirable, but looking good is of the utmost importance. The pageant precludes the notion of subjective beauty. Instead, it operates under the assumption that there exists an objective metric with which a woman's beauty and, by extension, the very essence of her femininity can be measured. By presenting an unattainable image of the ideal woman, Miss America not only reinforces noxious gender roles and stereotypes, but also implies that a majority of women have failed at womanhood itself.

Works Cited

Deam, Jenny. "There She Goes Miss America." *The Denver Post*. 11 Oct. 2005. Web. 2015.

Ferrari, Michelle. "Miss America." *American Experience*. Dir. Lisa Ades. Prod. Lisa Ades and Lesli Klainberg. PBS. GPB, 27 Jan. 2002. Television.

"Miss America History." *Miss America: Miss Americas History*. Web. 2015.

"Miss America of 1921 Wed." *New York Times.* 1925-11-16.

Peiss, Kathy Lee. *Hope in a Jar: The Making of America's Beauty Culture*. New York: Metropolitan, 1998. Print.

Perota, Joe, dir. "Episode #1.18." *Last Week Tonight with John Oliver*. HBO.

    21 Sept. 2014. Television.

Riverol, Armando. *Live from Atlantic City: The History of the Miss America*

    Pageant Before, After, and in Spite of Television. Bowling Green,

    OH: Bowling Green State U Popular, 1992. Print.

Sinclair, Rachel. "Yolande Betbeze Fox: Alabama's First Miss America

    Reflects on Title more than 60 Years Later." *AL.Com*. 09 Sept. 2014.

    Web. 2015.

"Timeline: Miss America." *PBS*. PBS, Web. 2015.

Farrah Agha

Dr. Carmen Comeaux

ENGL 1102

7 February 2015

Sexism in "The Free Radio"

Salman Rushdie's "The Free Radio" reflects the heavy gender bias of twenty-first century rural India. Rushdie's narrator recounts the tale of a animated rickshaw driver, Ramani, who is misled into agreeing to a vasectomy in exchange for a state-sponsored free radio; yet the radio never arrives, and Ramani seems to become slowly disillusioned with his reality. Ramani's path is purportedly chosen for him by the woman whom he eventually marries, a widow who desires no more children. Although ultimately both the widow and Ramani are, in many ways, powerless, suffering poverty and great hardship, it is the widow who is repeatedly blamed for Ramani's seemingly exponential misfortune. The widow is vilified due to her unconventional independence and initiative.

The narrator, an old man obviously colored by the sexism of his time, introduces the widow as an almost unstoppable, destructive force. She appears almost inhuman, described as having "claws" or "hooks," and as lurking in the shadows, waiting for the opportune time to strike. When out with her five children, they are depicted as a pack, with the widow ahead, leading her brood. When the widow begins to pursue Ramani, this imagery is heightened, as older women courting younger men are often, quite sexistly, viewed as predators. Yet, this initial characterization is not truly due to the widow's actions, but rather to her perceived identity as a tainted woman.

The widow possesses none of the characteristics of the stereotypical, upright woman in the 1900s. In a nation where widows were once burned following their husbands' deaths, the widow wholly retains her independence and is able to support her five children through her own means, as her husband "left her not one new paisa." She is no longer innocent, and in taking up with Ramani, she proves herself not to be chaste either. Her perceived worldliness and independence prove quite controversial for the setting.

Though the narrator presents her as somewhat wild and freewheeling, it is starkly evident that the widow is simply attempting to provide for her children and save herself from greater hardship. Struggling to support her large family, the widow is barely able to feed her children; the narrator decides that she is able to afford "three grains of dahl." Though the narrator is not entirely reliable, he even claims that the widow has resorted to prostitution to sustain her family. Certainly, any woman desperate enough to take such a path cannot be said to be in a position of power. The widow must demean herself and suffer in her children's name, but she is ultimately condemned by conservative society for her self-reliance.

When the widow later enters into a relationship with Ramani, the narrator depicts her as cruelly manipulating the young man, twisting his will in an effort to provide a better life for her family. However, while Ramani is often clueless, it is quite hard to believe that he does not understand the burden of six mouths to feed. "He was not such a fool that he didn't know" his own value, or the price he would pay in committing to this woman. The widow can only do so much to coax him into a relationship; Ramani is an adult, and, at some point, he becomes responsible for his own actions.

Though the widow receives the entirety of the blame, Ramani is as accountable, if not more so, for his own fate as she is. When Ramani proposes, she declines, as she cannot afford to bear more children. Still the two are eventually married, and Ramani joyously declares that he has "made it possible for [him] to marry [his] woman," in reference to his recent vasectomy. In marrying Ramani, the widow has, in a way, done what is expected of her by tying herself to a man. However, her actions are still fervently criticized, as she is still the one to hold the power in the relationship; she initially pursues Ramani by hailing a rickshaw, and she possesses an intellect that he lacks. This initiative and awareness causes her to be regarded with fear and distrust.

Yet the widow is not wholly condemned until it is revealed that Ramani undergoes a vasectomy in order to be with her. In supporting and quite likely instigating Ramani's actions, the widow is perceived as depriving a young man of his bright future, for the benefit of only her own shameful indulgence. However, the widow is attempting to protect her family; they are hungry, and she cannot sustain another child. Therefore, she has to sacrifice her morality in the name of her children's survival.

It is somewhat unexpected, however, that the widow's marriage to Ramani garners her only louder and more widespread disapproval. Generally, independent women are forced to suffer society's criticisms, hailing claims of selfishness and the like, while, on the other hand, women who tie themselves to a man satisfy the perceived criteria for a good life and are commended for their sacrifice. The widow's story, therefore, presents the ultimate sexist paradox: she is condemned for both her independence and her willing dependence.

Though the widow seems to be the prevailing force in her marriage, ultimately, she is still a woman in a highly conservative, sexist society: how much power can she truly hold? While she does prompt Ramani's vasectomy and their later move to Bombay, she is eternally weighed down by her many burdens: her history, her children, and even her gender. She appears intelligent and capable, but her power and position are strictly limited.

Due to her gender, the widow is deprived of many freedoms, but most glaringly, she is denied an identity. Her name is not given in the text, only her role in relation to a man. First, she is a widow, then a wife. Though she is singularly self-reliant, the widow's independence is not deemed to be appropriate, and so, it is not recognized; she remains a shadow of the man she is with. She is continually degraded because she dares to be a woman, alone.

The widow is condemned because of her status as a self-sufficient woman. Though she suffers greatly to ensure the survival of her family, she cannot overcome the stigma of her independence as a woman. While her story is specific to the political turmoil in India in the 1970s, the expectations and judgments placed on the widow as a woman are universally applicable. Regardless of how progressive a society claims to be, women are quite often expected to be only so independent and eventually to surrender their lives and settle down. However, each woman is free to shape her own future regardless of society's expectations. Just as the widow found herself fat and happy in Bombay, every woman is able, if truly willing, to have control over her own life.

Works Cited

Rushdie, Salman. "The Free Radio." *The Bedford Introduction to Literature.* Ed. Michael Meyer. Boston: Bedford/St. Martin's, 2008. 696-701. Print.

CHAPTER ELEVEN

Michael G. Moran Electronic Portfolio Awards for 2015–2016

Michael G. Moran Awards for 2015–2016

Beginning in 2007, the First-year Composition Program began recognizing the excellent work being done in electronic portfolios for English 1101, 1102, and 1103 by presenting three portfolio awards. Named in honor of Michael G. Moran, a former director of FYC who did much to shape and improve the program, the awards consist of cash prizes and publication in the *First-year Composition Guide* required of all students registered in our courses and on the FYC site at: https://english.uga.edu/fyc/pages/11.

English 1101

Student: John Henline

Allow Myself to Introduce. . . Myself

Life's journey will sometimes take you back along a path you've taken before. Which is not to say that the starting point is always the finish line, but you might find yourself returning to familiar territory every once in a while. And that's fine; what we do between the start and finish are the important bits. I like to believe the journey is more important than the finish.

This is my portfolio biography, the introduction to the finale. A fitting venue, then, for talk of starts and finishes. It is also the final first assignment to the first college-level writing course of my entire life. Not such monumental news, really. I'm sure, to professors of First-year Composition, since that it is the standard you see every semester. How should I set my biography apart from all the other students' submissions, then? I strongly considered going with an analogy about elephants returning to the place of their birth to die, but that seemed too dreary for an introduction. Instead, you get something we all love and enjoy, retro 80s pictures!

That's me on the right, circa 8-bit Nintendo and Reaganomics. I am what you might consider "thirty-five years old." If you are among the peers with whom I spend the majority of my day, you'd probably shorten that to just plain "old." I never stop marveling at this notion, of my being a colleague and cohort with a crowd I could consider "just a bunch of kids." Which is actually really awesome since I love feeling like a kid. I get to do it as much as I want these days! Previous to this semester, I was a normal, middle-class office employee with exactly the type of responsibilities you would imagine. Before that, I was in the Army, living a life where every minute of every day was planned weeks in advance (usually without my consent). Before that, I was the same type of post-high school kid that I call my peer today. The same kid sitting next to me in English 1101, just fifteen or twenty years removed and with a little less hair on top. In my high-school years and before, even as far back as kindergarten, writing was what I wanted to do with my life. That is likely a sentiment you see way too often in First-year Composition portfolios, but bear with me for one minute. English professors love a book worm, I know, and I'm not here to butter you up with my love for literature. I do remember reading my first word, though, or at least I remember the first time I saw letters on a page and recognized them for what they were: "the." I guess, in terms of English Composition autobiographies, this is as good a place to start as any.

There I am, in kindergarten or first grade or sometime around then, and I can read. Pretty cool, right? I even liked reading! I did a lot of it, any time I could, really. In school, at home, with friends, basically any time I had to myself, I was turning a page or returning a stack of books to the library dropbox. By the sixth grade I was a locust, devouring Madeleine L'Engle and Stephen King with reckless abandon. I started to write for myself, too, penning short stories and songs but nothing serious. I felt, at that time, like my real talent and passion were in editing the work of others. You know that feeling when you see a typo in some random trade paperback, probably in its tenth or twelfth printing, and you wonder at all the people who glanced over it in all the years of that book being written and revised and republished? I loved that feeling, knowing that you found the error that everyone else read past. This was my plight in the world at age twelve: to eradicate the paperback typo.

As is the case with childhood passions, I soon found time for other things in life, and my love for literature waned on my way into middle school. I was still reading, but not so often for myself. In fact, I was reading quite a bit as a result of my schoolwork, which rubbed me the wrong way: who were my teachers to decide what I was going to do with my time? Writing assignments left me feeling the same sort of sourness, leading to my doing the bare minimum and achieving even less. I took to creative writing easily through high school, but I lacked the passion to look at my assignments as anything more than chores. Ultimately, I graduated with decent grades and enlisted in the Army shortly afterward. I find it interesting in retrospect, because I had literally the entire scope of military careers to choose from, everything from infantry rifleman to nuclear engineer, and after not liking schoolwork so much, I still chose to be a reporter. I decided that I would write structured, serialized, standardized assignments all day long, the very thing that soured the taste of writing for me in high school. But I knew I had a knack for it, and it seemed to suit me well. I didn't so much mind the work as much as I imagined.

After leaving the Army, I was again faced with that always-daunting life decision: how was I going to earn a living? To keep a long story short, I got a job writing. Yes, of all things, writing. I accepted an entry-level Quality Assurance position at a small software company, writing step-by-step processes, test cases, and help pages for our customers and employees. All very much in-line with what I had been doing in the Army, and almost exactly what I claimed to loathe about writing for the previous decade of my life. But, I saw an opportunity to progress in my career, and I had found that I didn't so much mind the mundane side of writing: it was easy work, and I didn't have to put forth much effort to get decent content released and to keep the boss happy. Within five years, I had transitioned into the company's newly-established training department as a technical trainer and course developer (even more step-by-step exercises and user manuals), eventually moving into a position where I could dictate the content of the coursework I was writing. Now things would be different; I was the person in charge of the mundane assignments! I was even living my childhood dream, editing other writer's typos all day long. Such a glorious life, am I right? Well, after a few years of my dream job, I decided it was time for something new. I thought to give college a try (albeit a few years late), and here I am.

Just a fresh-faced freshman in English 1101, surrounded by a classroom of peers in the same unfamiliar, uneasy position. To be honest about it, the majority of them are miles ahead of me in the things that really matter, things like MLA formatting and identifying appositives. I am hoping my portfolio will tell a story, but it may be the same one being told by everyone else in my class, the same one you will read a hundred-some-odd times before getting to start your holiday break. Because while I learned a hell of a lot in this class, this semester of study has taught me that I have a long way to go before I am the best writer I can be. Having said that, here is my best work from this semester; I'm hoping that you won't have to deal with too many typos.

Another Day, Another Rhetorical Device

I am in a unique position as a First-year Composition student in his mid-thirties: I have a vast amount I would like to say about myself and the world, yet I lack the technical and rhetorical prowess to express myself efficiently. So, while I may have a lot to say, I don't have the skills necessary to say much of anything. At least, this was my position in August of this year, at the start of the semester and at my introduction to college-level writing.

For as long as I can remember, I have always been a big proponent of the written word. I have been a lover of books and writing for my entire life, and learned the "Dos" and "Don'ts" of writing through my exposure to books. Which is to say, I might be a damn good reader, but good readers don't necessarily make the best writers, at least not in the sense of proficiency. I find it interesting, then, that my first aspirations for gainful employment came at a young age and were geared immediately towards writing as a profession. At around the age of twelve, I forewent the traditional soldier/policeman/fireman/doctor route and boldly professed my intention to be an editor. Not a writer, but a technician in rhetoric all the same. Throughout my public schooling I took to writing naturally, but did not invest very much in improving my abilities. I instead relied upon the experiences I gathered as a reader in order to direct my writing, and as a result, I believe I had (and perhaps still have) an unnecessarily elevated opinion of my writing skill.

My continued love for literature post-high school still pushed me towards writing as a career, but at the time I thought I knew everything

I needed to know about the subject. Already having a good sense of English grammar and sentence structure meant I was able to form complete, coherent thoughts on paper. That's all there is to it, right? For my chosen career path as a technical writer and training course developer, it was almost enough. I am technical-savvy, and can understand advanced computer networking concepts. I have the skills needed to translate this information into technical literature about a specific topic. But I was still by no means an "expert" in rhetoric. Ten years later, despite a decade of professional, full-time employment as a technical writer, I am still severely lacking in any real rhetorical or literary expertise. At the start of this semester, I could not differentiate between simple and complex sentences, nor explain a transitive vs. intransitive verb, nor did I understand any but the most simplistic rhetorical devices. In other words, I lacked the *rhetoric* of rhetoric.

Consider this: you bring your vehicle to an auto mechanic to resolve an issue, and you are attempting to explain in mutually-understood terms where the problem lies. The mechanic may have the most advanced knowledge possible in his or her field. He or she will be able to diagnose your issue using expensive, specialized equipment, and be able to draw upon years of experience to do so. Yet, as the owner of the vehicle, and someone with no technical knowledge in this field, it is still up to you to attempt to explain to the mechanic where to start looking for the problem.

"It makes a noise when I turn left," you might say.

"What kind of noise?" the mechanic asks, "Like a grinding noise? A bumping or knocking sound?"

You're at a loss, but stammer out, "It kind of goes, 'Whirl-whirl-whirl-whiiiiirl,' and makes a grinding sound, then goes away once I straighten out the steering wheel."

Without skipping a beat, the mechanic replies: "It sounds like a bad wheel bearing to me, shouldn't take but an afternoon to fix."

In this example, the mechanic uses a combination of technical and practical experience to diagnose your problem, even though you have only provided a very elementary list of symptoms. In other words, only basic language and a fundamental knowledge are required to describe the problem, but finding the solution requires real experience and expertise. I started this semester feeling very much like the customer in this example: I knew my writing had problems, and could perhaps go so far as to point out the problem to an expert in the field, but could not explain in technical or specific terms why my writing didn't "sound right."

It is a curious situation, though, because I adore writing (both the process and the results, but mostly the results). Especially creative writing. Not my own writing very often, but the entire concept of literature: I loved the idea put forth to us this semester which likened writers to time travelers, able to affect the past and the future through their words. This level of writing is not something that comes to me naturally, despite what I thought at age fifteen (and, perhaps, still think at age thirty-five). Nowadays, the more I read great prose, the more I feel akin to Ta-Nehisi Coates in his series of articles from *The Atlantic*:

Every time he brought me before a great poem I was injured, because I knew that I would never say anything that beautiful.

. . I was injured because this was one less beautiful thing in the world waiting to be written, and even though I knew there were many others, I would never get to write them. (Coates 4)

This is how I feel everyone should look at writing. I am the type that cannot stop revising what I write, even at a detriment to overall quality. I just can't resist going back to try and make my finished work the slightest bit better. To start this semester, we first focused on concision, something I struggled with from the very beginning as a result of my love for over-editing. Our assignment, to expound upon silence as a precursor to action or inaction, was at the time both the most personal and the most difficult thing I had ever written. It required that I throw out the majority of the "good" writing I had learned in my life and instead focus on my own writing and on how to improve it. I have included this essay as an example of my revision process, and in it you will see a deliberate change in the way I approached the assignment: my first draft reads like the writer I am, while my final draft reads like the writer I want to become. It is my first attempt at taking a writing assignment 100% at face value, and I was very pleased with end result.

This semester also marked my first real attempt at understanding complex grammatical structures. I have always been decent at grammar, but I never knew much about it from a technical standpoint. For example, at the start of the year I understood that an adverb here and not there might make a certain sentence easier to read, but couldn't explain why a split infinitive can lead to trouble for a reader. Our second assignment dealt with exactly this type of shortcoming, calling upon us to organize and analyze a sample from a famous author and a sample from our own writing. This assignment required intimate knowledge of sentence types, verb types, sentence structure, common syntax issues, and the parts of speech. We were tasked with breaking down our writing into its most basic form, and analyzing what makes up our own personal writing style. This assignment was also very eye-opening for me, giving me first an idea of how far lacking I was in this type of literary knowledge, and second, an avenue to get caught up with my studies. I learned more about the English language in this three-week span than I did throughout all of my prior schooling, and I think this shows when comparing my early and later analysis.

Towards the end of the semester we moved into more complex writing and analysis, something I enjoyed quite a bit. Our final essay asked us to provide an analytical response to one of three technical essays, using cited work and standard MLA format. At the time, I was completely unfamiliar with MLA format and the intricacies of formatting essays. My first exposure to MLA format was in this class, actually, and I look at this third essay assignment as the litmus test for my ability to move forward in college-level writing. This assignment required very specific formatting, a bibliography of works cited, and footnoting of sources, all of which were new to me a few months ago. Additionally, the assignment itself was a difficult one: "respond to an expert's analysis with your own analysis, and don't look like an idiot in the process." In retrospect, I see this essay as my first attempt at writing a traditional college paper and have included it in my portfolio to show my progress towards that goal.

Over the last few months, I have found that I need to work at writing in order to become a better writer. I need to study grammar, rhetoric, sentence structure, and other related concepts, even though I already have a passing familiarity with them. A technician in any specialized field must have the ability to communicate to other specialists, and the field of specialized writing is no different. I realized this semester that a passing familiarity with "good" writing will not by itself lead to my becoming a better writer. I am now finding myself feeling more and more like a rhetorical mechanic, and no longer the ignorant customer.

Works Cited

Coates, Ta-Nehisi. "Preface to a 30-Volume Love Note." *The Atlantic*. Atlantic Media Company, 12 Aug. 2013. Web. 02 Oct. 2015.

John Henline

Professor Camp

English 1101 1:25

12/6/2015

Exploring Silence: Portfolio Draft

Rarely will I not have anything to say, even when there's nothing to be said.

I get this from my Mom.

She is the most personable person I know.

The woman who raised me and my two brothers always has a lot to say, when it needs to be said.

She's outspoken, well-spoken, and chooses her words carefully.

She is a leader.

Someone you might take for granted, and recognize when they are gone.

A person you turn to when you are in trouble.

Or when you need to bend an ear.

She is also a felon, but more on that later.

I should mention that I have never known my real dad.

I remember meeting him once, after my grandfather passed away.

His father.

I was five or so.

I remember it was the first time I had ever worn a suit.

He arrived for the wake at my grandfather's house, after the service.

The place I had spent every summer of my life.

We would gather pecans under the lumbering backyard shade trees.

My grandma was Scottish, and made sure I was, too.

Grandpa would wake me at dawn for our Sunday flea market trip.

We'd rush to browse before the crowds arrived, and while the heat was bearable.

My grandfather had been "Poppy" to me.

His wife had been my "Granny."

I remember that it was autumn, the last time I went to Poppy's house.

Suddenly, he was there.

We were in the backyard, and pecans littered the ground around us.

They matched the brown of his hair, longer than you'd usually see.

I remember that I was glad I had worn my suit.

Afterward, he drove my two brothers and me to Radio Shack.

Let us each pick out a video game, and bought us a Nintendo.

I remember thinking he must be wealthy.

It is my first and last memory of him.

My mom remarried some time later.

I remember I was the ring bearer in the wedding.

It was the second time I wore a suit.

Her new husband was younger, just 19 at the time.

He worked construction, when there was work.

My mom, the accounts-payable manager for a large real estate firm.

The "Bread Winner."

She raised us in the hours between dinner and bedtime.

She taught me how to cook, how to do laundry, how to balance my checkbook.

To treat others as I would like to be treated.

He is important, though, my step-father.

He taught me about cars, music, and how to tell a joke.

He was a drinker, a drummer, and a fighter.

He played fast music and longed for a fast life.

He liked to spend money and complained that we didn't have much.

Sometimes he would fight with my mom and us boys.

If things escalated the police might come, and we wouldn't see him for a few days.

Either because my mom had taken us to stay somewhere.

Or because he left, either to jail, or to a bar to cool off.

But he is important, as I mentioned.

He eventually cleaned himself up.

Right around the time that I started Junior High.

He stopped drinking, started getting more steady work.

He opened his own business.

We seemed to be doing well as a family.

We had some extra money, and my mom was more herself.

They started another home business together.

At first glance things were looking up for us.

Something seemed to lurk under the surface, though.

A new kind of tension had replaced the old, familiar one.

And my step-dad started doing drugs.

I found this out later, but I think I knew at the time as well.

He also started buying things, expensive things.

A huge piece of California real estate for a motocross track, to start.

Motorcycles, trucks, jet-skis, motor homes, drugs.

Expensive things.

This is the part of the story where words start to fight me.

Let it be known that silence and I are not on great terms.

When one of us enters the room, and the other is present, we get anxious.

The space between us shrinks until there is no choice but for one to concede.

I'm usually quick to fill that void where the silence persists.

It's against my nature that I find talking about the next part difficult.

When I try to start, I begin to understand what it means to hate someone.

And I don't like thinking that way about family.

I blame my step-father for what happened to my mom and our family.

Sometimes I wonder what may have been, had my mom never met him, never fallen in love with him.

Because she did love him, I recognize that now.

She would have done anything for him.

She stuck by him in the bad times, even when he wasn't there for her.

She gave up our stability, so that he might start a future for us.

When his business was struggling and he needed money, she found it for him.

As a real-estate accountant, her firm's checkbook was her checkbook.

So, she wrote some checks to my step-dad's construction business.

A lot of checks.

Approximately $750,000 worth of checks.

Enough to buy motorcycles and a race track, trucks and trailers, utilities and maintenance, labor and tools, and everything else one might need to start a successful business.

She did this for him, but also for our family.

She wanted him to succeed, to be the bread-winner, the head of our household.

She also embezzled close to a million dollars in the process.

Right around the time that I was graduating High School, my mom and step-dad went to prison.

I think I have experienced a good amount in life, despite a fairly vanilla existence.

I am your average American by most accounts.

I was raised and destined to be middle-class.

I enlisted in the military, like my real father, and his father.

I've made a career and a living for myself.

I vote.

I'm personable, like my mom.

People tell me I am a natural leader.

I've never met a stranger.

And I always have something to say.

When I meet people, or start a new job, or give the obligatory first-day-of-class introduction, I tend to leave out a few details about my family and my formative years.

People ask about my parents, and I say that my mom is an amazing lady.

That she is the strongest woman I know.

I skip over the five golden years she spent at Chowchilla Women's Facility.

I leave out that, given the chance, I wouldn't mind fighting my step-father.

But these things are a part of me, just like my ability to cook Mexican food and fold laundry, or my tendencies towards fast cars and loud music.

My mom has great stories about prison, just ask her.

The people she met, the things she did to make the most of her time there.

How she got to be popular for her jailhouse burrito recipe.

Coincidentally meeting a high-school friend of mine on her first day inside, and how they became unconventional friends.

Doing the other inmates' hair, their black-market makeup operation.

Those are the stories she tells us, anyway.

The rest of my family talks openly about these early years, too.

Her trial, visiting her upstate.

The funds they raised for restitution to get her sentence reduced.

Pros and cons of the California criminal justice system.

I don't usually have a lot to add to these conversations.

I'd like to say something, but the words are hard to come by.

It's like that part of my life is not a part of Me.

As if the silence and I are at an impasse.

We notice each other, and I quietly step back.

Though I'm not ashamed of my mom; I am proud of what my family has become.

Certainly her having a criminal record lends me some kind of street cred.

I very well could flaunt it.

John Henline

Professor Camp

English 1101 1:25

12/7/2015

Personal Finance of Cultural and Social Capital: Portfolio Draft

Pierre Bourdieu's 1986 article "The Forms of Capital" lays out a detailed analysis of the ways in which economic ideas of capital and investment translate to social and cultural situations. In his article, Bourdieu concludes that social and cultural capital are linked in their very nature to economic capital, and that many of the same rules that govern Capitalism as an economic system also govern the flow of social and cultural capital from society to an individual (and, from one individual to another). Accordingly, many standard practices of personal finance can be applied to the management of social and cultural capital. Using Bourdieu's theories of investment of labor-time in social and cultural settings, an individual is capable of securing for themselves a successful start in society while maintaining a diversified, forward-thinking portfolio of social and cultural investments.

Bourdieu's analysis in "The Forms of Capital" finds that individuals have at their disposal numerous forms of capital separate from, and in addition to, economic capital. Two distinct forms of capital emerge alongside traditional economic capital in Bourdieu's theory:

> [C]ultural capital, which is convertible . . . into economic capital and may be institutionalized in the forms of educational qualifications; and . . . social capital, made up of social

obligations ('connections'), which is convertible . . . into economic capital and may be institutionalized in the forms of a title of nobility. (Bourdieu 98)

Cultural capital includes the capacity to imbibe, retain, use, and transfer cultural and institutional knowledge on an individual basis, whereas social capital refers to the sense of self in society, connections people make with others, and the ideals they carry with them when forming into groups. These two non-traditional forms of capital carry many of the same rules and best practices from the capitalistic economy, namely the investment of time and labor, the accumulation of wealth, transferring of wealth in exchange for goods or services, the conversion of capital from one form to another, competition among consumers and manufacturers, supply and demand, free markets, business ethics, and capital gains from investments. These forms of capital are inherently linked to economic capital, and "the most material types of capital-those which are economic in the restricted sense-can present themselves in the immaterial form of cultural capital or social capital and vice versa." (97) Essentially, social and cultural capital can be treated identically to economic capital in many ways, and can be earned through the conversion of economic capital and/or investment labor-time. "The Forms of Capital" goes so far as to offer some best-practice approaches to certain social and cultural settings, specifically the weighing of time and energy against expected future gains, speculation of the market in making financial decisions, and the importance of connections in investment planning. This parallel led me to consider the possibility of applying all forms of financial planning and economic guidance to the capital of society and culture.

In thinking about this problem, I found myself relating my personal situation as a student at the University of Georgia, as well as the financial management experience I have accumulated over the course of my life, to the concept of social and cultural investment. A college student such as myself must effectively manage all aspects of his academic, social, cultural, and financial needs, and most don't have the luxury of relying upon a financial planner or life coach along the way. According to Bourdieu, "ability or talent is itself the product of an investment of time and cultural capital" (98) and, "[c]apital is accumulated labor." (96) In order to gain new talents, experiences, knowledge, or abilities, a person must invest time and/or labor into the process. Bourdieu's "accumulated labor" is referencing time and energy, so one might say capital itself is the direct result of a time and energy investment. A diversified investment portfolio is needed to succeed in this way, or more to the point, a person must take from one form of capital (usually, economic capital) to pay for gains in another form. Capital, in the various forms, can flow from one such market to another to fulfill this need; however, the conversion itself also requires an investment of accumulated labor:

> Profits in one area are necessarily paid for by costs in another
> (so that a concept like wastage has no meaning in a general
> science of the economy of practices). The universal equivalent
> . . . is nothing other than labor-time (in the widest sense); and
> the conservation of social energy through all its conversions

is verified if . . . one takes into account both the labor-time accumulated in the form of capital and the labor-time needed to transform it from one type into another. (106)

In terms of social capital, college students have almost limitless opportunities for investment of their accumulated labor. It is clear that Bourdieu recognizes the importance of social affluence as well, stating that it "provides each of its members with the backing of the collectivity-owned capital, a 'credential' which entitles them to credit, in the various senses of the word"(103). Individuals spend this social 'credit' throughout their lives, from the first semester of school to their retirement from the workforce and beyond. It stands to reason that social capital, and the accumulation of it at an early age, is paramount to a successful existence (not merely a successful career). He explains in very direct terms that this "network of relationships is the product of investment strategies, individual or collective, consciously or unconsciously aimed at establishing or reproducing social relationships that are directly usable in the short or long term." (103) When choosing avenues for the investment of their accumulated labor, college students are certainly free to choose social investments as the sole market for their accumulated labor, foregoing the accumulation of cultural capital and traditional economic capital in the process. However, this strategy will result in a one-dimensional portfolio, focusing only on one very high-risk investment. A heavy investment in social capital requires that the student's funds are taken from other investments such as academic advancement, cultural gains, and furthering their economic position. Finally, the return on the student's social investments will come much later than those from traditional economic investments (107). The student runs the risk of poor academic performance, finding himself unable to sustain his budget due to a lack of available accumulated labor-time. While this single-prong approach to college finances may result in a fun and exciting few years of university, it is not a viable long-term strategy for success, and the delayed return on social investments means a more balanced portfolio is required for overall success.

Cultural capital is earned by an individual in a number of ways, starting at a young age within the home and continuing throughout a person's life. It is a multi-faceted marketplace, with many opportunities for investment:

Cultural capital can exist in three forms: in the *embodied state*, i.e., in the form of long-lasting dispositions of the mind and body; in the *objectified state*, in the form of cultural goods (pictures, books, dictionaries, instruments, machines, etc.). . . and in the *institutionalized state*, a form of objectification which must be set apart because, as will be seen in the case of educational qualifications, it confers entirely original properties on the cultural capital which it is presumed to guarantee. (98)

Accordingly, an individual's cultural capital includes her academic qualifications, and earning this should be at the forefront of a college student's list of priorities. After all, the accumulation of knowledge should be the crux of a student's desire to attend university, as this knowledge is directly related to obtaining critical qualifications which, "cannot be transmitted instantaneously (unlike money, property rights, or even titles of nobility) by gift or bequest, purchase or exchange" (99). Academic learning "depends on the cultural capital previously invested by the family. Moreover, the economic and social yield of the educational qualification depends on the social capital, again inherited, which can be used to back it up" (99). One aspect of this relationship is the student's ability to delay the accumulation of economic capital in lieu of more cultural pursuits, an ability that depends on the family's supporting the student financially. The same sentiment holds true for virtually every college student: tuition acts as a form of investment, and the return on this monetary investment is the degree provided by the university (and, to a lesser extent, the knowledge obtained while attending). If a student is unable to pay her tuition, she must then choose either to delay her cultural investments, or to forego social investments in lieu of finding a job or some other way to pay for her schooling through economic means. Doing so may limit the total amount of cultural capital (and associated academic credentials) the student is able to accumulate over the course of her education, and further limit the conversion of her cultural capital to economic capital in the workforce. Indeed, having specialized skills and education means being more in demand, as "any given cultural competence (e.g., being able to read in a world of illiterates) derives a scarcity value from its position in the distribution of cultural capital and yields profits of distinction for its owner" (100). Once again, having such a narrow focus and ignoring other forms of capital may place the student at a detriment in the future, and "the investments made (in time and effort) may turn out to be less profitable than was anticipated when they were made." (102)

What can a student do, then, to ensure a successful start to her various capital investments? Ultimately, it demands an element of balance in your investment portfolio, including enough startup capital (both economic in the form of money, and social/cultural in the form of time) to sustain a living while your investments mature. Bourdieu makes it clear when he says "the transformation of economic capital into cultural capital presupposes an expenditure of time that is made possible by possession of economic capital" (106). That is to say, it takes money to make money. Investments in cultural and social capital also have a much longer timeframe for a return of capital gains, and will usually require an initial investment in economic capital to succeed. Once acquired, social and cultural capital can be converted to economic capital through various means, including social investments which may provide business connections, appreciation and collection of culture, study of foreign languages, and academic credentials that provide a person with distinction among her peers. Still, to expect a return on these investments the earner must have the ability to manage all forms of capital, and to maintain a balance in the flow of accumulated labor-time towards each investment strategy.

Works Cited

Bourdieu, Pierre. "The Forms of Capital." *The Sociology of Economic Life.* Eds. Mark Granovetter and Richard Swedberg. 2nd ed. Cambridge, MA. Westview, 2001. *Emma.* Web. 6 Nov. 2015.

Say What You Say

As far as fluid drafts go, my first essay of this semester was the Aquaman of the written word. It took on new forms like a hydra, and I struggled from the beginning with making it concise. This assignment was all about saying exactly what you want to say, no more, no less. As it were, I chose the toughest topic I had ever attempted, which made for many revisions before I got to the draft included in my portfolio. This was a very personal essay, and it marked my first time writing about my family. In the first draft, I opened my essay with some random thoughts about the prompt, some of which I cut and others that I moved elsewhere. What I have included below become the new introduction in the second draft and onward.

First Draft:

Rarely will I have nothing to say, even when there is nothing to be said.

And some will say this is a flaw, no doubt.

Myself included.

But, it is a skill that has served me well, and one that I have come to like about myself.

And there are so few of those things for most people.

I get this from my Mother, the most likeable person I know.

The woman who raised me and my brothers always had a lot to say, when it needed to be said.

She is always well-spoken, and chooses her words carefully.

She is a natural leader, someone you could easily take for granted, and miss entirely when they are gone.

A person you might go to when you are in trouble.

Or when you need someone to talk to, because the silence is too much.

She is also a felon, but more on that later.

I am not very proud of this paragraph's merit, but I like that it has emotion involved. It is the first draft I liked enough to keep writing more afterward. I almost immediately recognized the first and last sentences as holding their own, and those sentences stay the same throughout all coming iterations of this passage. Almost every other sentence gets significant edits going forward.

Second Draft:

Rarely will I have nothing to say, even when there is nothing to be said.

I get this from my Mother, the most likeable person I know.

The woman who raised me and my two brothers always has a lot to say, but only when it needs to be said. [1] I try to soften this line, not sure why.

She is outspoken, well-spoken, and chooses her words carefully. [2] I liked my usage of "outspoken" and "well-spoken" here, since the two are not always mutual. It had a nice ring to it in writing.

She is a leader, someone you could easily take for granted, and long for when they are gone. [3] This was better than the first draft, but still too cheesy.

A person you might go to when you are in trouble. [4] "Might" is a bad choice here, too conditional and not concrete enough. It makes my mom sound less reliable.

Or when you need someone to talk to. [5] Bad grammar and awkward. She is also a felon, but more on that later.

In this draft of my essay I placed the passage above as the lead-in to the first paragraph, and I think this helped the essay tremendously. It was a suggestion from a peer review, and a great one. At this point, I started to open up to myself about the topic at hand as well, and also to focus on fixing the stream-of-consciousness feel that the original draft showed. I took out the self-effacing speech at the beginning and instead brought the focus to my mom a lot faster. I liked this version well enough, but it seemed a bit cheesy and I wasn't happy with some of the word choices I had made. I went into my third draft looking to cut the fat and spice things up.

Third Draft:

Rarely will I not have anything to say, even when there's nothing to be said.

I get this from my Mom.

She is the most likeable person I know. [6] In the spirit of concision, I decided to try the second sentence as two shorter sentences and ended up really liking the result. It made the opening feel more terse, but more honest, also.

The woman who raised me and my two brothers always has a lot to say, when it needs to be said.[7] Back to the stern mother in this version, I liked it more this way.

She is outspoken, well-spoken, and chooses her words carefully. She is a leader. [8] Once again, shorter sentences according to the assignment, but it works well.

Someone you might take for granted, and notice when they are gone.

A person you turn to when you are in trouble. [9] Better

Or when you need to bend an ear. [10] Could be better.

She is also a felon, but more on that later.

This edit felt closer to what I was truly wanting to say, and I was reasonably happy with the way it had turned out. I felt that I could turn this version in and be fine with the results, but I still made one or two small wording tweaks before the final draft.

Final Draft

Rarely will I not have anything to say, even when there's nothing to be said.

I get this from my Mom.

She is the most personable person I know. [11] This was one of the most beneficial changes I made to the entire essay. In my first set of peer reviews from draft 1, a colleague suggested that "likeable" was the wrong word here, and I ignored her suggestion until this draft. As soon as I changed it to "personable person" I knew that "likeable" had been wrong all along, and having it this way set a completely different mood for my next few remarks.

The woman who raised me and my two brothers always has a lot to say, when it needs to be said.

She's outspoken, well-spoken, and chooses her words carefully.

She is a leader.

Someone you might take for granted, and recognize when they are gone. [12] I chose to use "recognize" instead of "notice" on account of it having more of a precedent. As in, you don't just notice my mother, you RECOGNIZE her. With gifts of frankincense and myrrh.

A person you turn to when you are in trouble.

Or when you need to bend an ear.

She is also a felon, but more on that later.

Peering In

I was excited to learn, at the start of the semester, that we would be doing graded peer reviews in English 1101. Not only do I enjoy this type of work, but I consider it among my few raw talents, and always appreciate the insight that a fresh set of eyes can provide. I have never held a negative opinion of peer reviews, though I sense that the majority of my new classmates might.

Very simply put, I am a lazy writer. I tend to procrastinate and skip early drafts, then edit as I go along, and revise too much after I think I'm finished. Structured peer reviews help to mitigate these problems in my writing process by providing me with a second opinion very early on. The peer reviewer acts not only as a stoplight to guide my writing, but also as the proverbial wall against which I can test new ideas and experiments. I also feel that my experiences and insight are beneficial to other writers, and I take this type of feedback seriously. The following is one such review that I provided to a fellow student, a strong-visioned writer with great ideas, albeit some lingering issues in the formal side of things. In this review, I focused on restructuring his own words into stronger, more convincing sentences, and in correcting the recurring issues seen in his grammar and punctuation. My comments are shown in blue text, with suggested additions highlighted in yellow, and suggested omissions stricken through.

IRE- The game is no harder than the process

When I started English 1101 at the beginning of the semester, I was intimidated and dreading it as I never considered myself a writer. In order to demonstrate how the game of baseball correlates with writing, each of my essay topics and what I learned during the writing process encompass the idea of critical thinking skills that go along with the game of baseball, this idea or motivation I have found also goes along with writing, the main objective being to win the game.

I wanted to make a more in-depth note here to work on the first two sentences specifically, because they are really important to setting the stage for the rest of the essay. The first sentence has everything you need to make it run smooth and hook me in, but the ordering is kind of weird, so I would suggest making it more about you and less about English 1101. You have yourself as the subject, but it's conditional right off the bat, so let's make you the central focus:

"I was intimated and dreading English 1101 at the beginning of the semester, as I had never considered myself a writer."

Same sentence, same wording, but a little simpler overall. We talked about the next sentence and it being a good thesis, so I will just add in the changes we talked about already:

"~~In order to demonstrate how the game of baseball correlates with writing, e~~Each of my essay topics from this semester, and what I learned during the writing process along the way, encompass the ~~idea of~~ critical thinking skills that go along with the game of baseball.(new sentence) ~~this idea or motivation~~ I have found this same idea also goes along with writing, the main objective being to win the game."

In this one we took out the quantifier at the beginning and made it into two sentences.

~~However, since English and the game of baseball are similar, it allowed me to start improving and becoming a better writer.~~ Whenever I step onto the field, regardless of whether I am confident in my ability to perform or not, there is a sense of urgency that goes through my head.*I love this sentence for its imagery, but the ending could use some fixing up. Instead of saying "there is a sense of urgency," try it make it more about your feelings at that exact point in time. As it is now, to me it sounds like the entire stadium has a sense of urgency around it, which may be the case but I want to know how you felt personally! "...*

whether I am confident in my ability to perform or not, my head still runs wild with the need to _____ (fill in the blank)." Much more colorful, and it brings me into your thoughts like you're wanting to do.

Everyone has a job on the field~~;~~ ;I have to make sure I do my part as my teammates have to do their part. ~~Having to rely~~ Relying on my instincts has paid off in game situations ~~throughout the game has paid off~~, but not always. Taking on ~~the~~ this class was like starting a new game~~,~~ : my classmates were my teammates, the teacher was my coach, and the overall objective was to win (or in other words: pass). I found there ~~is~~ are a few things you have to do to win any game, that is to better yourself by instruction from your coach, to learn from your teammates, and to do your part. *- Note: when making lists, you don't always have to have "to" or "an" or "the" before each entry, but if you start the first entry with one added, make sure the rest of the list matches.* I found that I take on the task of writing my papers much like I take the field during a game~~.~~ : I listen to what my teacher has to say~~;~~ ,apply it to my writing the best I can, and use any constructive criticism I can get to better my writing skills. *- I think this last sentence could work well with a colon and the list of examples afterward, but if you prefer two sentences here I can see it that way also.*

While writing my first paper, personal essay, I wasn't given a specific topic like in all of my past high school assignments *- We talked at length about this one, but after another read through I think its just fine as it is.* For the first time I had free will to write about anything I wanted ~~to~~. I focused on organizing my writing for the first time; passion and emotion ~~is something~~ were elements I could now put into my writing. Whereas before I was assigned a topic which I felt that didn't serve a purpose, I now felt that someone could read my work and actually gain something from it. Immediately iIdeas immediately started to come into my head, and the brainstorming process began as soon as I received the prompt. I wanted to make a statement, and now I was able to do it. It - *I feel like you're talking about the assignment prompt here, but the last sentence was referring to your being able to make a statement with your writing, and the "It" in this sentence coming afterward lost me a bit. I would maybe try to use a stronger, more descriptive noun in this sentence so that the subject is better defined; it is a really important part of your essay (starting to show your passion for writing, and I want to see more of that) so help out the reader and give us the subject we are looking for here. What specifically opened up this new form of expression for you?* allowed me to express my own ideas that were my own and opened up a new way to express my emotions other than the baseball field.

Before, the only way for me to express my emotions was by playing ball, but writing now gave me a new way to show emotions while I'm not on the field - *Two things here: first, instead of using "emotions" a second time in this sentence, see if there is another word or phrase that says what you mean more accurately (ie, which new emotions were you feeling now that you were getting a feel for writing?). Second, be careful not to over-use key phrases like "on the field" when you are making a broad analogy like this. They are very quickly worn out on the reader, so if you can find an area (like this one) where the baseball analogy can stand alone without being spelled out, take out the reference and save it for another time* . Starting a new paper, I would get the same feeling as if I were about to start a game. For me, writing wasn't about not having good ideas, but executing them ~~in the way I need to~~ in order to form a proper essay. This would happen on the field as well~~;~~ :I would think in terms of how to make a game-changing decision, but at times I wasn't sure if I was making the right choice, or if I knew exactly how to execute it to perform what I intended it to do. I would sit thinking about a million ideas getting absolutely no where *- I think the phrase you used here is just too clichéd to be effective. You know what I would like to see here? Some sort of metaphor about baseball, maybe some drills you did in practice that you hated, or having a long inning where you just can't get the third out. This is the perfect spot to reinforce the baseball analogy.* , then I started writing down all the important ideas ~~and~~ that I some*(no space here)*how wanted to incorporate in my essay. I soon had enough ideas that connected with one another and dove right into my writing with rare excitement ~~which was rare~~. Like reading a pitcher as I was up to bat, each pitch was a little different, but they all have pattern tendencies and there I make my connection. The pitcher may think he has me on a guessing game, but once I focus on what is actually happening, he is now a part of my game. Throughout my first essay, I threw out *- this is a little iffy, having "throughout" and "threw out" so close to one another. I would change one or the other (probably this one)* the ideas that I had even if they didn't make sense. As a writer and a baseball player, I feel ~~like~~ that by addressing my papers in the same perspective as I do for the game that I love, I maintained the passion throughout my writing.

My second paper, analytical ~~analysis~~, focused on attention to detail ~~details~~ and what makes a specific style of writing "your" style. ~~When receiving the prompt~~ - *It's that passive voice again. Try to make you, the writer, the center of this sentence: "I was more than a bit intimidated after receiving the prompt..." works a lot better here.* it was more than a bit intimidating as I had to include the different sentence types, sentence structures, and clauses. Then, I had to describe the patterns ~~the writers~~ each writer used in their writing to portray what they were trying to say. My writing process was messy as it required me to constantly speculate about the authors' style, and to move around sections of my paper until I had created an order I thought was the most effective. Messy is a understatement~~,~~ ; I was completely lost, as I was the first time I ever went to a showcase, or a state invitational, and saw all of the talent that took the field. I was always in the top five of players on my team and now I was in a dugout full of top-five players. Sitting in my English 1101 class with my professor and peers was a whole new game. I had had great teachers in high school, but just like my coaches, their level of greatness is relative to ~~the area~~ their surroundings. In the end, I was rewarded with seeing how I was capable of depicting someone's style and able to make a final product.

When creating my wild card, I knew that I wanted to incorporate the emotion ~~that~~ which shows my love for the game of baseball. I included a memoir that could be about any experience. It ~~described~~ describes a sense of humor, and sometimes when you're down you just need a friend to get you back to what you were doing before~~,j~~ . Just like in baseball: always moving forward. While playing the game

I loved, it was always about having fun and sometimes when things didn't go your way, you had to proceed; move forward onto the next game without replaying the last move in your head. New day, new plan.

When looking at the work I have created this semester in English 1101, I realized I have came a long way in the writing process. I am far from mastering the skill, but as the semester went on the topics made ~~you~~ me think more; really forcing ~~you~~ me to get out of ~~your~~ my comfort zone. I now feel more confident in the work I create, and like in baseball, when you ~~play~~ face opponents that play at a higher level than you, there ~~is~~ are two options: learn to play at their level, or get left behind. I have taken that perspective into English 1101 this semester ~~and I began to execute my ideas.~~

And here we are, back at the beginning again. This was my very first journal entry for the class, and it might be the one on which I spent the most time.

Things to Avoid When Writing Good

- More than one punctuation mark at the end of a sentence is too much!!

- Ending a sentence with a preposition never sounds as good as you think it.

- Sentences that are written in passive voice have been known to cause issues with verifying validity.

- "When quoting someone or using dialog, ALWAYS specify who is speaking," he said.

- Clichés are to be avoided like the plague.

- Overly using adverbs will subtly, quickly, and completely discount your point entirely.

- The Oxford comma: use them, love them and never forget them.

- Keep it simple; if you can say the same thing with less words, less punctuation, or a simpler format—i.e. easier to read—: do so.

- Aint no place in composition for slang or shorthand.

- Try not to give too superfluous an explanation, meaning you shouldn't over-do your examples or treat your reader condescendingly (talking down to them, basically).

- You're pronouns, possessives, plural, and numbers should always matches there context.

- Never start or end a sentence with and.

- And finally, know your audience!

    Sincerely, your loving nephew,

    Jay

Akilah Alexander

Writer | Producer | Director

Akilah Rasheeda Alexander was born in Georgetown, Guyana to Tricia Hughes, a humble bank teller. Before she was three months old, Akilah was given books as gifts. Her mother read to her every night before bed, and at the age of three, Akilah learned to read. With this new talent, she was left to her own devices, and while other children itched to go outside and play, Akilah wanted nothing more than to find someplace quiet to read her favorite books. She developed such a strong love of the language she heard everywhere around her. After she and her mother immigrated to America, she quickly adapted to the new society that welcomed her and her unique background. Her distinct "Guyanese" accent was lost within a week of attending Kindergarten classes because she found it much easier to communicate with her classmates when they could understand her. It was her appreciation for language that helped her assimilate ... See full bio below »

However, despite how well she fit into her new culture, Akilah remained proud of her country of origin and continued to view it as the place where she discovered that words could be brought to life. It goes without saying that in time, she developed yet another talent: the ability to paint with her words and shape whole new environments out of varying sentence structures. She was introduced to writing through online video games, where she was able to create her own characters and develop them thoroughly. At the age of twelve, she found a community of writers, like herself, and delved into a world she created with her friends—friends of various backgrounds.

Although her writing was far from perfect in the beginning, like a sponge, she soaked up any opportunity she had to improve. In high school, English became her favorite subject. "I never shied away from essays like my other classmates did. Even if I did procrastinate more than a few times, I always saw in-class essays as a challenge and an opportunity. I wanted my teachers to know that I was more than capable of expressing my ideas," she states.

Nonetheless, her confidence was dashed when she received her first English 1102 essay grade in professor Turula's class. With her grade came the realization that she was far from being a skilled writer. So, she buckled down and opened her mind—determined to perfect her talent and bring her ideas to life.

Before the Big Screen

Development

On Monday, August 17th, 2015 at approximately 3:35 P.M., I encountered my first foe—the woman who would later drive me to insanity and break my heart: Sarah Turula. I entered English 1102 with boundless confidence in my ability to weave my ideas together into a unified argument. To me, the writing process was like filmmaking, and I wanted nothing more than to receive the highest award for my efforts: an Oscar—or a big, fat 100%, in my case. In hindsight, I believe my professor took pleasure in dangling that goal right in front of my nose. I felt like the Leonardo DiCaprio of English 1102, always nominated but never awarded. However, rather than giving up, I worked and worked to better myself. I became my biggest critic and discovered my fatal flaw: my writing was too vague. By comparing my writing process to the progression of creating a movie, I was able to assess my strengths and weaknesses. I became acutely aware of how significant point of view was in regards to filmmaking and realized that it was just as significant to my writing process. Entering English 1102, I was certain of my writing prowess, but being in this course has taught me that writing doesn't have to be a lone endeavor. In fact, I've learned that my writing, in particular, thrives on the perspectives of others.

Pre-production

I can clearly recall my professor's omen: "Writing these essays will be difficult," and I remember how I smiled to myself at her kind warning. To me, her statement could be translated into, "You've got a tough crowd, that 'tough crowd' being me." Yet, somehow, I had enough confidence in my ability to sway a difficult audience; I had assumed that my first essay would be a blockbuster, and that the other two would be just as successful. I was wrong, of course. My first essay flopped miserably. While I didn't actually fail the assignment, I didn't receive the grade I was striving for, and that was a shocker for me. For one thing, I chose to analyze a poem I had already familiarized myself with: Sylvia Plath's *Mirror*. I thought doing so would give me the upper hand in piecing together an argument that wasn't just some immature thought I came up with because I was pressed for time. In retrospect, I realize I shouldn't have taken the easy way out for my first essay. I loved so much to be challenged, yet I deliberately chose the poem I had already covered in my twelfth-grade AP English Language and Composition class because I thought no one would be able to tell me my ideas were wrong. I began my journey into becoming a better writer by running away from critique.

Filming

My thesis for my first paper stated, "Plath's characterization of the mirror as truthful, faithful, and meditative aids in the reader's ability to understanding its sincerity and the important role it plays in reflecting the lives of those that look into it. This description of the mirror's reliability serves to create the theme of humans' fear of aging and death." It was a very undeveloped and elementary thesis. My entire introductory paragraph lacked the "so what" factor that was necessary to explain exactly why my argument was relevant. I failed in describing what the mirror in the poem was "faithful and meditative" towards, and did not delve into what role the mirror had in the poem. My introductory paragraph was a shallow gloss over what could have been an in-depth analysis, and frankly, I was surprised that I received an 88 on this paper. My professor was too kind. If I were to grade myself now, I would give my first essay a 79 at best. Similar to how I approached my final essay, I made the mistake of being so comfortable with my poem of choice that I forgot my audience might not have the same context I did for supporting my argument. I was blindsided by the fact that my audience was not me, and although my argument might have sounded sophisticated, it was much too vague. However, I didn't come to this realization until my third essay was graded. That was when I realized how important perspective was when it came to essay writing.

The assignments leading up to the second paper and the second paper itself will always be remembered as my worst nightmare. I barely had enough time to recover from the blow I'd received after getting my grade on the first essay before I was catapulted into the second one. There was no quiet lull before the storm. I blinked and I came face to face with a hurricane of essays and short stories I had no hope of comprehending, but instead of remaining optimistic, I immediately gave up. In fact, I sent my professor an email stating that I was worried that my paper wouldn't be as good as I want it to be. I was beyond ready to receive the lowest essay grade I've ever gotten. Little did I know that my desperation would become a blessing in disguise. Because I had reached out and admitted that there was a task that I lacked confidence in completing well, I received something priceless from my professor: perspective. With her advice, I was able to change my writing into something mature and refined. Rather than presenting my audience with an attempt at gathering my ideas together, I gave them depth. I gave them perspective. That was the first and only essay I had ever made an A on in the class, but although I had improved, I still hadn't learned. However, in the process of writing this particular essay, I did go through my most significant period of growth which is why I've chosen to present it as one of my final revisions. I also utilized my second paper's introductory paragraph in my revision exhibit to show the progression of my ideas throughout the course of writing.

When the time came for me to write my third and final paper, I can honestly say I put every ounce of my soul into that essay, but I made a crucial mistake. My confidence blinded me yet again, and I sought no opinions from those that would tell me where my writing needed improvement. Rather, I received words of encouragement from close friends who were much too biased to approach my paper objectively like my professor would have. In her review, she wrote, "I like the details from the movie you have included here and there's a lyrical tone to your descriptions that is very nice. But there is a real problem in that you seem to take for granted that your reader knows what the point and theme of the movie is." When I read that, it struck me that, once again, I had assumed that my audience had the same level of understanding I did. It was heartbreaking, not because I didn't receive the grade I was hoping for but because I completely understood why I didn't deserve that grade. I avoided constructive criticism because my ego somehow managed to convince me that I was right and that my limited, two-dimensional essay was profound—a work of art. For my portfolio, I've chosen this essay as my second final revision because I know it has the potential to be more than what my limitations turned it into. After all, it was my second paper that inspired me to think of my writing process as filmmaking. I want to do it justice and show it in its best light. I want it to get the recognition it deserves.

Post-production

When I reflect on the difficulties I faced in my English class during the course of this semester, it eases my mind to know that my struggles were not just my own. I believe it goes without saying that my writing would never have improved as much as it did without the input I received from not only my professor but my peers as well. Being meek and timid in a social sense never helped when it came to the writing or the communicating with others. I was selfish as well and prided myself on the notion that my writing surpassed those around me, but as a result of taking this course, I've learned the importance of humbling myself. I've seen my writing soar to new heights with a gentle push in the right direction, and I've had ideas bloom in my head from the suggestions I've received from my classmates. Without them and without their perspectives, my writing would never be where it is now.

Release

I'd like to believe that I've learned since first entering English 1102. Although I do take pride in my ability to create new worlds with my writing, I'm now aware of the fact that doing so doesn't have to be a solitary experience. To me, writing is like filmmaking, but what makes a movie great is not the plot itself. Rather, it is the plot, camera techniques, actors, scene directors, makeup artists, and much more that turn ideas into reality. When a film wins an Oscar for Best Picture of the Year, a whole team of individuals take to the stage, and I've come to realize that the best writing is a collaborative experience. What makes writing a living, breathing thing is what I've finally stopped running away from: perspective.

Script Breakdown

Before actors are able to portray the characters that have been written for them on the big screen, they come together for a script reading. The process works like proofreading, in which the cast is able to pick out parts of the script that seem off in a way. Sometimes, they may even request for certain parts of the script to be emphasized in order to give the audience more insight into the message of the film itself. The script is critiqued in a sense and goes through a number of edits, some involving actual deletions and insertions of material.

Editing essays until they're clear and concise enough to be submitted to Emma is much like taking apart a script. My first drafts are usually characterized by a cluster of ideas that are in dire need of being fleshed out, and the journey I make from my first draft to my final draft—one that is worthy enough for my professor to set her eyes upon—is usually one filled with nail-biting, hair-pulling anxiety. Much of my time, when revising, is in fact spent glaring at the screen of my laptop.

For my revision exhibit, I chose to show the progression of my second assigned essay because it is the most accurate portrayal of how my writing evolves as a result of being critiqued. The sequence in which I edit my drafts is also very similar to the way I have changed as a writer. I entered English 1102 with little care for organizing my thoughts. I only wished to be heard (through my writing of course), and so much of my beginning work was a jumbled mess. Only when I finally accepted constructive criticism and advice regarding how to improve did I see a change in my writing for the better.

<u>Key</u>

>Issues<

>Additions<

>Thesis<

In Albert Camus' *The Rebel,* Camus claims that a rebel is "a man who says no, but whose refusal does not imply a renunciation." In Camus' opinion, a rebel is one who says yes and no simultaneously by rejecting the invasion of a value that is of great significance to him and affirming the existence of a boundary that has been crossed. The Misfit in Flannery O'Connor's "A Good Man is Hard to Find" is a prime example of an unconventional rebel. While, at first glance, The Misfit seems to be motivated by his resentment for mankind, it later becomes evident that The Misfit is acting against society's general belief that every man is capable of being "good" no matter what they may have done in the past. Multiple facets of Camus's description of the characteristics of a successful rebel are in harmony with the characteristics of The Misfit in "A Good Man is Hard to Find." Despite the Misfit's generally questionable morals, he is actually advocating every man's right to free will because every man is born into sin and punished for crimes he may not even remember committing.

- The key issue with my first draft was that I gave no background on the short story I was analyzing. I dove right into talking about how the short story connects with Camus's characterization of the "Rebel" without giving the audience some context on what the story was about.
- My thesis is also very broad and does a poor job of explaining the theme which I'll be describing throughout the essay.

Flannery O'Connor's *A Good Man is Hard to Find* tells the tale of a family's unfortunate run-in with a criminal and murderer called The Misfit. While, at first glance, the Misfit seems to be motivated by his resentment for mankind, it later becomes evident that the Misfit is acting against society's general belief that every man is capable of being "good" no matter what they may have done in the past. In Albert Camus's *The Rebel,* Camus claims that a rebel is "a man who says no, but whose refusal does not imply a renunciation" (Camus). In Camus' opinion, a rebel is one who says yes and no simultaneously by rejecting the invasion of a value that is of great significance to him and affirming the existence of a boundary that has been crossed. The Misfit in Flannery O'Connor's *A Good Man is Hard to Find* is a prime example of an unconventional rebel. Despite the Misfit's decision to kill in retaliation to the unjust punishment mankind receives for their natural inclination towards sin, he is actually advocating [ ] every man's right to free will.

- This introductory paragraph is much better than my previous one. Unlike before, I used one sentence to give my audience a bit of background on Flannery O'Connor's short story, which made all the difference in the coherence of the paragraph itself.
- My thesis is also completely different from my first version. This time, I give the audience enough detail to cement the reason for my argument. This way, my thesis comes off as more sophisticated and developed than it did at first.
- The issues in this draft are primarily grammatical errors that hinder the flow of the paragraph.

Flannery O'Connor's *"A Good Man is Hard to Find"* tells the tale of a family's unfortunate run-in with a criminal and murderer called The Misfit. While, at first glance, The Misfit seems to be motivated by his resentment of mankind, it later becomes evident that The Misfit is acting against society's general belief that every man is capable of being "good" no matter what he may have done in the past. In Albert Camus's *The Rebel*, Camus claims that a rebel is "a man who says no, but whose refusal does not imply a renunciation" (Camus). In Camus's opinion, a rebel is one who says yes and no simultaneously by rejecting the invasion of a value that is of great significance to him and affirming the existence of a boundary that has been crossed (Camus). The Misfit in Flannery O'Connor's "A Good Man is Hard to Find" is a prime example of an unconventional rebel. Despite The Misfit's decision to kill in retaliation against the unjust punishment mankind receives for its natural inclination towards sin, he is actually advocating for every man's right to free will

- The final draft for this paragraph includes the corrected grammatical errors. The flow of the paragraph has greatly improved due to the minor alterations, and because of this, the ideas that support my general argument fit together almost seamlessly, ultimately serving to keep the audience aware of what they will be looking for in my body paragraphs.

Akilah Alexander
Turula
English 1102

I Am a Sinner. Digital image. *Quotesgram*. N.p., n.d. Web. 9 Oct. 2015. <http://media-cache-ak0.pinimg.com/736x/a6/a3/3b/a6a33b252347a3ec477ad3a844b66bc6.jpg>.

Madman or Rebel?

Flannery O'Connor's *"A Good Man is Hard to Find"* tells the tale of a family's unfortunate run-in with a criminal and murderer called The Misfit. While, at first glance, The Misfit seems to be motivated by his resentment towards mankind, it later becomes evident that The Misfit is acting against society's general belief that every person is capable of being "good" no matter what he or she may have done in the past. In Albert Camus's *The Rebel*, Camus claims that a rebel is "a man who says no, but whose refusal does not imply a renunciation" (Camus). In Camus's opinion, a rebel is one who says yes and no simultaneously by rejecting the invasion of a value that is of great significance to him and affirming the existence of a boundary that has been crossed (Camus). The Misfit in Flannery O'Connor's "A Good Man is Hard to Find" is a prime example of an unconventional rebel.

Despite the Misfit's decision to kill in retaliation for the unjust punishment mankind receives for their natural inclination towards sin, he is actually advocating for every man's right to free will.

To understand how Flannery O'Connor manages to present the Misfit as a rebel, one must examine the typical traits that are observed in a rebel. Camus states that, "In every act of rebellion, the rebel simultaneously experiences a feeling of revulsion at the infringement of his rights and a complete and spontaneous loyalty to certain aspects of himself" (Camus). This characteristic is shown in The Misfit's repulsion at Jesus's decision to bring the dead back to life. He feels as though it was not right for Jesus to do what he did because it set everything "off balance" (O'Connor 1185). Because he was not there to witness such a thing, The Misfit seems conflicted about whether it is the right decision to "throw away everything and follow Him" (O'Connor 1185). This confusion grants The Misfit an awareness of the fact that he is capable of acting of his own will. While The Misfit feels empowered by his right to free will, he is disgusted by the naiveté of people who choose to follow God blindly. A prime example of this mentality is shown by the grandma, who ironically pleas for her own life rather than the life of her family when she realizes her life is at stake. As the family is later murdered in cold blood, it becomes clear to the audience that if the grandmother had not "sinned" by hiding the cat in the car or lying about where the old house was, the family might have lived. The Misfit resents the self-absorbed hypocrisy of the grandmother and anyone else who blindly follows God. By taking the lives of anyone despite their age or gender, he is retaliating against this behavior while simultaneously showing others that they can make decisions for themselves and act on their own impulses without being controlled by the word of God because it is part of their nature to sin.

One can argue that The Misfit cannot be a rebel, but he is actually resentful because a rebel does not derive pleasure from the pain of others, and The Misfit actually states that there is "no pleasure but meanness" (O'Connor 1185). Ross Wilson states in his essay that The Misift maintains the philosophy of both the rebel and the one who resents: "Interestingly, both of these philosophies apply to The Misfit in some respects and provide an interpretive framework through which The Misfit's motivation and desire to sin and commit atrocities can be understood" (Wilson). Despite his claim, however, the tone of voice in which The Misfit speaks when he says this implies that he does not agree with this view. This is evidenced by the narrator's description of The Misfit's voice as "almost a snarl" (O'Connor 1185) which implies that The Misfit is actually disgusted by the way that people can derive pleasure from hurting each other. Later, near the conclusion of the story, The Misfit addresses his accomplice

Bobby Lee when he states, "It's no real pleasure in life" (O'Connor 1186). Because this takes place after the grandmother's murder, which he would have considered "meanness", it becomes evident that The Misfit did not take pleasure in killing the old woman. This is a characteristic of the rebel, whose actions are not driven by the need to satisfy his own selfish desires, but are instead used to further the advocacy of his rights which have been infringed upon by either society or another oppressive individual.

Camus claims that "rebellion is not realistic" (Camus). This is a rather obvious characteristic of Flannery O'Connor's short story, which falls under the category of Southern Gothic literature. Short stories that fall under this category usually have a theme which can be found beneath the dark, gloomy, and sometimes morbid tone that the author sets. In "A Good Man is Hard to Find," The Misfit appears to be a criminal in the eyes of the other characters present, but it is later revealed that The Misfit is somewhat like a prophet. His beliefs, if considered closely, are not warped, but actually align with the morals of someone who would consider his or herself a realist. His explanation of what motivates him to kill as a way to take advantage of the free will that God has given mankind is what makes the grandmother realize that they are more similar than they are different. Despite the pride that the grandmother takes in being an honorable, godly woman, she realizes that they are both flawed sinners. If she hadn't lied about the old house being in Tennessee, and if she hadn't snuck the cat into the family car, her family would never have encountered the Misfit. With the realization of this, the grandmother also realizes that The Misfit is killing because he wishes for people to accept their inherently sinful nature and stop living as slaves to man-made conceptions of right and wrong. He believes that society's view of what is good and bad is inaccurate and unjust because a good deed does not override what a man truly is: a sinner.

While rebellion may not be motivated by resentment or "malice," Camus believes that "we must consider the idea of rebellion in its widest sense on pain of betraying it; and in its widest sense rebellion goes far beyond resentment" (Camus). This characteristic of rebellion is shown in the feeling of betrayal that the Misfit feels in being able to act of his own accord and even sin despite the claim that he should be following God. He feels as though people are wasting their time in trying to experience salvation or get to Heaven because they are given the option and the power to do things like kill each other. To The Misfit, people will always be unjustly punished for being born into sin. Although Jesus is the only one that can bring a person back to life, The Misfit believes that He has put everything off balance by doing so. Death is part of the natural order of things, and by bringing someone back to life, Jesus has tipped the scales of normal perception. Before, people would assume that death was finite and one's soul would either transcend to Heaven or descend to Hell. Reviving the dead only resulted in confusion for mankind, creating the border between believers and non-believers. Knowing this, The Misfit has witnessed many good people die, including his father, and he knows that since Jesus has not saved them, no man can be pure enough to save. The Misfit kills to dissuade people from going against their sinful nature in an attempt to attain the unattainable, which is God's grace and mercy.

The Misfit does not care about tarnishing his image because he is aware of the fact that he was born tarnished. With this knowledge, he has created a new name for himself and has taken on a mission, one where he grants people mercy by killing them. While this may not line up with the conventional good morals that one might assume a rebel should have, it is The Misfit's love for humanity, no matter how warped, that drives him to take lives.

Works Cited

Camus, Albert. *The Rebel: An Essay on Man in Revolt*. Vintage, 2012.

O'Connor, Flannery. "A Good Man Is Hard to Find." *Making Literature Matter: An Anthology for Readers and Writers*. Ed John Schilb and John Clifford. Sixth ed. Boston: Bedford/St. Martin's, 2000. 1174-186. Print.

Critical Reception

Nothing makes a director's heart beat faster than the anticipation of waiting for the reviews of movie critics. Before entering English 1102, I had never actually reviewed another classmate's writing in a formal setting. So, when I was told to swap my work with someone for the first time, I conveniently forgot how to speak. My writing was my baby; it was my greatest creation, and although I had confidence in it, I was not very fond of sending it out into the world for people to scrutinize. It was a silly mentality to have at the time, but since then, I've come to realize the importance of the peer reviewing process. While I had been reluctant to share my opinion at first, as I gradually watched my writing flourish from the criticism I received, I became more honest in my peer reviews. I was no longer scared of hurting feelings because I was aware of how much of a difference I could make with my words.

For my peer review exhibit, I decided to display the review I did of my classmate Paul's final essay. Because I was already so excited for my own essay to be reviewed, I tried my best to approach his paper with an open mind. I wanted to help him improve because I had already seen how my writing evolved after being critiqued. This peer review reflects how I learned to embrace criticism and view it as a chance to develop my writing into something with more depth, and while I may not have made the grade I wanted to receive on this assignment, I hope my advice helped Paul shape his ideas in some way.

IMDb > Life (2015/I) > Reviews & Ratings - IMDb

Reviews & Ratings for

Southpaw   More at IMDbPro »

14 out of 17 people found the following review useful:

Draft 2 Paper 3

In a year that filled theaters and box offices with astounding films, one film that stood above the rest was the release of *Southpaw* in late July. Directed by Antoine Fuqua, this emotion-packed redemption drama attracts attention of all ages with its incorporation of action in the form of brutal boxing, the love story of a father and his daughter, and even the acts of criminal injustice. Actor Jake Gyllenhaal stars as boxer Billy Hope in this motivational redemption drama that could inspire even the weakest of hearts. A life filled with fame and glory, a loving wife, and a daughter to cherish: all lost in the blink of an eye. [1] This bit seems kind of unnecessary, like filler sort of. Through utter despair and self-destruction, Billy Hope (Gyllenhaal) gives it his all to redeem himself to his daughter, the world, and ultimately himself by changing his life and positioning himself to become the fighter he once was praised for. This act of redemption, along with the character types, the love shared between Hope and his daughter, and the goals in desire to achieve, all serve to show how the film successfully conformed to the genre type of a redemption drama.[2] This is a 3-part thesis it seems, so you may run into some trouble and end up limiting yourself to just these 3 ideals rather than actively developing your argument.

Billy Hope (Gyllenhaal) stars as the undefeated light weight champion of the world, and it appears that nothing could strip him of his glory. During a celebration to glorify Hope, opposing boxer, Miguel Gomez, decided to call out Hope and downgrade his fighting skills. "You've never been hit by a real man." Stated Gomez. These words between Hope and Gomez soon turned to fists flying and managers of both fighters in an all-out brawl. It wasn't until the gun shot sounded, and Hope's wife, Maureen (Rachel McAdams), is left motionless on the floor, that Hope's actions began to change. [3] This must be a huge shift in the movie. You should expand on this part a little more and connect it back to your thesis. It seems like Hope's character changed after this event; you can relate this to character development. From that moment on, everything within the film changes. Hope (Gyllenhaal) loses match after match until he goes overboard with his temper and strikes a referee, therefore becoming suspended from boxing. Being outside of the ring, no money coming in, no wife to tell him everything will be fine, Hope slowly loses all sense of desire to live, and with his fearful daughter, Leila, played by Oona Laurence, under his protection, things inevitably fall apart. He turns to alcohol and drugs and ultimately loses everything. From his house to his championship belts, it isn't until he loses custody of his daughter to child protective services that he realizes it is time for a change.

Living on the streets, he begins searching for a job to simply get by, when he stumbles upon a gym run by retired boxer, Tick Wills (Forest Whitaker). Soon, that relationship turns to a partnership between the two, and Willis promises Hope the chance to train in his gym as well as the chance to earn his life back. Frequent visits to child protective services to see, Leila, Hope's daughter played by Oona Laurence, becomes a hopeless encounter as Leila has lost all hope in her father ever changing and ever winning her back. Countless hours of hard work and sacrifice between training, sobering up, and becoming a stronger man, the time came for the match of the century. Hope earned the chance to fight Miguel Gomez for a chance at the world light weight championship, and nothing was going to stop this determined father from reclaiming the glory he deserves. A gruesome battle between the two, with glorifying action shots of battle that related to such scenes from celebrated movies like Rocky and Cinderella Man, with spit flying, blood dripping, and fans cheering. [4] The comparison and the imagery used in this sentence is great! Maybe give a little brief background on what makes those movies so popular. Countless rounds having passed, the bell tired of ringing, Billy Hope gains what little strength he has left, finds an opening, and takes the punch, knocking out Gomez with a style and brute power rarely witnessed in the ring. Billy Hope, now champion of the world, daughter Leila back in his arms, and life back to where it should be Billy Hope is the ultimate comeback kid.

A great redemption drama is one that places emphasis on the comeback story of the protagonist. It's a genre of film where failure and loss are a normality in life, and in order for the main character to be happy with him or herself, a change within the character must occur. Character dramas such as this always possess the same character types. There's the protagonist, who at the beginning of the film seems invincible and possesses everything he or she could have ever wanted, but then falls short of something and loses all. Just as Billy Hope lost everything, from his wife, his home, to even his daughter. There is the woman character, or the love interest, in this case Hope's daughter Leila. [5] Really good connection to the themes present in character dramas. Maybe talk about how unconventional it is that the "romantic interest" or the "object of the protagonist's affections" is his daughter Leila. In most character dramas the love interest is a person of similar age in which intimate feelings are shared between the two. However in *Southpaw*, Leila serves as the girl who has infatuated Billy Hope into changing his everyday life for the reclaiming of her love. There is also the bad guy, epitomized by foe boxer Miguel Gomez alongside two-timing manager, Jordan Mains, played by 50 Cent. Each character plays a major role in how the main character feels about himself, life, and how successful he is in accomplishing his goal of redeeming his name and all that he once was. [6] With this statement, you could delve into the relationship between Hope, the antagonist, and other supporting characters.

Alongside character types, another characteristic of the redemption drama are the conflicts that could potentially prevent the character from achieving his or her goal.   The biggest factor, or theme revealed in this genre is man versus himself. [7] Really important sentence! I think after this bit, you should go into how Hope epitomizes that "man vs. self" conflict. It is ultimately up to the character to decide how important their goals are and to do whatever need be to accomplish them. There's always that temptation to backslide into who they were before from other characters and people's action around them. In this case, the media plays a huge role in Hope's potential to backslide, due to their negative comments on him and his livelihood. The story line rests on this idea that a man has all the glory, messes up, loses all his glory, and then comes back in the end to redeem himself and reclaim his glory. The backbone of a genre is not to be changed simply to entertain the audience in some new way. The audience wants a boxing movie that appeals to the emotions of the viewer while also exciting them with scenes of brutal fighting, love, and relatable aspects of life that can connect the audience to the film in its entirety. [8] What are the emotional scenes like? This film was a success to me, and was definitely a success by its accordance with the overlaying aspects of what a redemption drama should be.

The redemption drama epitomizes the "Comeback kid" idea. [9] Try to give a little background on the "Comeback kid" theme. Great fighting movies such as *The Karate Kid, Rocky*, and *The Fighter* are all wonderful examples of this drama in the way that they each share similar characteristics that define them. From the character types, to situations such as death and crime, to the introduction of a love interest, to the goal of achieving glory, fame, respect, or love, to finally the ending scene of the protagonist achieving their goal, all negatives turn positive, and a happy ending to leave the audience motivated and happy. *Southpaw* is more than a cliched boxing movie. It's a heart-pounding, soul-wrenching, nail-biting story that will leave audiences on the edge of their seats with the inspiration that life is theirs for the taking.

I think you've got a lot of strength in your arguments to describe how the film conforms to the genre, but it may serve you well to provide a genre characteristic and then an example from the film that fits that characteristic. I can see where everything belongs. It just needs to be ordered well, and you'll have a winning argument! :)

Akilah Alexander

English 1102

Turula

"So It Goes With God"

A boundary is defined as "the line or plane indicating the limit or extent of something," and it comes in many different forms: physical, emotional, and social, to name a few. Yet, one can discover things that have been hidden to them by crossing these boundaries and, as a result of doing so, may also experience a feeling of profound enlightenment. Ang Lee, the director of *Life of Pi* dared to go farther than the boundary of the film's genre. Through its use of breathtaking 3D imagery and its haunting soundtrack, the film adaptation of Yann Martel's best-selling novel *Life of Pi* manages to push beyond the standards of an average character drama by immersing the reader in a tale that redefines mankind's limits, capabilities, and strengths.

From the very beginning of the movie, Lee wastes no time in establishing the importance of the setting. The viewer is shown a montage of various animals residing within a zoo, yet the environment the animals live in is so spacious and peaceful that one might not believe that the animals are living in a manmade "cage" per se. The opening scene is accompanied by a rather melodious song that is coincidentally titled "Pi's Lullaby" in the soundtrack. Before the audience is even introduced to the protagonist of the film, they are given a glimpse into his life. By doing this, Lee manages to create a bond between the audience and the protagonist and makes himself appear much more engaging as a fellow human being. The third thing the audience associates with the protagonist, besides the zoo and the lullaby, is his voice. After the writer asks if he was raised in a zoo, Pi replies, "Born and raised," before moving on to tell the intriguing, yet comical tale of how he came into the world of Pondicherry: what he calls "the French part of India." The origin of Pi's namesake is also explained within the beginning of the film; he was named after a French swimming pool, Piscine Molitor, in which his uncle taught him how to swim. During one of their lessons, he explains to Pi that a "lungful of water will not harm him", and Pi recounts that his uncle's lessons would later save his life. This exposition is very different from the introduction of the main character in average character dramas. Usually, the audience gets to decide whether or not the protagonist is the audience becomes aware of Pi's humble beginnings and charming personality. That alone is a significant strategy Lee uses to imprint the image of a man that is not unlike us into our brains, and it makes the struggles that Pi faces throughout the movie that much more engaging.

Pi encounters his first challenge as a young boy, trying to find his place within the world he was born into. He recalls the order in which he discovered three religions: Hinduism, Christianity, and Islam. Being raised a Hindu, Pi recalls that he viewed the Hindu gods as "superheroes" and often found himself in awe of their power. It is by chance, that he is dared by his brother, Ravi, to go "drink the holy water" from a Christian church when they are on vacation in the mountains. The priest of the church finds Pi and offers him a glass of water before generously answering Pi's many questions about Christ, the son of God. He recounts the tale of how Jesus Christ sacrificed himself to atone for the sins of mankind. Pi discovers that he admires Christ's selflessness, and he later finds peace within himself and his surroundings through Islam. Rather than facing more tangible obstacles, as the hero of any other character drama might do, Pi realizes that his open-mindedness is an obstacle because others cannot understand his rationale behind following all three religions although he claims that he "just wants to love God." His father criticizes Pi's decision by stating that "believing in everything at the same time is the same as not believing in anything at all", and although Pi's mother attempts to defend him by claiming that Pi is "still finding his way," she does not explicitly say that she supports Pi's decision to follow all three religions.

Some may say that it is Pi's naiveté and willingness to accept everything he is told that causes his next dilemma. He attempts to feed the zoo's new tiger, Richard Parker, by hand, solely acting on the belief that animals have souls like humans do. However, before he can do so, he is reprimanded by his father and is later forced to witness Richard Parker gruesomely kill a goat as a "lesson". After that, Pi states that "the world had lost some of its enchantment." Like any other protagonist in a character drama, Pi goes through a slump where nothing seems to appeal to him anymore-that is, until he meets Anandi the dancer. Their relationship allows him to feel alive again, but his happiness is short-lived when he learns that his family will be moving to Canada. Despite Pi's protests, the family uproots itself and boards a ship to sail from India to North America. It is while they are sailing over the Mariana Trench, commonly known as the "deepest spot on earth," that the family encounters a furious storm that changes the course of our protagonist's life. The storm is so rough that it damages the ship, effectively flooding the lower decks and cutting Pi off from the rest of his family. Desperate to find help for them, he begs the other crewmates to follow him, but they only throw him into one of the ship's lifeboats. The rope that secured the lifeboat loosens, and the boat falls into the rough ocean below. Pi, and a crazed zebra that had managed to dive onto the boat, escape the ship just before it sinks below the water. What makes this sequence of events ironic is that the water that Pi had learned to be so comfortable in is what took everything away from him. It can be inferred that the theme of the movie may be man versus nature, but Ang Lee incorporates many themes into the film. Because of this, the audience is able to choose the theme that resonates with them personally.

The next scene, and the music that accompanies it, epitomize the purpose of the genre: to elicit an emotional response from its audience. When Pi is knocked into the water, he ducks under it just in time to prevent a huge wave from crushing his skull. The camera follows him as he swims past ravenous sharks and drowning zoo animals, only pausing when the sunken ship comes into view. The lighting in this scene is eerie, and Pi's expression is conveniently hidden from the audience, but the complete stillness of his body communicates to the audience that he is shocked, to say the least. It is after Pi breaks the water's surface that we see his expression. Although one might have expected to see the devastation on his face, that doesn't stop it from making our hearts ache for him. Pi has become so relatable and charming at this point that we can only imagine how heartbreaking it would be to lose our entire family in such a terrible way. However, the acute feeling of sadness that the audience feels towards Pi's loss is brief. Once the storm passes and the sea calms, Pi and the audience are faced with their next challenge: How will he survive long enough to find his way back home? In most character dramas, while the protagonist is challenged, the challenge itself is usually realistic, with the only obstacle being the hero's own mind. Despite the surrealism of the situation Pi finds himself in—trapped in a boat with a tiger—Lee somehow succeeds in keeping the audience hooked. Although we are all aware that Pi lives to tell the tale of how he survived under those circumstances, we aren't sure how. The combination of knowledge we have and the surrealism of the film is what stops us from looking away. It is what stops us from claiming that the film is "something we've seen a thousand times."

Years ago, filmmakers were incapable of creating immersive movies such as *Avatar* or *Gravity*. Before, people would think it was impossible to have someone interact on set with an actual Bengal tiger, but Lee managed to create a world that, while we knew was not real, still succeeded in pulling us in. We didn't feel as though we were at home in our couches, watching everything unfold on a screen. No, we were on the Tsimtsum when it sank, we were there with Richard Parker on the lifeboat, and we pulled ourselves to the shore with hardly enough energy to stand. When the movie ended, we were proud of ourselves and our resilience because we survived. This is the feeling that *Life of Pi* elicits from its viewers and why it was praised by many reviewers. The movie went beyond everyone's expectations and redefined its genre by using immersion. It gave us that same exhilarating feeling we experience when reading a book, except that this time, we could see, feel, and hear everything.

Works Cited

Life of Pi. Digital image. *Hitfix*. N.p., n.d. Web. 13 Nov. 2015.
   <http://s3.amazonaws.com/images.hitfix.com/assets/1828/5lifeofpi.jpg>.

Life of Pi. IMDb. IMDb.com, 21 Nov. 2012. Web. 13 Nov. 2015. <http://www.imdb.com/title/tt0454876/>.

Movie Score

Whenever I would watch films, the thing that stood out to me the most was not how vivid and realistic the scenes and characters were, but rather, how strongly the music resonated with me. To me, a song could paint a better picture than anything else could. Without it, scenes would lack a vital part of what brings them to life: emotion. Even if I would forget what happened in a movie I'd watched only days before, I would never forget the music that accompanied the most powerful scenes.

For my wild card, I chose to paint a picture of some of the most significant moments in my life, using five emotionally-stirring musical pieces as my guide. I wanted to combine my love of music and language while also painting a picture of the person I've become through my experiences. I've always been hesitant to open myself up, so my wild card serves as a small peek into the best and worst parts of me. To get the full effect, I encourage anyone reading this to listen to the song that corresponds to each story.

https://www.youtube.com/playlist?list=PL8-hwFKQhplJCRBsUqLgFqVFfNr9Kgb1

Arrival of the Birds

The Cinematic Orchestra

There was something beautiful about being whisked away in the dead of night, especially when I knew I was being saved. I could only stare, wide-eyed, at my home as my grandfather drove farther and farther away from it, and I could only stare, wide-eyed, at the ground below me as it grew smaller and smaller the higher our plane rose in the sky.

Black clouds soon turned pink as sunlight spilled onto them, and I thought of the warmth of my mother , whom I had missed dearly. I thought of the last goodbye I said to her before she left for America, leaving me alone for five months. I thought of the anger of my father and tears in my eyes. I thought of how happy I was to be plucked from my bed at the young age of five to be brought God knows where.

Anywhere but here.

I thought of her and only her, wishing she'd be there when the plane landed.

She was.

Thank God she was.

My mother and me after moving to America

Domestic Pressures

The Theory of Everything

New York City was unlike anything I had ever seen in my entire life. There were no palm trees, no gravel, no shabby wooden houses, and there were certainly no mangoes or bananas hanging from the boughs of the few trees I saw scattered here and there. Gray buildings towered over my mother and me, and an unfathomable number of bodies knocked against my own, no matter how closely I stuck to her side. With every breath I took, I inhaled stale cigarettes, honey-roasted peanuts, and what at the time smelled like month-old garbage.

I remember crowds of people pouring into subways, my mother's firm hand on my back as she guided me past row after row of cold, hard faces. And when I realized that I was invisible in this new world, just like everyone else, a smile spread across my face. I was in a world full of people who had yet to learn of my existence, and I loved it.

Me grinning widely on my 7th birthday

Autumn Love

Thomas Bergersen

I can vaguely remember the days leading up to the birth of my little brother, and yet, funnily enough, I can hardly remember life without him. I do recall begging for a sister, as though my parents could miraculously choose which genes they wished to give to their unborn child. I wanted someone soft like myself: someone who would join me in the corner of my bedroom, someone I could read to. Somehow, I was aware of the fact that a brother would only bring chaos into my peaceful life.

Before he even left the womb, my brother would bully me relentlessly. He would only kick when I laid my head upon my mother's stomach, and coincidentally, her morning sickness would worsen whenever she looked at me. My brother kept me away from the one person I wanted to know that I existed. I never wanted my brother; before my brother was born, I had already resented him.

Still, when my mother gently passed him over to me as I lay in the hospital bed, I felt my breath catch in my throat. I was aware of the fact that I held a tiny menace in my arms, but in an instant, all of his sins against me were forgiven.

Holding my brother for the first time

To Build a Home

The Cinematic Orchestra

There was something heartbreaking about being whisked away at the beginning of summer, especially when you knew you would never see your home again.

I waved goodbye to the tall skyscrapers and the broken roads and the hooting pigeons—and my old life. In my mind, I kissed every cold face I saw and hugged every corner store clerk. And I felt my soul weep and weep, hearing the faint splash of its tears against the gray pavement beneath my small feet.

"If the sky isn't blue when you reach your new home, you will never be happy there." I promised myself this.

When we arrived in Georgia, my eyes found the trees, the little birds, the red clay, and my family.

I will always regret looking up at the sky that day. I will always regret making that promise.

I wish . . . .

I wish it had been blue that day.

My family and me one winter in Georgia

Love Hurts

Yiruma

In the summer of 2015, my new world fell apart. I lost the peace I had, and I lost part of my soul. The summer before I began my first semester of college, love fled from my home, and my parents went their separate ways. I fell out of touch with my family and friends, and I hid myself, ashamed of myself for existing.

That summer changed me completely. I tread upon the ground for months as an empty, smiling vessel, and when I was alone, I wept silently.

I mourned for my parents and my brother and my family and for the part of me that died in those months.

It still pains me to talk about it, but this experience, just like all the others, is part of who I am.

English 1102

Student: Andrea Morrison

(Me, Andrea Morrison, as of November of 2015)

How We Killed the Loch Ness Monster

Biography

Every summer, my brother Christian and I perform the same ritual: we turn my room into a large fort of pillows and blankets, stock up on snack supplies, and sit for hours on end playing a computer based role-playing game called *Wizardry 8*. This routine might seem trite, but *Wizardry 8* has been an integral part of our lives for well over a decade.

When our father first introduced the game to us, he created our first team to help us get started. He named all six of our characters after family members, and he let Christian and me choose which characters would be named after us. I chose to be a whimsical engineer with a knack for picking locks and pockets alike, while my brother wanted to be a gladiator who could strike devastating blows to all who opposed us. Using our father's original party, my brother and I spent hours upon hours playing *Wizardry 8*; we worked together to better our team, solve extensive puzzles, and survive challenging battles. One of our toughest battles was against a giant sea monster comically named

"Nessie." Time after time, she defeated our party, and every time she did, Christian and I were forced to reload and try again. Each time we restarted, we employed a new strategy to help us defeat her. During one of our sessions, as we played through the night and into the early hours of the morning, our party had been reduced from six characters to two; my brother and I were the only ones left. However, we had weakened Nessie quite a bit, and a well aimed strike from either of our characters could finish her off. We were the closest we had ever been to winning the battle, and as Christian and I sat huddled around the computer, afraid to start the next round of combat, we took a deep breath and reminded ourselves that if we didn't win that time around, we would simply try again.

We would persevere, and perseverance, like many of the skills *Wizardry 8* taught me, has been invaluable in my every day life. Games may be primarily for fun and entertainment, but many games also encourage players to develop versatile, indispensable skills. A game taught me patience and diligence, and that the inability to do something once didn't mean the inability to do it *ever*. A game showed me the role of process in progress by encouraging me to make observations and apply them to problem solving. A game helped me see how well a team could function when they worked together and used their individual strengths to help each other.

But what does any of this information have to do with killing the Loch Ness Monster? It's simple. By honing our skills and testing new methods, we were able to defeat her with a shot from a tinkerer's gun and a blow from a warrior's sword.

(Left to right: Christian, age 3, and Andrea, age 5)

The Portfolio Manual

Introductory Reflexive Essay

The first morning of class, I arrived at Park Hall an hour before the building opened. I am a commuter student, and it was the first time I had driven to the University of Georgia. I gave myself time to get lost, time for traffic, and time for the bus, but in all the time I had given myself, I hadn't given myself time to prepare adequately for the first day of English 1102. I assumed that college writing would be akin to high school writing, and that I would simply begin planning and writing essays as soon as they were assigned while spending little to no time worrying about them. However, I was proved very, *very* wrong, and for the first time in my life, I was pretty happy about being wrong. During the first few class periods, Ms. Hittel stressed the importance of the writing process, but like many students, I figured I could pull through the class without using this process. However, as we delved into our first assignment, I noticed that I had seen this process before—just under different circumstances. As an avid gamer who's played my fair share of role-playing games, I realized that the writing process was quite similar to how I worked through games. Surprisingly, there are actually many similarities between writing and gaming.

In most role-playing games (RPGs), the player sculpts their own worlds and characters. Because of the endless possibilities for gameplay, every gamer plays the game differently. Will the star of the show be a rogue with a penchant for thievery? Or perhaps a hero who protects even the meekest of creatures? Truly, a character's traits depend on the gamer's choices, and each gamer uses their own unique brand of logic and reasoning to make these determinations. Even when changing the characters of a game, a player still explores and experiences the main story line. I followed this same approach when I illustrated the core themes and values of George Bernard Shaw's play *Pygmalion* while changing key elements in order to adapt the play to a film, which is exactly what Ms. Hittel asked us to do for our Drama Project. I used my own perspective and preferences to craft my adaptation of *Pygmalion*, which features Eliza Doolittle living as a Mexican woman in Baton Rouge, Louisiana, during the 1930s. Changing Eliza's ethnicity, as well as the setting of the play, allows me to capitalize on Eliza's imposed inability to have both freedom and esteem. My adaptation proves that Shaw's commentary on women applies to more than just twentieth-century England and also mimics the process of character and world creation that is essential to RPGs.

However, character creation is only one step in the RPG experience. Once a character and a world are established, a player must actually *play* the game. Most RPGs require players to make observations and use their acquired information to solve problems and puzzles throughout the game. Often, a player will encounter an obstacle that seems impossible to conquer and must look back at their observations to find a solution. Every major quest in a game is part of the bigger picture, and it's not until the player has enough experience that they can begin to decipher this picture. They have to examine every scenario they face from a multitude of angles, and certain pieces of the overarching puzzle may not fit where they appear to. This idea of keeping an open mind to new perspectives is essential in my Poetry Project. Throughout the project, I examine how terms that appear mutually exclusive can be used to analyze the same poem. My main focus is the ambiguity of beauty and tragedy and how different observations of the same poem can lead readers to form different conclusions. With most games, there are many paths to victory, and with the poems in my anthology, there are many paths to forming a perspective. Not everything is as it appears at first glance, and as a reader and a gamer, it's important to refrain from forming opinions too soon.

One of the most efficient ways to maintain perspective is to incorporate new information as it presents itself. In my experience with RPGs, one of the most crucial aspects of a game is to improve a character. As the player progresses in the game, their character must adapt to fit new situations. They often need to develop new skills while simultaneously improving upon old ones. Essentially, a player must edit their character. A beginning character is akin to the first draft of an essay: the basics are present, but they need to be fleshed out and developed. A writer must successfully integrate new material into old material, sometimes keeping previous sentences, sometimes changing them, and sometimes omitting them entirely. As a gamer learns new information and explores new areas of a game, they may find that skills that once seemed important are now utterly useless. Similarly, a writer may find that a sentence or paragraph that they once felt was essential to their essay now seems to be inconsistent with their work. When playing a game, a player must modify their character as they go along, just as a writer must modify their paper. No character starts off with the ability to complete a game, and no first draft perfectly portrays the arguments a writer makes.

To get from one draft to the next, writers often need advice from their peers. Similarly, many RPGs have online or multiplayer components to enhance gameplay. Each player serves as the protagonist in their own story, but they work together and cooperate with other players in order to reach a common goal. Often, a player provides information and materials that are helpful to the other players. However, they can't play the game for them. Similarly, in the peer reviewing process, peers aid each other's "gameplay" without taking control. When playing an RPG and writing an essay, it's easy to overlook minor errors and occurrences. Luckily, this problem can be solved by communicating with peers. One person's strength may be another's weakness, and vice versa. By communicating with each other and using their strengths to their advantage, gamers can help each other overcome obstacles, and writers can help each other bolster their arguments. Since no two gamers play a game the same way, each can recount the unique information they've collected. Likewise, with no two writers having the same perspective, they can use their differences to round each other out.

As I've gone through English 1102, I've had to do a lot of rounding out for myself. This entire semester has been a journey of self-discovery and self-acceptance, and while it hasn't always been easy, it's definitely been worth my time. My Wild Card, entitled *The Evolution of Knightly Sinclair*, reads as a small look into my personal life and history. As a predominant character in most of my playthroughs of the RPG *Wizardry 8*, Knightly embodies my uncertainty in my own life. She has never quite fit into my party, and yet she's always there. She has a lot of potential, but neither she nor I have quite figured out what is to become of that potential.

English 1102 has been an exciting and impactful experience. Like any RPG, the obstacles were challenging but not impossible, and it was only when I trusted myself and my peers that I could truly succeed. I've learned my strengths and weaknesses as a writer, and as the protagonist in my own life, it's up to me to decide what I'll revise and what I'll keep the same. I've learned to treat life as an RPG: to keep an open mind, to not be afraid to change, and to ask for help when I need to. Without English 1102, I don't think I ever would have thought to apply these strategies to my life, and I've got to say, I think I'm a better person with them than without them.

Andrea Morrison

Ms. Hittel

English 1102

5 December 2015

Creation

Exhibit One: Drama Project

Iceberg: Beneath the Surface

(Scambos)

Introduction

On the surface of the water, icebergs often appear small and non-threatening. However, the true scope of an iceberg's power and magnitude hides beneath the surface—beneath visibility. Similarly, a woman's true potential is masked by superficial features such as race, attire, and language. In his play *Pygmalion,* George Bernard Shaw confronts English society's attitude towards women, specifically calling attention to the upper class's predilection towards ignoring a woman's feelings and only accepting her value if she presents a convincing facade painted with beauty and ignorance. The female protagonist in his play, Eliza Doolittle, must give up her independence in order to get society to see her as an acceptable, respectable woman, as evidenced by her telling Henry Higgins, the male protagonist, that "you've made a lady of me [and now] I'm not fit to sell anything [other than myself]" (Shaw 48). Concurrently, Higgins spends the entirety of the play reforming Eliza to be fit for high society, but he sees her "only as an object for experiment" (Lihua 41). In order to demonstrate the significance of Shaw's commentary on the role women in society, I am adapting *Pygmalion* to a film of a different time and place, transforming Eliza Doolittle into a Mexican immigrant in Baton Rouge, Louisiana. By creating an adaptation with an ethnic element, I expand upon Shaw's initial commentary and show the additional struggles of women of color as well as add a visible representation of Eliza's transformation.

Context and Setting

As a Mexican woman in the 1930s in the American south, Eliza Doolittle faces many struggles regarding her race and gender. Her family adopted the last name Doolittle in an attempt to assimilate into American society, meaning that Eliza and her father speak with a heavy accent that limits their employment and status potential. In the beginning of the adaptation, Eliza works as a flower girl, and because of her accent and the indignity associated with her job and heritage, many people refuse to hire her. Eliza hopes that by learning to speak as a southern debutante, she will be able to get a stable job.

Henry Higgins, on the other hand, remains truer to Shaw's original character. He is British and makes a living as a phonetics expert. However, in order to explain his involvement in America, the film adaptation shows that his mother has retired to Baton Rouge in hopes of the warmer weather easing her arthritis pain. Higgins has a manor in Baton Rouge so that he may check on his mother from time to time, as well as learn more about the dialects of the American south. In the context of the film, Higgins and Pickering have arranged to meet at Higgins's study in Baton Rouge.

Time Period

The film takes place in the mid-1930s. During this time, immigrants living in the United States (particularly Hispanic immigrants) were forced to pass a literacy requirement ("Timeline of Important Dates"). Several years later, the United States government placed a limit on the number of immigrants allowed into the United States and simultaneously created Border Control to prevent these immigrants from entering the country. In addition to these events, the United States was just beginning to recover from the Great Depression. This time in history allows for the greatest struggles, for Eliza as a Mexican woman in America: she knows English, but she doesn't speak it very well, and people will only accept her in society as an inferior member of the proletariat. Eliza initially believes that correcting her accent means enhancing her prestige, but upgrading her social status doesn't change the inequality she faces. With the United States healing from the Great Depression, businesses and proprietors won't hire a woman to do a man's job, and they won't allow a Hispanic woman to hold the same position as a white woman. With a new accent, she's respected, but she's no longer free.

Place

This particular production occurs in Baton Rouge, Louisiana for two primary reasons. The class issues are often extreme (even if dramatized) in the American south, which will allow the director to capitalize on the hardships Eliza faces as a poor, Hispanic woman. In addition to the class issues present, there are many dialects there that would attract Higgins and Pickering such as typical southern dialects, Cajun English/French, and creole.

Sets

The scene takes place entirely in the study of Higgins's manor. The appearance of the room very closely resembles the description given in the written play at the beginning of Act II, especially in having the basic amenities of a drawing room such as a fireplace and an easy chair while being mostly cluttered with work materials such as "a phonograph, a laryngoscope, a row of tiny organ pipes with bellows, [etc.]" (Shaw 14). There are two large windows facing the front of the house that allow the audience to see that this scene occurs at night, and that it is raining.

Lighting

The central source of lighting for the scene comes from the hearth. Just before this scene occurs, Higgins turns off the main lighting to the room, completely oblivious to Eliza's presence. The hearth acts as directional lighting in order to cast dark shadows and create heavy contrast, which adds ambiance and ominousness to the set (Zettl 160, 162).

Furthermore, changing which character is better illuminated throughout the scene allows the lighting to allude to the battle for equality between Eliza and Higgins.

Camera Shots and Angles

At the beginning of the scene, the audience sees Higgins with a low angle shot, which gives him a sense of power and dominance (Freer). The low angle shot of Higgins pairs with a high angle shot of Eliza to showcase Eliza's perceived inferiority. Furthermore, having the camera angles capitalize on solely Eliza or solely Higgins demonstrates their differences (Marcotte). As the scene continues, the camera angle adapts to an eye-level shot that features Eliza and Higgins together in order to give the audience a subtle hint of Eliza's rise to equality.

Music

The selection below plays quietly in the background as the scene progresses. The slow tempo and somber tones of the selection give the audience a heightened sense of sorrow and fragility, which mimic Eliza's feelings during the scene. The long, full notes allow the music to add to the scene without overpowering it, and the tempo and melody of the music embody the essence of the intense argument between Higgins and Eliza.

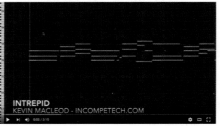

https://youtu.be/gkSU5RPeh-o
(*Intrepid*)

Furthermore, rain and thunder sounds improve upon the tension of the moment. Rain often signals despair and discontinuity, two sentiments that epitomize this scene, and the thunder adds power and anger to their argument by providing loud, chaotic bursts of noise. Furthermore, Eliza and Higgins first met in the rain, so adding rain to their argument gives the idea that their relationship has come full circle and shows that a relationship cultivated from desperation can only end in desperation.

https://youtu.be/5fNLEPrNi2A
(*Thunder Sound FX*)

Costumes

Eliza Doolittle

Eliza is wearing very extravagant attire. However, during this scene, she realizes that becoming a well respected woman in society means losing her independence and her identity. To demonstrate Eliza's torn feelings between her freedom and her social standing, she rids herself of extravagances throughout the scene. She takes her jewelry off and gives it to Higgins. Her hair begins in an updo at the beginning of this scene so that she can tear it down as she realizes she has been viewed as a doll. She may *look* better off under Higgins's teachings, but because of how society functions towards women and towards Hispanics, he takes more from her than she's willing to lose, and her exterior finally begins to reflect her emotions instead of the desires of society.

(*Photograph of Hair*)

(*Photograph of Jewelry Set*)

(*Evening Dress*)

Henry Higgins

Based on the fact that Higgins has no manners or subtlety, not having a sense of style will enhance his character by providing a visual demonstration of his apathy towards social protocol. Throughout his conversation with Eliza, he remained poised. While Eliza discovers herself and her worth, he fails to discover anything. Higgins has given Eliza what she wanted, but he has not helped her, and he does not understand her feelings of inequality because he is not in the same situation as her. His position in society is secure, and unlike Eliza, he doesn't have to choose between independence and respect. He doesn't have to "dress to impress." In order to reflect his static characterization, his appearance, while not fashionable, remains fairly tidy and consistent throughout the scene.

(Murawski)

(*Vintage Smoking Jacket*)

(*Men's Slippers*)

Actors

Eliza Doolittle

(*Photograph of Odette Annable*)

Odette Annable speaks Spanish and English fluently, so she can easily demonstrate Eliza's vocal transformation by turning a heavy

Spanish accent into a proper English one. Furthermore, her appearance can be easily altered (with the help of makeup) to place emphasis on her more Hispanic features or on her more Caucasian features. The more "sophisticated" Eliza becomes, the more "white" she appears, demonstrating that social status, especially in the American south, is predominantly based on race. This modification of her appearance acts as a visual representation of Eliza losing her identity. The more Caucasian Eliza looks and sounds, the more value the average person sees in her because many people of this time and place have been conditioned to view "white" as synonymous with "better." In addition to these characteristics, Odette Annable is fairly tall for a woman, and with the heels she will be wearing in the scene, her height advantage gives her leverage to help illustrate her desire for and rise to equality.

Henry Higgins

(*Photograph of Hugh Laurie*)

Henry Higgins is straightforward, pretentious, and insensitive; he is not quick to anger, does as he wishes, and has no manners. Hugh Laurie portrays his character on the television program *House, M.D.* with these exact characteristics, as seen in the following clip:

https://youtu.be/3s09m8ZoHP0
(*Video of Hugh Laurie*)

Furthermore, as an Englishman who can give credence to a variety of English accents and dialects (including American English), Laurie can easily portray a phonetics expert with the ability to teach Eliza how to speak like a proper southern belle.

Conclusion

The fact that a film adaptation can embody the same core values and ideas Shaw established in his play *Pygmalion* (even when key elements are modified) proves how universally these issues are ingrained into human society. The elite class only views Eliza as a woman of value when she tailors her accent, presents herself as a possession to be acquired, and becomes suitable for "the Governor-General of India or the Lord-Lieutenant of Ireland, or somebody who wants a deputy-queen" (Shaw 55). Unfortunately, according to many societies and cultures throughout history and throughout the world, a valuable woman is not allowed to be an independent woman. To be accepted as a woman of worth, Eliza must accept a role as an inferior, which epitomizes global attitudes towards women as, at best, secondary. Often, the genteel members of society only value a woman based on how she appears while her true, hidden potential is allowed to wither away. She is an iceberg obscured by the water—strong and powerful, but only valued based on the small portion of her that her observers can see. Eliza Doolittle is determined to change this perspective. She is determined to prove that freedom and respect aren't mutually exclusive, and she proves her point by standing up to the man who turned her into an object, by standing up to Henry Higgins, and consequentially, standing up for all women.

Works Cited

Evening Dress. 2015. Photograph.

Freer, Ian. "Film Studies 101: The 30 Camera Shots Every Film Fan Needs To Know." *Empire Online*. Empire, 16 Dec. 2013. Web. 19 Nov. 2015.

Intrepid. Prod. Kevid MacLeod. *Incompetech*. *YouTube*. Creative Commons, 17 Sept. 2015. Web. 20 Nov. 2015.

Lihua, Chen. "A Feminist Perspective to *Pygmalion*." *Canadian Social Science* 2.2. (2006): 41-44. Print.

Marcotte, Kathryn. "Making a Film." Personal interview. 6 Nov. 2015.

Men's Slippers. Photograph. Kohl's.

Murawski, Joseph J. *Yellow Tuxedo*. Photograph. Etsy.

Photograph of Hair. 2015. Photograph. Coafuri Mireasa.

Photograph of Hugh Laurie. 2014. Photograph. Sn-z.

Photograph of Jewelry Set. 2014. Photograph. Hodress.

Photograph of Odette Annable. 2012. Photograph.

Scambos, Ted. *Iceberg*. 2006. NSIDC. *National Snow & Ice Data Center*. Web. 15 Nov. 2015.

Shaw, Bernard. *Pygmalion*. New York: Brentano, 1916.

Thunder Sound FX. Prod. Grant Evans. *Sound Bible*. *YouTube*. Attribution 3.0, 30 May 2011. Web. 20 Nov. 2015.

"Timeline of Important Dates." *Latino Americans*. PBS, 2013. Web. 14 Nov. 2015.

Video of Hugh Laurie. *YouTube*. N.p., 5 Aug. 2009. Web.

Vintage Smoking Jacket. Photograph. Gentleman's Emporium.

Zettl, Herbert. *Video Basics 7*. San Francisco: Cengage Learning, 2013. Print.

Observation

Exhibit Two: Poetry Project

Drawn in Pencil: An Anthology on the Obscurity of Boundaries

(Photograph of Shark Fin)

Is it ever alright to lie? Some people believe that mild fabrications are completely acceptable. Others have determined that deceptions, regardless of the circumstances, should never be told. Little white lies, as these meek inaccuracies are often called, have the capability to cause damage, but it is not clear if this harm is in the inherent nature of the lie, or if it is only engendered when the lie stretches beyond its capacity. This boundary-this ill tension between help and harm-is indeterminate, and lies demonstrate only one of many examples of issues that conjure up opposing views. Conflicting ideas such as those of life and death, joy and sorrow, and beauty and tragedy rarely fail to appear without their antithetical companions. One always lurks in the mind of the other. So where, exactly, is the line between these abstracts? Does such a line even exist?

The poems in this anthology show that a boundary doesn't always exist between concepts that are seemingly polar opposites. After examining an abundance of works, pinpointing the poems that invoked a deep sense of amazement, sorrow, loss, and wonder proved easy. These poems allow the reader to visualize-and thus to question-the "boundaries" presented between the aforementioned antithetical notions.

In the first poem, "Child Burial" by Paula Meehan, the speaker is so distraught over the loss of her child that she wishes he had never been born, insisting she never would have felt such overwhelming pain if she had never had him to lose (Meehan 779). Although dealing with a grim subject, this poem demonstrates that intense pain can only stem from passionate love, establishing the unbreakable ties between beauty and tragedy and giving the reader a new way to view a bleak situation.

Matthew Sweeney also explores new perspectives in his poem "The Volcano." Sweeney challenges the negative destructive connotations of lava by introducing ideas of preservation. In the poem, the speaker mimics the natural reaction to run from and fear the volcano, only to be amazed by "a herd of donkeys, galloping, / and the sky filled with crows" (Sweeney 717). He observes that the volcano is actually evacuating the mountain to protect the inhabitants and conserve the land, turning their belongings "into sculptures / that one day [they'd] come back and see."

However, "Ter Conatus" by Bernard O'Donoghue, takes a completely different tone in regard to conservation. The poem features two siblings growing old together who, in all their years, haven't learned to care for one another. When the sister grows ill, she never tells her brother, and he never asks. It's heartbreaking that he never "embraced her with a brother's arm" before she died, but the knowledge that he would change their estrangement if he could inspires great awe and sorrow because the brother is motivated to change, but it is already too late for his change to impact his relationship with his sister (O'Donoghue 539). O'Donoghue tinkers with ideas of regret-the should haves, could haves, and would haves of remorse. By advancing the brother's feelings from ostracization to affection, O'Donoghue proves that regrets and mistakes, as terrible as they can be, are the driving forces behind breathtaking improvements.

This sense of regret and remorse is featured in Eavan Boland's "Quarantine," especially in the lines "In the morning [the man and his wife] were both found dead. / Of cold. Of hunger. Of the toxins of a whole history," implying that the couple featured in the poem didn't have to live or die in the tragic way they were forced to (Boland 490). Boland demonstrates love as defined by westernized wedding vows, by inherent antitheses: for better, for worse; for richer, for poorer; in sickness and in health. The despair in this poem allows Boland's true, harsh definition of love to shine through: until death do us part.

Death, featured prominently in "The Soul Kisses Goodbye" by Enda Wyley, turns into a beautiful but heartwrenching dance between body and soul, bringing forth the idea of a deep, lifelong connection now severed. The soul talks to the body it has abandoned and returns to it time and time again because it cannot bear to be separated. Death, while appearing to silence the body, allows the soul to express the love and gratitude it couldn't before. Death finalizes many endings while simultaneously creating new beginnings, contradictory ideas necessary for mutual continuation.

All of these poems present their subjects as both tragic and beautiful, terms that are not as exclusive as they might appear to be. These works discuss varied topics but still embody the essence of boundary ambiguity. Together, they show that while black and white may be idealistic, they're certainly not realistic. Good and bad, light and dark, beauty and tragedy: in every scenario, there is more than meets the eye, and it is important for the reader to examine these scenarios from a multitude of angles before forming their own opinion. The entirety of a picture is more than the sum of its parts, and every piece may not function the way it initially appears to. When answering the question "Is it ever alright to lie?" a yes or no answer may not suffice.

(Photograph of Gold Fish with Fin)

Beauty and Tragedy

Paula Meehan

(Photograph of Paula Meehan by D. Meehan)

Paula Meehan was born in the inter-city districts of Dublin, Ireland (Davis 773). Throughout her life, she has written a wide variety of plays and poems for audiences both young and old ("Paula Meehan"). Her poems most notably handle the inner, personal depths of everyday situations (Davis 773).

Paraphrase

Your tiny coffin is so elaborate. Everything you have been buried with and in has been chosen as a reflection of you. You will be alone, and you will not know where you are. There will be no one there to show you the ways of the world and the beauty it possesses. There are so many things you will never know, my child. If I could, I would reverse time, go back to a time when you were alive and healthy inside of me. I would go back further, to the night you were made, the night you became a twinkle in my eye. Instead of having you and subjecting us both to this pain, I would give you back to the world just as you came.

Summary

I carefully chose every detail of your burial to make you feel comfortable and protected. There are so many concepts I will never teach you and you will never learn. I would rather you never have been born than have suffered this fate.

Analysis

The eldest of six children, Paula Meehan was born in Dublin, Ireland in 1955 (Carty). She attended a variety of schools in her youth, but since education wasn't deemed a necessity for women at the time, it wasn't until later in her adulthood that she decided she would use her writing to "stand up for the word" (Meehan qtd. in Carty). Writing about everything from plays to poetry, her topics of choice tend to cover "deeply personal [terrains] in which the imagination charges ordinary occurrences . . . with transcendental significance" (Davis 773). As such, Meehan has been known to write about the "terrain" of her surroundings as opposed to writing about herself. Following this observation, and given that Meehan has not had any children of her own, it is unlikely that "Child Burial" stemmed from personal experience, but whether it spouted from her imagination or an observation is unknown.

"Child Burial" is an elegy written from a mourning mother to her deceased son. This narrative gives the poem a sense of intense privacy and has the reader intruding on the speaker's most intimate thoughts. The speaker freely expresses the emotions that she truly feels, regardless of the opinions others might form. Meehan uses this point of view to address an often hidden side of human nature, beautifully conveying the speaker's bare emotions in the face of tragedy. To further illustrate the speaker's severe depression, the author has composed the lament of heterometric couplets that do not abide by a rhyme scheme. The lines often end in enjambment, which adds to the chaotic nature of the poem and gives the poem a hint of quick, sporadic movements. Thoughts pour fluidly into each other, giving the poem an essence of raw honesty. The beginning lines, "Your coffin looked unreal, / fancy as a wedding cake," compare two events that have vastly different connotations (P. Meehan 778). This comparison invites the reader to see another side of this tragic event; weddings mean looking forward to a happy life, while funerals mean looking back on a life well lived. Funerals wouldn't embody such sorrow if the life preceding them didn't embody equivalent joy.

The speaker then shifts from this evoked antithesis into describing the clothing she buried her son in, such as "[his] favorite stripey shirt,

// [his] blue cotton trousers" (P. Meehan 778). These descriptions allow the reader to see the child through his mother's eyes; these descriptions make the child real, and the more palpable the reader's image of the child becomes, the more pain his absence causes. To best elicit a sense of sorrow in the audience, the author must remind them that the loss of a child is dependent on the existence of a child. Meehan continues to tap into the reader's sympathy as the speaker says that she had picked "a gansy of handspun wool, // warm and fleecy for [him]. It is / so cold down in the dark" to show that even though her child is not alive, the mother still has a strong desire to protect him and to keep him safe and comfortable (P. Meehan 778). While the speaker's deep affection for her child demonstrates the astonishing depths of maternal love, the audience is forced to come to the realization that this love is now missing a recipient. Meehan proves that maternal love does not die with death. The speaker's desire to protect her child transcends death; she still wants to help him develop, to answer the questions he never got a chance to ask, as proven when she says to him:

> No light can reach you and teach you
> the paths of wild bird,
>
> the names of the flowers,
> the fishes, the creatures. (P. Meehan 778)

She implies that her son was a bright, inquisitive boy and illustrates the joy that this kind of blissfulness brings while also showing the heartbreak that results when this joy vanishes. Teaching a child is a beautiful process, and being robbed of that experience is tragic.

She follows her saddening realization by addressing her son with a variety of animal cub names: "my lamb, my calf, my eaglet, / my cub, my kid, my nestling, // my suckling, my colt" (P. Meehan 779). Her narration has many meanings; she uses these terms as expressions of youthful innocence and to show that the bond of motherhood exceeds the bond of species. The loss of her child speaks to her identity as a mother more than any other aspect of her existence. She presents herself as a mother, and she unites herself with the universal definition of motherhood. A key aspect of being a mother is having a child, and losing him means losing a piece of herself.

From this poignant point on motherhood, Meehan delves into "alternate reality," a popular topic of hers (Davis 774). Davis claims the author "[probes] the moment of infinite possibility just at the cusp of tragedy, trying to imagine alternate stories, but often colliding with the stony reality of inevitability," and this claim is seen in the last half of "Child Burial" when the speaker wishes she could "spin // time back . . . through nine waxing months" and "cancel the love feast // the hot night of [his] making" (P. Meehan 779). True to Davis's observation, this "alternate reality" ends in the way it "inevitably" would; the speaker says:

> I would travel alone
> to a quiet mossy place,
>
> you would spill from me into the earth,
> drop by bright red drop. (P. Meehan 779)

Her writing here can mean one of two things: instead of creating the child, his potentiality would leave her in a menstrual cycle, and she would never know the pain of losing him; or, knowing the devastation caused by his birth and subsequent death, she would have killed herself there and then to spare herself from the pain of his loss. The speaker's thoughts can be classified as selfish, but the reader must remember that these thoughts were not expressed with the purpose of being shared. Her reflections are raw, which contributes to their grimness. However, the speaker would not have known this kind of torment if she had not borne a deep, eternal love for her child. A pain this consuming can only come from a love just as fulfilling, and while it is horrible to imagine this mother's sorrow, her sorrow can only deflate her as low as her happiness elated her. This tragedy could not exist without its eternal sister, beauty, and when this kind of beauty exists, it *always* has the possibility of ending in tragedy.

Preservation and Destruction

Matthew Sweeney

(Photograph of Matthew Sweeney)

Born and raised in Ireland, Matthew Sweeney himself says that his poems often showcase a form of "imagistic narrative" he refers to as "alternative realism" ("Matthew Sweeney"). A common concept he employs in his writings is "simplicity," or getting as much use as possible from as few words as necessary (Davis 706).

Paraphrase

The volcano near us is erupting, so we grab our valuables and leave for safer ground. We are afraid we won't make it, but soon we are running as fast as we can go, being filled with the sights, smells, and sounds of the volcano. We are reckless and our pet monkey panics, so I calm him down and try to get a sense of the impending danger we are in. But instead of seeing the horror I expect, I see a beautiful landscape filled with the animals that the mountain is personally evacuating. Time slows down, and I realize the volcano is nothing to fear. The volcano will not destroy our home; the lava will preserve it.

Summary

We flee from the volcano in fear, and as we flee, we observe the beauty of the mountain's evacuation. The volcano is not destroying; its lava is preserving.

Familiar and Estranged

Bernard O'Donoghue

(Photograph of Bernard O'Donoghue)

Born in County Cork, Ireland, O'Donoghue says he has always had an interest in written and oral linguistics (Davis 529). He credits this to his upbringing in rural Ireland and the historical prevalence it brought to his life, which he often uses in his own poems and in his interpretations of poetry (Davis 530).

Paraphrase

A brother and sister were estranged growing up. She developed a mysterious illness that she mistook for a common, recurring pain. By the time she went to the doctor, she could not do anything about her cancer. She never intended to tell her brother, but the pain made it difficult for her to do common tasks. Still, she refused his help when he offered it. It was the first time he had tried to help her, and he didn't know how to. Instead, he chose not to try. She died, and there was a funeral. All the funeral attendees wanted to know what the brother was thinking. He was thinking that for once, he should have tried something new instead of sticking to what he knew.

Summary

A brother and sister were so distant that she could not tell him when she got sick, and he could not help her when he should have. She died, and he was filled with regrets.

Love and Despair

Eavan Boland

(Photograph of Eavan Boland)

While born in Ireland, Boland's upbringing was mostly divided between New York and London ("Eavan Boland"). As she blossomed into a young Irishwoman, she noticed that there was an absence of prominent woman in both Irish culture and in Irish history (Davis 470-471). She addresses and challenges this absence through her poetry.

Summary

During the potato famine, a married couple tried to find a better life. They died because they were in the wrong place at the wrong time, but their love-true love -was proved through their actions toward one another in a period of darkness.

Life and Death

Enda Wyley

(Photograph of Enda Wyley)

Enda Wyley, born in Dublin, Ireland, began her writing career at a very early age (Davis 844-845). Her poems tend to focus on love and seeing mundane objects from hidden angles.

Summary

I, the soul, am so deeply connected to you that your death represents my own. You were my everything, and you treated me so well in life, so I will treat you well in death.

Works Cited

Boland, Eavan. "Quarantine." *An Anthology of Modern Irish Poetry*. Ed. Wes Davis. Cambridge, MA: The Belknap Press of Harvard UP, 2010. 490. Print

Carty, Ciaran. "Paula Meehan: The Poet at 60." *The Irish Times*. 28 Feb. 2015. Web. 23 Sept. 2015.

Davis, Wes. *An Anthology of Modern Irish Poetry*. Ed. Wes Davis. Cambridge, MA: The Belknap Press of Harvard UP, 2010. Print.

"Eavan Boland." *Poetry Foundation*. Poetry Foundation. Web. 21 Sept. 2015.

"Matthew Sweeney. "*Poetry Foundation*. Poetry Foundation. Web. 21 Sept. 2015.

Meehan, Dave. *Photograph of Paula Meehan*. n.d. *Paula Meehan*. Irish Times, 2015. Web. 21 Sept. 2015.

Meehan, Paula. "Child Burial." *An Anthology of Modern Irish Poetry*. Ed. Wes Davis. Cambridge, MA: The Belknap Press of Harvard UP, 2010. 778-779. Print.

O'Donoghue, Bernard. "*Ter Conatus*." *An Anthology of Modern Irish Poetry*. Ed. Wes Davis. Cambridge, MA: The Belknap Press of Harvard UP, 2010. 538-539. Print

"Paula Meehan". *Wake Forest University Press*. Wake Forest University Press. Web. 21 Sept. 2015.

Photograph of Bernard O'Donoghue. n.d. *Bernard O'Donoghue*. Huffington Post UK, 2012. Web. 21 Sept. 2015.

Photograph of Eavan Boland. n.d. *Eavan Boland*. Poetry Foundation. Web. 21 Sept. 2015.

Photograph of Enda Wyley. n.d. *Enda Wyley Image*. Australian Broad-
     casting Corporation, 2015. Web. 21 Sept. 2015.

Photograph of Gold Fish with Fin. n.d. Google, 2013. Web. 7 Dec.
     2015.

Photograph of Matthew Sweeney. n.d. *Matthew Sweeney*. Poetry Foun-
     dation. Web. 21 Sept. 2015.

Photograph of Shark Fin. n.d. Palm Springs News Wire. Web. 7 Dec.
     2015.

Sweeney, Matthew. "The Volcano." *An Anthology of Modern Irish Po-
     etry*. Ed. Wes Davis. Cambridge, MA: The Belknap Press of
     Harvard UP, 2010. 717. Print

Integration

Revising and Editing

In a role-playing game, gaining experience and leveling up characters is crucial. In most games, a player can improve upon their characters' skills once their characters have gained enough experience points. However, many of these same games also allow characters to improve their skills as they use them. For example, a character who fights with a sword can enhance his combat skill by engaging in more battles. As a younger gamer, I used the "leveling up" approach as my only method of bettering my characters' abilities, but I quickly noticed that my characters would easily be outperformed by other characters of the same level. At that point in time, I knew I needed to develop a different progression strategy.

Similar to this process, I once viewed revising and editing as merely finding the errors in my writing. I didn't view it for what it really was-a tactic to *strengthen* my writing. In my experience before English 1102, I simply skimmed my essays for basic grammatical errors and made sure Point A got connected to Point B. I never really focused on *how* to connect these points; I just assured that the connection got made. I saw revising and editing as a one and done deal, not as a constant, ongoing process.

My revising and editing process has changed a lot throughout this semester. First of all, I've stopped trying to make the elusive "perfect draft" from the beginning. I now write what comes to mind first, and even if it doesn't sound quite right, or I know that I'm missing something, I write it, anyway. As I revise, I mark off areas of interest with brackets so that I can easily find them later. Typically, these points cover big ideas such as "explain more" or "incorporate xyz idea," but they also call attention to small edits such as punctuation problems and ineffective repetition. A coordinated highlighting system further breaks down my initial revisions and emphasizes which type of revisions I need to perform. In addition to this revising and editing process, I often include a section in red text at the beginning of my project entitled "Overall Fixes" that focuses on the global revisions I need to pay attention to when drafting the next version of my project. As I sculpt my new draft, I remove the highlighting and the brackets, and I integrate my new ideas into my old ones, similar to how I now integrate skill practice into my gameplay.

The following highlighting strategy was used for the entire revision process regarding the introduction of my Fiction Project:

Something needs to be added.

When a phrase is highlighted in purple, it means I have nothing to work with initially. I know I need *something* there to better my paper, but I am currently not sure what that something is.

Different word/phrase.

If a word or phrase is highlighted in green, it typically means that it is serving as a placeholder. I know the idea I am trying to convey, but I don't want to forget it while trying to think of the proper way to phrase it.

Reword sentence.

Blue highlighting indicates that an entire sentence need to be reworded. The sentence could be faulty because it is riddled with grammatical errors, worded confusingly, or inconsistent with the rest of the paragraph.

Punctuation.

Any marks or comments highlighted in red mean that I have used incorrect punctuation.

Citations.

Anything highlighted in yellow is related to citations. A citation is either incomplete or incorrect, and I need to fix the citation for my next draft.

Draft One

Overall Fixes: Find a better way to explain Stokols' theory. Furthermore, the organization is, well, *not organized*, and that's a problem. I'm jumping around from idea to idea, and I need them to flow into each other. I'll need to reorganize some of my thoughts.

[A REAL INTRODUCTION, PLEASE - MAKE IT SNAZZY]

Disillusionment, as defined by Daniel Stokol, occurs when reality does not live up to expectations (Stokol ??). This can happen through either personal or neutral thwarting on behalf of the [THING] a person is becoming disillusioned with (Stokol ??). [AWKWARD SENTENCE] The [PERSON] either feels their expectations were not met because of uncontrollable circumstances or because they were personally victimized (Stokol ??). While one may simply be told to lower their expectations; this will not change that disillusionment is an inevitable part of life that [WE] are all predisposed to experience. Building expectations out of common occurrences is natural to human behavior, but it is simply unreasonable to assume that all of these expectations can be met all of the time. Perhaps, then, [WE] should examine where these expectations come from.

[TRANSITION; In XYZ year...] Psychologist Jean Piaget theorized that children undergo a self-centered stage, where they only view the world in terms of themselves (McLeod). They develop certain expectations that their surroundings will adapt to their wants and needs (given that the parent has generally provided these) [AWKWARD SENTENCE]. Generally, this is considered a healthy exploration of self and surrounding. However, some caretakers have difficulty with forcing their children to experience this disillusionment, which can lead to more traumatic experiences [down the line - OR THE LIKES OF]. For example, young children are typically fed by their parents, but as they get older, most realize that they can no longer expect their parents to feed them and must begin feeding themselves. However, if the parents continuously ensure that the child never has to make their own food, the child may be very surprised and confused when a friend's parent asks them to make something on their own [BETTER EXAMPLE]. Either way, this is a [MILD] form of disillusionment [BECAUSE THE CHILD HAD HIGH EXPECTATIONS THAT WERE NOT MET].

Analysis

Having my character practice once doesn't perfect their skills, and revising my project once doesn't make it suitable for submission. Whenever I return to my project to edit it, I have had more time to think about the ideas I am trying to explore and express. When looking back at my first draft, I often find that it appears childish and ineffective. However, I can still identify the concepts I am trying to explain, and I have a better understanding of how to explain them. My second draft doesn't solve each of the individual problems with my first draft. Instead, it acts as a comprehensive solution. By making my global revisions first, many of my local revisions become obsolete. I have new words and sentences to work with, so abiding by all of my original revisions would be impossible. The following draft is the result of adding my initial edits and revisions. The highlighted portions of this new draft illustrate the revisions I plan to employ when crafting my third draft.

Draft Two

Overall Fixes: I *really* need to incorporate *The House in Paris* earlier. Does Stokols's definition still make *sense* in this context? I also need to work on my transitions; it gets a little choppy sometimes. Where, exactly, is my thesis?

An old adage says to "hope for the best, prepare for the worst, expect nothing, and you'll never get hurt" (CITE??). While these words may seem to provide sound advice, they can be contrasted against Alfred, Lord Tennyson's "'Tis better to have loved and lost / Than never to have loved at all" (Tennyson). [TRANSITION] While [ONE] may simply be told to lower their expectations, [THIS] will not change that disillusionment is an inevitable part of life that humanity is predisposed to experience. Building expectations out of common occurrences is natural to human behavior, but it is simply unreasonable to assume that all of these expectations can be met all of the time. [BUT] where do these expectations come from?

In 1936, Psychologist Jean Piaget theorized that children undergo a self-centered stage, where they view the world only in terms of themselves (McLeod). It was Daniel Stokols who explained how [THIS] could be problematic later in life. According to Stokols' "Toward a Psychological Theory of Alienation" disillusionment is when a person "begins with high levels of involvement and expectation only to arrive at, or be jolted into, an extremely unfavorable situation" (31). [TRAN-SITION] There are two paths to becoming disillusioned. The first path "involves a *neutral thwarting* – that is, one which does not emanate directly from [O], is not specifically directed at [P], and is perceived by [P] as being unintentional" whereas the second path "involves a *personal thwarting* – that is, one which stems directly from [O], is specifically directed at [P], and is perceived by [P] as [intentional]" (Stokols 32, 33). Furthermore, [IT IS STATED] that each of these paths – *neutral* and *personal thwarting* – has two potential outcomes depending on "the salience of desirable alternative relationships" (Stokols 34). A person who feels that salient alternatives are available to their current status will have an "adaptive" strategy to problem solving (Barber 161). According to Stokols, the potential outcomes of disillusionment with regard to types of thwarting and alternatives are as follows: isolation, reintegration, subjugation, or rebellion (35).

Analysis

As I finish making my second round of revisions, I notice that my paper feels much more unified than it did originally. When I look at my third draft to see if it functions efficiently enough to become my final, I have much less to revise and edit than I did with my first or second drafts. For the most part, I have all the pieces I need, and I simply have to worry about rewording certain sentences and phrases so that they better add to my overall argument. My second round of revisions have been applied to this next draft, and the highlighted portions illustrate the final edits I plan to make before my paper is ready for submission.

Draft Three

Overall Fixes: How much of Stokols's theory is *necessary*? I should better tie my thesis - as well as my general introduction - into *The House in Paris*. Also, I use passive voice a lot, and I should probably do something about that.

An old adage says to "hope for the best, prepare for the worst, expect nothing, and you'll never get hurt". While these unattributed words may seem to provide sound advice, [THEY CAN BE EASILY CONTRASTED AGAINST] Alfred, Lord Tennyson's "'Tis better to have loved and lost / Than never to have loved at all" (Tennyson). Expressed truthfully, to love is to be exposed, to be vulnerable; to hurt and be hurt, but also to forgive and be forgiven. Love, by all standards, defies the notion of preparation simply because love is not rational. Contrary to [THIS], many people, such as Karen Michaelis and Max Ebhart of Elizabeth Bowen's *The House in Paris*, grow up believing that love is supposed to "be safe" and easy like "furniture or the dark" (Bowen 87, 159). To grow up, to grow into oneself, is to develop expectations and have them quickly crushed. The process of disillusionment is an essential element of the human experience, one that cannot be avoided with any amount of preparation.

To understand why disillusionment [CANNOT BE EVADED], it is important to accurately define what it means to be disillusioned. According to Daniel Stokols' "Toward a Psychological Theory of Alienation" disillusionment occurs when a person "begins with high levels of involvement and expectation only to arrive at, or be jolted into, an extremely unfavorable situation" (Stokols 31). Stokols states that there are two paths to becoming disillusioned. The first path "involves a *neutral thwarting*—that is, one which does not emanate directly from [the cause of disillusionment], is not specifically directed at [the disillusioned person], and is perceived by [the disillusioned person] as being unintentional" whereas the second path "involves a *personal thwarting*—that is, one which stems directly from [the cause of disillusionment], is specifically directed at [the disillusioned person], and is perceived by [the disillusioned person] as [intentional]" (Stokols 32, 33). Furthermore, it is stated that each of these paths—*neutral* and *personal thwarting*—has two potential outcomes depending on "the salience of desirable alternative relationships" or, essentially, "the extent to which [the disillusioned person feels] 'caught' or 'trapped' in an unsatisfying situation" (Stokols 34; Barber 155). A person who feels that salient alternatives are available to their current status will have an "adaptive" strategy to problem solving (Barber 161). According to Stokols, the potential outcomes of disillusionment with regard to types of thwarting and alternatives are as follows: isolation, reintegration, subjugation, or rebellion (Stokols 35).

Analysis

Upon fixing the last few errors present within my third draft, I arrived at my final version of my Fiction Project introduction. My thesis is clearly visible in my final edition, and my introduction efficiently explains the scope of my project. As I have built up my characters through practice, I have built up my writing through revisions. The process doesn't happen all at once, but the step-by-step nature of revision and practice is what makes them effective.

Final

An old adage says to "hope for the best, prepare for the worst, expect nothing, and you'll never get hurt." While these unattributed words may seem to provide sound advice, Alfred, Lord Tennyson's "'Tis better to have loved and lost / Than never to have loved at all" distinctly contrasts against them (Tennyson). Expressed truthfully, to love is to be exposed, to be vulnerable; to hurt and be hurt, but also to forgive and be forgiven. Love, by all standards, defies the notion of preparation simply because love is not rational. Contrary to this truth, many people, such as Karen Michaelis and Max Ebhart of Elizabeth Bowen's *The House in Paris*, grow up believing that love is supposed to "be safe" and easy like "furniture or the dark" (Bowen 87, 159). Max and Karen spend the entirety of the novel being disillusioned about love because the prominent figures in their lives have groomed them into ideal dolls instead of real people. They are forced to learn that the disillusionment process is an essential element of the human experience, one that cannot be avoided with any amount of preparation.

To understand why Max and Karen cannot avoid disillusionment, it is important to define accurately what it means to be disillusioned. According to Daniel Stokols' "Toward a Psychological Theory of Alienation," disillusionment occurs when a person "begins with high levels of involvement and expectations only to arrive at [...] an extremely unfavorable situation" (Stokols 31). Stokols states that there are two paths to becoming disillusioned. The first path "involves a *neutral thwarting*—[which] is perceived by [the disillusioned person] as being unintentional" whereas the second path "involves a *personal thwarting*—[which] is perceived by [the disillusioned person] as [intentional]" (Stokols 32, 33). Furthermore, it is stated that each of these paths – *neutral* and *personal thwarting*–has two potential outcomes depending on "the salience of desirable alternative relationships" or, essentially, "the extent to which [the disillusioned person feels] 'caught' or 'trapped' in an unsatisfying situation" (Stokols 34; Barber 155). A person who feels that salient alternatives are available to their current status will have an "adaptive" strategy to problem solving (Barber 161). According to Stokols, the potential outcomes of disillusionment with regard to types of thwarting and alternatives are as follows: isolation, reintegration, subjugation, or rebellion (Stokols 35). By following Max and Karen's development throughout the novel, the reader can identify the causes of their illusion and their subsequent paths to disillusionment.

Communication

Peer Review

The online world hosts a variety of role-playing games where players can interact with each other. Every gamer plays the protagonist in their own story, but they often ask their fellow gamers for guidance and help. Players can provide information and advice regarding gameplay, side quests, and strategies to better each other's gaming experience. Likewise, a writer serves as the main contributor to their own work, but that doesn't mean that they can't ask their fellow writers for input. Initially, this perspective wasn't the stance I took when I envisioned the peer reviewing process.

When I learned that English 1102 would require peer editing, I expected it would be nothing new. However, early in the class, I discovered a problem with my peer reviewing strategy: in my high school peer revision process, I had developed a tendency to edit my peers' work to reflect my voice instead of theirs. Furthermore, I wasn't accustomed to having people edit and critique *my* work. As the valedictorian of my high school, my classmates had constantly asked me to look over various essays, projects, and assignments. It wasn't until I took English 1102 that I understood why they *really* asked me to review their work: rather than helping my peers strengthen their arguments, I would supplant their words with my own. Essentially, I had played the game for them. Instead of telling my peers to find evidence, I would provide it, and instead of suggesting that they reword a sentence, I would rework it for them. I didn't aid my peers' growth; I stunted it, and they simultaneously stunted mine by never seriously reading and reviewing my papers. Upon my realization, I became determined to improve this peer reviewing strategy (at least on my end) to reflect what it should be-a peer *review*.

For me, changing my peer reviewing approach meant starting with global revisions. In red text at the top of each document I reviewed, I created a section entitled "Overall Comments," where I placed all of my opinions concerning the bulk of the project. I always made sure to start this section with a positive comment because I knew that my peers had put a lot of hard work into their projects, and that work deserved to be acknowledged. I then moved onto evaluating the organization of the project, as well as the overall tone and the development of my peers' ideas. These comments differed from praise to advice to simply calling attention to some problem areas. Once I was satisfied with my commentary on the global level, I skimmed for possible local revisions. For most of the local revisions, I could utilize Emma's Markup section to express what I felt my peers could add to better their assignments. However, in certain cases, I would insert a note in order to suggest potential options regarding word choice or phrasing. Once content with my local revisions, I would read the entirety of the assignment aloud. This tactic had helped me when I had been writing my valedictorian speech; I had discovered that reading aloud made it easier for me to identify minor errors in the writing. As long as I paid attention to each word I spoke, I could better identify errors within individual sentences as well as evaluate the effectiveness of the flow, transitions, and syntax. I began to provide advice instead of leadership, and I discovered how to help their characters succeed without doing the job for them.

The following is an example of my new and improved peer revision process. Since I cannot replicate Emma's commentary, I am instead using coordinated highlighting to demonstrate my process.

Peer Revision

Overall Comments: Your project is very well done! It accurately and exceptionally portrays your vision of this adaptation! Your sections are well defined, but perhaps you could work on the flow between sections? Sprinkling in a few references to previous sections might help with this!

With a Little Flare(1) *and Fun: The Importance of Being Earnest* *"Re-done* by Zachary Durden:

The Importance of Being Earnest, written by Oscar Wilde, is(1) a satirical play of the Victorian Era. In his play, he(1) relentlessly mocks and berates his audience's views on marriage and other Victorian ideals like(2) being earnest, honest, and polite(1) (Spininger 50). My favorite scene from *The Importance of Being Earnest* is the "Tea Scene" between Gwendolen and Cecily because it is so(1) humorous and full of great dialogue. However, I wish to change the context of the scene and have it occur during 2015. By doing this, I prove that *The Importance of Being Earnest* can be shifted to any time when supported with proper context, can still rely upon current themes, and play on "earnest" qualities present.(1)

For the adaptation(1) of this scene, I need a city that is aesthetically pleasing and full of culture. New(1) York is a beautiful city regardless of the era present(2) day New York is a cultural melting pot, which makes it the perfect place to base my interpretation. With such diversity present, it makes a diverse cast feasible and the twist I will add possible. However, while the overall setting of the play takes place in New York city(3), the scene of which(1) I am producing will be in the Hamptons. Seeing as how Jack was, "Ernest in town and Jack in the country," the country in my adaptation is the Hamptons (Wilde). The Hamptons acts as a getaway for many rich New Yorkers, like Jack, to leave the busy city. By Jack having property both in the Hamptons and New York City, he is able to maintain the two separate identities and thus maintain a pivotal part of the play.(2)

In my adaptation(1) of *The Importance of Being Earnest,* Algernon will be gay. And(1) by changing Cecily to Carter, a gay romance can be created though it will not follow stereotypical gendered roles(4). This relationship can bring modernity and authenticity to my adaptation while honoring Wilde, who, at the time, could not be open about is(2) sexuality. Also, the relationship further enhances the comedic scene between Carter and Gwendolen. Not only are they arguing about who really has Earnest, but they will(5) also question whose love he really has.

Beautiful: I include this section in my peer reviews to assure that I provide comments on exemplary aspects of my peers' work. Not all comments have to point out something the author should change.

(1) Your structure here is amazing!

(2) This definitely brings your thesis full circle.

Wrong Word: Every now and then, the author will use an incorrect word. This error usually occurs when a writer accidentally misspells a word or, every now and then, when trying to distinguish between tricky homonyms.

(1) I think you mean "flair" instead of "flare."

(2) His?

Extra Space: I've noticed that Emma has a problem with occasionally adding extra spaces between words, and while I don't always catch it, I try to help others correct it.

(1) You accidentally put two spaces here!

Suggestion: I offer this category purely based on my opinion. There is nothing technically wrong with the way the author has written the following words or phrases, but there might be a more efficient/appropriate way to express their meanings.

(1) Maybe replace "he" with "Wilde."

(2) "Like" is colloquial. "Such as" might work better with your tone!

Omit: Usually, this section is reserved for when a word either takes away from the writer's mean idea or simply adds nothing to it.

(1) You could omit this word!

Special: Essentially, this group is my "miscellaneous" category, discussing specific issues that only occur once. Any of the issues below would get their own category is they were an ongoing problem.

(1) Work on the parallel structure in this sentence!

(2) You need a conjunction here.

(3) Capitalize "city."

(4) You need something to set this phrase off! Maybe a comma or parentheses?

(5) You changed from present tense to future tense here, so keep

an eye on that!

Repetition: Any instance of repetition gets its own category because using the same color to point out multiple instances of ineffective repetition would be, well, *ineffective*.

(1) You might want to change up your transitions between paragraphs! This one is a bit repetitious.

Expectation

Wild Card

The Evolution of Knightly Sinclair

(*A screenshot from Wizardry 8*)

Every time I play through *Wizardry 8*, I create a character named Knightly Sinclair. Despite the many different options for character creation, I find that my party simply isn't complete without her. I'm not sure where she came from, but every time I start a new game file, she's there, and she's waiting for an adventure. As a rogue, Knightly can wield daggers and use her unique "backstabbing" ability to cause extra damage. She can pick locks as well as she can pick pockets, and she has always been essential in maintaining my party's financial standing (even if she keeps a little for herself every now and again). She has the stealth of a ninja and the agility of a cheetah, and as a rogue, she can use some of the best weapons and armor in the game.

To me, Knightly has always represented the ideal character because of her ability to be a jack of all trades. During the beginning of every game, she would easily outshine her teammates and prove to be the most useful character. However, as the game progressed, she would slowly fall farther and farther behind the other members of her party. She went from being essential to being essentially useless. Sure, she could inflict decent damage, but her daggers were no match for a warrior's swords, and her ability to use a bow and arrow left much to be desired when compared to an archer. She couldn't pick locks as well as an engineer or pockets as well as a bard, and her dexterity, while suitable, didn't make up for her shortcomings. The characteristics that had attracted me to the rogue had also alienated me from her. Because of her mediocrity, I worked with her less and less as I focused on improving her peers' abilities. When the game ended, Knightly Sinclair was nothing more than a side note.

However, there was a large gap of time between my first run through with Knightly and my second, and it appeared that I had forgotten my wrongdoings with her initial characterization. I began to fall into the same pattern of development. Fortunately, this time around, as her teammates began to leave her in a trail of dust, I decided to do something about it. Initially, Knightly had become useless because I had stretched her beyond her capabilities. She had many skills, but she had few skills that, individually, couldn't be better performed by a specialist. I needed to narrow her scope and focus on one attribute at a time.

Why did I *really* want Knightly on my team? I could leave the lock picking to an engineer and allow a monk to be my master of stealth, but what made *Knightly* important?

Looking back, I find that Knightly Sinclair embodies my college experience. In high school, I was adept at nearly everything. I performed excellently in all of my classes, had plenty of time to be involved with extracurricular activities, and never had a problem finding time to spend with my friends and family. However, as my high school years quickly transformed into my college years, I found myself trying to exceed at everything just as I always had, only this time, *I couldn't do it*. I saw everyone around me blossom into beautiful, well-rounded people while I seemed to wither and cave beneath the weight of my own expectations. I had become Knightly Sinclair, and like Knightly, I was no longer the star of the show.

At UGA, I wasn't the best writer, or the best note-taker, or the best student, and for me, if I wasn't the best, I wasn't anything. I had once cried at the thought of potentially being my school's salutatorian, as if that title was somehow representative of failure. But now I realize that my high school version of my self was simply my "first draft" so to speak. It was a good draft-an excellent draft, really, and at the time, it suited my needs. However, since then, I've acquired more experience and learned more about myself and my surroundings, and I've had to undergo some serious personal revisions.

Sure, I may not be the best at everything. But now I finally get the chance to ask myself that pesky little question that can cripple any argument: *so what*? What does it matter if I'm not the best writer in my class? It doesn't mean that I can't write efficiently. Not being the best note-taker doesn't mean that my notes aren't sufficient, and not being the *best* student doesn't mean that I'm not a *good* one. I can't focus on everything anymore; I need to decide what's really important to me and focus on that.

The only problem is that I don't *know* what's important to me. Everything used to be important, and now I'm realizing that some of my previous concerns are actually fairly trivial. Some problems just aren't worth worrying about, and I no longer know what those issues are. However, I'm not terribly worried about it. I'm confident in my ability to figure it out. I figured out where Knightly stood in my party, and I'm sure I can figure out where I stand in my own life. It's not going to be easy, but what's that old expression? Nothing worth having comes easy.

Part 2

Signs: A Grammar Handbook

by Allison D. Smith

Section I — Word Level: Basic Grammar

1   Articles
2   Nouns
3   Pronouns
4   Pronoun/Antecedent Agreement
5   Subjects
6   Verbs
7   Subject/Verb Agreement
8   Modifiers: Adjectives
9   Modifiers: Adverbs
10 Modifiers: Prepositions

ARTICLES

Articles (*a, an, the*) are a type of determiner or adjective and function as noun markers, in that they always occur before nouns. Articles are also part of the larger noun phrase, so if another determiner or adjective, such as *one* or *red*, occurs in the noun phrase, the article is placed at the beginning of the noun phrase. See Chapter 2 for more information on nouns and noun phrases.

→ **A** sign of good health can be rosy cheeks.

→ **The** one obvious sign of a fever is rosy cheeks.

→ **A** red nose is often a sign of hay fever.

1a   Indefinite articles

An indefinite article is used when it marks a singular count noun that is indefinite or unspecified. This means that the writer has not given enough information to identify the noun. Context plays an important role in determining whether to use indefinite or definite articles. When the writer is introducing something for the first time or does not have a particular noun in mind, he or she will use an indefinite article to mark the noun. For instance, in the previous sentence, *an* is used to mark the noun phrase *indefinite article* because I did not choose which indefinite article (*a* or *an*) to which I was referring.

Be sure to use *a* before a consonant sound and *an* before a vowel sound.

➔ A sign of good health can also be bright eyes.

➔ An eye that is blurry can be a sign of a sty.

When determining whether to use *a* or *an*, consider the vowel sound that follows and not the alphabet letter.

➔ She put the for sale sign in front of a house that was not for sale.

➔ She only had an hour left to sign the papers.

Did You Know?

Do you *loathe* grammar rules? One person you can blame is an eighteenth-century grammarian named Robert Lowth, who, in 1762, wrote *Short Introduction to English Grammar*, one of the most influential grammar books of its time, which went into at least 22 editions during the eighteenth century. Lowth is responsible for rules prohibiting double negatives and prepositions at the ends of sentences, to name a few.

1b Definite articles

The definite article *the* is used with count and non-count nouns that have been identified or are about to be identified by the writer. (See 2c for information on count and non-count nouns.) This identification can come in different ways: in the sentence itself, earlier in a paragraph or the text, from general knowledge, or from the superlative.

Count noun identified within the sentence➔ As I came to the corner, I saw the signs for First Street and Elm Avenue.

Non-count noun identified within the sentence➔The happiness that I felt when I reached her street brought tears to my eyes.

Identified earlier in the text➔ When she gave me directions to her house, she said that I would arrive at a large magnolia tree about five minutes down First Street. I saw the tree and turned right.

Identified through general knowledge➔ The president said that the stock market bounce was a sign of economic recovery.

Identified with the superlative➔ Last week, the stock market had its best day ever.

Non-count nouns, plural count nouns, and proper nouns do not have to take either the definite or indefinite article.

Non-count noun➔ Happiness about the recovery slowly evaporated.

Plural count noun➔ Signs of the economic recovery include the stock market bounce and fewer foreclosures.

Proper noun➔ Even though the economy is recovering, California may be in a recession for a while.

EXERCISE 1

Directions: Fill in the blanks with the appropriate articles.

In __ hills around Los Angeles sits ____ sign known all over ____ world: HOLLYWOOD. __ classic icon of Tinseltown was first constructed in 1923, although ____ original sign read HOLLYWOODLAND. With letters fifty feet tall by thirty feet wide and lit by 4,000 light bulbs, ____ sign proclaimed the glitz and glamour below, drawing would-be stars to ____ town. In 1932, ____ aspiring actress, 24-year-old Peg Entwistle, brought the sign even more publicity when, in despair over her rejection from ____ biz, she jumped from the top of ____ letter H to her death. (Ironically, ____ letter arrived for Peg ____ next day informing her that she had been cast in ____ leading role as ____ woman who commits suicide.) Unlike Peg, the town's marquee, originally intended to last only ____ year and ____ half, survived—although barely—to 1949, when ____town removed ____letters L-A-N-D and restored ____remaining nine letters, including ____recently fallen H. This renovation would last for almost thirty years, until ____sign again fell into disrepair in the 70s, requiring ____city to completely rebuild the landmark for $250,000 in 1978. Aside from ____ fresh paint job in 1995 and increased security in the 2000s, the sign has sat untouched in ____ Hollywood hills, continuing to represent ____ center of ____global film industry.

Above paragraph obtained from: http://www.hollywoodsign.org/history.html

NOUNS

A noun names a person, a place, a thing, or an idea. Nouns can have suffixes such as the –s in *cats* or the –'s in *cat's*. However, nouns can also take on endings that may be more familiar to you for other word classes, such as the –*ing* in *fishing*. Be sure to look at both the form and function of a word before you determine whether it is a noun.

2a   Singular or plural nouns

Singular nouns signify one person, place, thing, or idea.

> **Singular nouns →**   student, classroom, desk, theory

Plural nouns represent more than one person, place, thing, or idea.

> **Plural nouns →**   students, classrooms, desks, theories

Only count nouns can be pluralized (see 2c). Thus, the word *happiness* cannot be made plural.

Did You Know?

Many languages add endings to words (called inflections) to change the word's form in a sentence. English has eight inflections, such as adding –s to make nouns plural, –ed for past tense verbs, or –er and –est for comparative and superlative adjectives. But many languages, including Russian and German, are highly inflected and require specific endings for all parts of speech depending on number (singular or plural), grammatical gender (male, female, or neuter), and its function in the sentence (subject, object, indirect object, possessive, etc.).

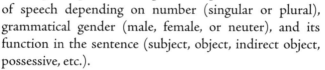

2b   Common or proper nouns

Common nouns name a general person, place, thing, or idea.

    Common nouns ➜   student, classroom, desk, theory

Proper nouns name a specific person, place, thing, or idea. Capital letters are used to identify proper nouns.

    Proper nouns ➜   Harry Potter, Biology Lab, Information Desk, Albert Einstein, Theory of Relativity

2c   Count or non-count nouns

Count nouns indicate that a person, place, thing, or idea can be counted. Only count nouns can take plural forms.

    ➜   I have only one sign left to put up.

    ➜   Many theories exist about why honeybees are dying out.

Non-count nouns indicate that certain things or abstract ideas cannot be counted.

→ I have only my patience to lose.

→ Water is all over the floor.

Some nouns can have both a count and non-count use, and this type of usage is continuing to grow, especially when non-count nouns are used in a type of classification system.

Non-count→ It will be easier to analyze nouns when you have more experience.

Count→ My experiences in the past have not been happy ones.

Non-count→ I usually have beer or wine with my dinner.

Count→ The grocery store is now stocking ten wines and twenty beers.

2d Concrete or abstract nouns

Concrete nouns name things that are tangible and can be seen, heard, tasted, touched, or smelled.

Concrete nouns → student, Harry, classroom, Biology Lab, desk, Information Desk

Abstract nouns name things that are not tangible or something that is an idea, condition, or feeling.

Abstract nouns → theory, Theory of Relativity, grief, hope

2e Possessive nouns

Possessive nouns usually signify ownership but can also mark a state of belonging.

ownership→ Jane's sign, the boy's desk

state of belonging→ the sign's color, the desk's legs

Add –'s if the noun does not end in –s.

→ Jane's sign, the boy's desk

Add –'s if the noun is singular and ends in –s or an s sound.

→ Janis's sign, Giles's desk

Add only an apostrophe if the noun is plural and ends in –s.

→ the boys' desk, the Smiths' house

When you are using proper nouns and want to show that something is jointly owned, mark only the last noun with the appropriate punctuation.

→ Jane and John's desk, Jane and Giles's desk

When you are using proper nouns and want to show that each individual has ownership, mark each noun with the appropriate punctuation.

→ Jane's and John's desks, Jane's and Giles's desks

EXERCISE 1

Directions: Change the description on the left to one that includes the possessive form of the noun.

Example: That book belongs to Jane. → *That is Jane's book.*

1. That song was written by Big Boi and Kanye West. → *That was _____ song.*

2. The cookies are made by Mrs. Fields. → *I enjoy _____ cookies.*

3. Please tell us two weeks before you resign. → *Please give us _____ notice.*

4. The profits on my investments are varied. → *My _____ profits are varied.*

5. The dog that ate my homework belongs to the Jones family. → *The _____ dog ate my homework.*

2f	**Collective nouns**

Collective nouns indicate a group or unit and are usually viewed as singular when they emphasize the group as a unit.

→ The audience is happy to see signs of life behind the curtain.

→ I saw my neighbor's family drive by with its luggage piled high on top of the car.

If you want to highlight the individuals of a group, then some collective nouns may be treated as plural.

→ The audience are happy that each of their chairs is draped with velvet.

→ I saw my neighbor's family drive by, each of them smiling widely.

EXERCISE 2

*Directions: Indicate whether the underlined nouns in these sentences are **common** or **proper**, **concrete** or **abstract**, and **count** or **non-count**.*

Example: Falling <u>leaves</u> are a good indicator that winter is around the corner.

Answer: common, concrete, count

1. In the depths of <u>winter</u>, I finally learned that within me there lay an invincible summer. –Albert Camus

2. If we had no winter, the spring would not be so pleasant. – Anne <u>Bradstreet</u>

3. One kind <u>word</u> can warm three winter months. – Japanese proverb

4. Winter is the <u>time</u> for comfort—it is the time for home. – Edith Sitwell

5. <u>February</u> is merely as long as is needed to pass the time until March. – J.R. Stockton

What is wrong with this picture?

PRONOUNS

Pronouns are words that are used in place of nouns or noun phrases. When a pronoun substitutes for a specific noun or noun phrase, the word or phrase that has been replaced is known as an antecedent. In the sentence below, *the daisy* is the noun phrase, and *it* is the pronoun that replaces it.

→ The daisy is a sign of loyal love; it also suggests gentleness and innocence.

Some pronouns can be used as articles or subjects, as with *this* in the following sentences.

Pronoun as article → This language of flowers was called *floriography* in Victorian times.

Pronoun as subject → This is a flower that is commonly called a *daisy*.

There are eight types of pronouns: personal, possessive, reflexive, relative, interrogative, demonstrative, indefinite, and reciprocal. Sometimes, possessive and reflexive pronouns are also described as personal pronouns.

3a   Personal pronouns

A personal pronoun indicates a specific person, place, thing, or idea. Personal pronouns are in nominative (subject) or accusative (object) case, depending on the function of the noun they are replacing. They are also described as singular (one person) or plural (two or more people).

Personal pronouns		
	Subject	**Object**
1ˢᵗ person singular	I	me
2ⁿᵈ person singular	you	you
3ʳᵈ person singular	he	him
	she	her
	it	it
1ˢᵗ person plural	we	us
2ⁿᵈ person plural	you	you
3ʳᵈ person plural	they	them

When a personal pronoun replaces a noun that is functioning as a subject, the pronoun will be in subject case.

> Subject ➜ The Victorians had hundreds of meanings for different flowers; they used flowers every day to express these feelings, not just on Valentine's Day.

When a personal pronoun replaces a noun that is functioning as a direct object, indirect object, or object of a preposition, the pronoun will be in object case.

> Direct object ➜   A Victorian male could woo his love by giving her a flower every day.

> Indirect object ➜   Not only did a Victorian male give his love a flower, but he also gave her the meaning of the flower

> Object of a preposition ➜   A Victorian male gave his love not only a flower, but also gave the meaning behind the flower to her.

3b   ## Possessive pronouns

Possessive pronouns indicate a state of ownership or belonging. They can occur in determinative form (before a noun) or in predicative form (after a verb), and they can also be singular or plural.

Didst Thou Knowest?

Some languages (such as Russian and French) have singular and plural second person pronouns—often used for informal and formal address. But did you know that English had them too? *You* was once the plural (formal) second person pronoun, while *thou* was the singular (informal). This distinction is noticeable in Shakespeare's plays and in the King James Version of the Bible, and it is still maintained in some English dialects.

Possessive pronouns		
	Determinative	Predicative
1st person singular	my	mine
2nd person singular	your	yours
3rd person singular	his	his
	her	hers
	its	its
1st person plural	our	ours
2nd person plural	your	yours
3rd person plural	their	theirs

Determinative➔ Victorian females gave flowers to their loves or friends.

Predicative➔ I wonder if that flower is mine.

Apostrophes are never used with possessive pronouns.

➔ The daffodil is my favorite flower; its petals are always so well formed.

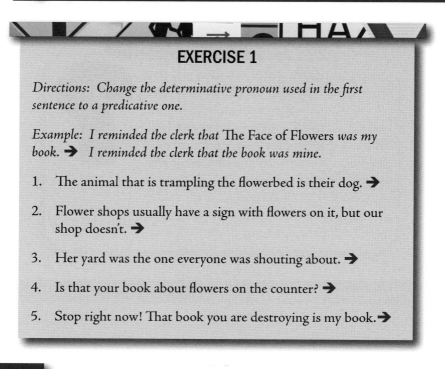

EXERCISE 1

Directions: Change the determinative pronoun used in the first sentence to a predicative one.

Example: I reminded the clerk that The Face of Flowers was my book. ➜ *I reminded the clerk that the book was mine.*

1. The animal that is trampling the flowerbed is their dog. ➜

2. Flower shops usually have a sign with flowers on it, but our shop doesn't. ➜

3. Her yard was the one everyone was shouting about. ➜

4. Is that your book about flowers on the counter? ➜

5. Stop right now! That book you are destroying is my book. ➜

3c   Reflexive and intensive pronouns

Reflexive pronouns are formed by adding *–self* or *–selves* to a personal pronoun. A reflexive pronoun can be an object (direct object, indirect object, or object of a preposition) or a subject complement.

Reflexive/intensive pronouns	
1st person singular	myself
2nd person singular	yourself
3rd person singular	himself
	herself
	itself
1st person plural	ourselves
2nd person plural	yourselves
3rd person plural	themselves

Direct object➔ To show that you love yourself, you could send flowers!

Indirect object➔ People can send themselves flowers but don't often do so.

Object of a preposition➔ Nowadays, sending flowers to oneself is not common.

Subject complement➔ My mother is being herself when she cries over red roses.

Reflexive pronouns are sometimes called intensive or intensifier pronouns when they are used to emphasize the noun or pronoun they are related to.

➔ I, myself, am allergic to most flowers.

➔ He brought the flowers himself when he was not busy.

EXERCISE 2

Directions: Fill in the blanks with the appropriate reflexive pronoun.

1. The florist wrote_____ a reminder about the new order.

2. She _____ told me many times that she forgot things without writing reminders.

3. When she gets orders in, she does most of the arrangements _____.

4. However, I _____ have a great memory especially in the work place.

5. I never have to remind _____ with lists or post-it notes.

3d   Relative pronouns

Relative pronouns that introduce dependent relative clauses include *who, whom, that, which, whose, whoever, whomever, whichever,* and *whatever*.

→ When floriography was at its peak, more than 400 flower language dictionaries, *which* gave a meaning for each flower, were available.

Use *that* to begin relative clauses that are restrictive (see **31d2**) and *which* to begin relative clauses that are non-restrictive. When using *which* for a non-restrictive relative clause, be sure to put commas around the entire clause to indicate that it is optional.

Restrictive (essential for sentence meaning)→ The flowers *that* I like are often too expensive to buy.

Non-restrictive (not essential for sentence meaning)→ I planted day lilies, *which* can come in a variety of colors, last spring.

Some relative pronouns are classified as nominative (subject) and accusative (object) pronouns. Be sure to use subject relative pronouns when replacing a subject noun, and object relative pronouns when replacing an object noun. *Whose* is a relative adjective that shows possession.

Relative pronouns			
	Subject	Object	Possessive
Personal	who	whom	whose
	whoever	whomever	whose
Non-personal	that	that	

Subject relative pronoun→ In 1718, Lady Mary Wortly Montagu, *who* had lived in Turkey before then, introduced the language of flowers to Great Britain.

Helpful hint

To determine whether to use *who* or *whom*, consider the word *who* or *whom* replaces or refers to.

If the noun would function as a subject, use *who*; if the noun would function as an object, use *whom*. Do not be fooled by the placement of the relative pronoun; it's the noun it replaces that matters.

Subject relative pronoun➔ In 1718, Lady Mary Wortly Montagu, who had lived in Turkey before then, introduced the language of flowers to Great Britain. (*Lady Mary Montagu is the subject of the inner sentence: Lady Mary Wortly Montagu had lived in Turkey before then*)

Object relative pronoun➔ Lady Montagu, whom her husband had taken to Turkey as part of an ambassador assignment, was enthralled by the language of flowers. (*Lady Montagu is the direct object of the inner sentence: her husband had taken Lady Montagu*)

EXERCISE 3

Directions: Fill in the blank with the appropriate relative pronoun.

1. In Turkey, the Montagu house, _____ was filled with flowers, became a symbol of what Lady Montagu wanted to take back to Britain.

2. The Montagu's staff, some of _____ came from England, replenished the flowers daily.

3. Floriography, _____ is the association of emotions with certain flowers, still exists today.

4. For instance, the black rose _____ is in the vase in the story "The Flower Game" represents death, hatred, or revenge.

5. Lady Montagu, _____ husband was assigned an important government post, became the more famous of the two.

Object relative pronoun➔ Lady Montagu, whom her husband had taken to Turkey as part of an ambassador assignment, was enthralled by the language of flowers.

Possessive relative pronoun➔ Lady Montagu, whose husband moved with her to Turkey, brought the language of flowers back to Great Britain.

3e   Interrogative pronouns

Interrogative pronouns are used to introduce questions. Some of these can also function as relative pronouns, but when they are used as interrogative pronouns, they trigger the use of a question mark.

Interrogative pronouns➔ who, whom, what, which, whose

➔   What is the name of the Navy plane that carries the president?

➔   Who is the pilot today?

➔   Whom did the president recommend?

> **Helpful hint**
>
> Note that *who* and *whom* take on the case of the word they are replacing. If the interrogative pronoun is replacing a subject, use *who*, and if it replaces an object, use *whom*.
>
> ➔   Who is the pilot today? (*Frank Smith is the pilot.*)
>
> ➔   Whom did the president recommend? (*The president recommended Frank Smith.*)

3f   Demonstrative pronouns

Demonstrative pronouns identify, point out, or point to people, places, things, or ideas, usually without naming the noun to which the demonstrative pronoun refers or marks. Demonstrative pronouns can function as noun replacements or as articles/adjectives.

Demonstrative pronouns➜ this, that, these, those

Functioning as article/adjective➜ That plane is the president's.

Functioning as noun➜ This is the ramp that should be moved to the plane.

3g Indefinite pronouns

Indefinite pronouns refer to unknown or unnamed people, places, things, or ideas. Some are singular, some are plural, and some may be used as either. Indefinite pronouns can function as either noun replacements or as determiners/adjectives.

Functioning as article/adjective➜ Several planes can fly the president.

Functioning as noun➜ Several can fly the president.

Indefinite pronouns

➜ all, another, any, anybody, anyone, anything, both, each, each one, either, everybody, everyone, everything, few, many, most, much, neither, nobody, none, no one, nothing, one, other, several, some, somebody, someone, something, such

3h Reciprocal pronouns

Reciprocal pronouns indicate the individual parts of a plural antecedent noun.

Reciprocal pronouns➜ each other, one another

➜ The pilot and co-pilot were talking to each other.

PRONOUN/ANTECEDENT AGREEMENT

When using pronouns to replace or refer to nouns, be sure that a pronoun agrees with its antecedent noun (the noun it replaces or refers to) in number, person, case, and gender. The following are some of the most common pronoun agreement problems that student writers have.

4a   Check if a noun is singular or plural

Use singular pronouns to refer to singular nouns, and use plural pronouns to refer to plural nouns.

➜ The **pilot** of Air Force One is on-call; **her** phone could ring at any time.

➜ **Pilots** of Air Force One are on-call; **their** phones could ring at any time.

4b   Check if a noun is definite or indefinite

Use a singular pronoun with an indefinite pronoun (see 3g).

Okay➜ Each has **his** own special call number.

Okay➜ Each has **her** own special call number.

Okay➜ Each has **his or her** own special call number.

Not okay➜ Each has **their** own special call number.

If you are unsure of which pronoun to use in this situation, it is always possible to rephrase the sentence to avoid the situation.

Okay→ Each pilot has a special call number.

Okay→ All pilots have their own special call number.

4c   Check if a noun is generic

Use a singular pronoun with a generic noun, a noun that is general or unidentified by name.

→ Each pilot has his own special call number.

→ A pilot of Air Force One must have her plane ready at all times.

4d   Check for compound antecedents

Use a plural pronoun to refer to antecedents that are joined with an *and*.

→ The pilots of Air Force One and Navy One work at the request of their president.

4e   Check for pronouns with correlative conjunctions

Use a singular pronoun to refer to antecedents that are joined with *either...or / neither...nor*.

→ Either the pilot of Air Force One or the pilot of Navy One will take his plane to the disaster area.

→ Neither the pilot of Air Force One nor the pilot of Navy One has his plane ready.

Use a plural pronoun to refer to antecedents that are joined with *both…and.*

→ **Both** the pilot of Air Force One **and** the pilot of Navy One will take **their** planes to the disaster area.

EXERCISE 1

Directions: Change any ungrammatical pronoun to a more appropriate one.

Tim, my boss, told the advertising staff today that she would be promoting one lucky person due to the success of the latest billboard design. This individual would be recognized at the end of the week for their hard work and dedication to their job, and they would also get their own private office. I thought it might be Sue, who had spent many of his nights and weekends diligently working overtime on the project. The employees were excited that one of its own would soon be working in administration, but it couldn't figure out who the lucky person might be. Since everybody had spent so much of his personal time on the ad campaign, everyone on staff felt he had a chance at the big promotion—and his own office. Unfortunately, the company had a policy of only promoting one of their staff members per year. Tim had a tough decision to make.

Chapter 5

SUBJECTS

The subject of a sentence includes all words that are part of the phrase or clause that is functioning as a noun. The subject is the part of the sentence about which something is said or described. Pronouns, nouns, noun phrases, and noun clauses can be the subject of a sentence.

5a   Pronouns and nouns as subjects

Single words—pronouns and nouns—can be subjects.

Pronoun➔ He can fly the plane.

Noun➔ Sheila can fly the plane.

5b   Noun phrases and noun clauses as subjects

More complex than single words, noun phrases and noun clauses can also be subjects of sentences.

Noun phrase➔ The flight attendant can fly the plane.

Noun phrase➔ The substitute flight attendant who is training to be a pilot can fly the plane.

Noun clause➔ That she can fly the plane is lucky.

A complete subject that is made up of a noun phrase includes all pre-modifiers and post-modifiers of the head or main noun. Note that *pilot* is the head—also known as the simple subject—of the following noun phrase, but that the entire noun phrase is the complete subject of the sentence.

➔ The unconscious **pilot, who had suffered a heart attack,** left the controls unattended.

5c Other parts of speech as subjects

When they are functioning as nouns, other parts of speech, such as verb infinitives or gerunds, can also be the subject of a sentence.

Verb infinitive phrase➔ **To fly the plane** is easy.

Gerund phrase➔ **Flying the plane** is easy.

Prepositional phrase➔ **In the courtyard** are two pilots ready to fly the plane.

5d Delayed subjects

In English, the subject occurs before the verb in most sentences since English has what is called an S-V-O (Subject-Verb-Object) language pattern. Some sentences, though, can have delayed subjects when a placeholder—*it* or *there*—occurs before the verb, and the delayed subject comes after the verb. Note that these placeholders occur with forms of the *to be* verb.

➔ **It** has been some time since the flight attendant went into the cockpit.

➔ **There** seems to be some problem in the cockpit.

The subject is also delayed in questions.

➔ **Where** is the river?

➔ **Why** are we losing altitude?

Although English allows for the subject to be delayed, this type of sentence structure, if not a question, is often referred to as wordy. Try to rephrase the sentence without using the delayed subject. If your re-

phrased sentence has the same meaning and emphasis you intended, then use the less wordy sentence.

Wordy➜ It has been some time since the flight attendant went into the cockpit.

More concise➜ The flight attendant went into the cockpit an hour ago.

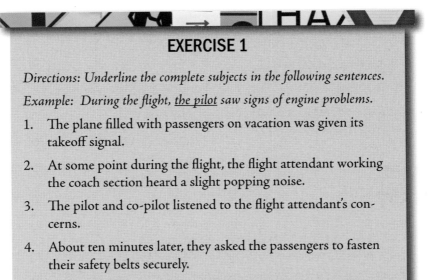

EXERCISE 1

Directions: Underline the complete subjects in the following sentences.

Example: During the flight, <u>the pilot</u> saw signs of engine problems.

1. The plane filled with passengers on vacation was given its takeoff signal.

2. At some point during the flight, the flight attendant working the coach section heard a slight popping noise.

3. The pilot and co-pilot listened to the flight attendant's concerns.

4. About ten minutes later, they asked the passengers to fasten their safety belts securely.

5. What the flight attendant had heard was the sound of a goose flying into one of the engines.

VERBS

Main verbs express action or a state of being, and auxiliary verbs (*be, have, do*) help conjugate main verbs for tense (present, past, future), voice (active, passive), and aspect (perfect, progressive). Verbs or verb phrases can sometimes function as other elements in a sentence, such as a subject.

6a   Main verbs

Main verbs can be divided into three different types: linking, transitive, and intransitive.

1. Linking verbs

Linking verbs link subjects to a noun (or noun phrase) or adjective (or adjective phrase) in the verb phrase or predicate. Sense verbs, such as *smell* or *taste*, and stative verbs, such as *seem* or *become*, also function as linking verbs. When a noun or adjective follows a linking verb, it is called a subject complement or predicate noun/predicate adjective.

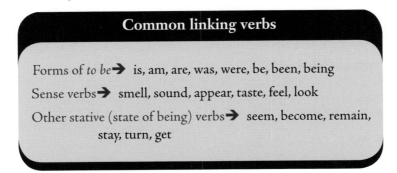

Common linking verbs

Forms of *to be* ➜ is, am, are, was, were, be, been, being

Sense verbs ➜ smell, sound, appear, taste, feel, look

Other stative (state of being) verbs ➜ seem, become, remain, stay, turn, get

→ Sally and John **are pilots** who have experience flying Air Force
  One.   N

→ Air Force One **is the call sign** for the president's plane when the
                 NP

  plane is a U.S. Air Force plane.

→ Air Force One **remains ready**.
                 Adj

Linking verbs can also connect subjects to prepositional phrases that are
functioning as adverbial complements, giving necessary information to
complete the sentence.

→ Air Force One **is on the ground**.
                 PP

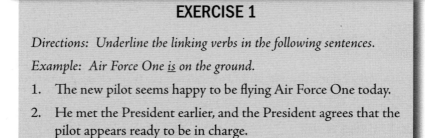

EXERCISE 1

Directions: Underline the linking verbs in the following sentences.

Example: Air Force One is on the ground.

1. The new pilot seems happy to be flying Air Force One today.
2. He met the President earlier, and the President agrees that the
   pilot appears ready to be in charge.
3. Pilots of Air Force One must be intelligent, steady, and reliable.
4. Air Force One remains standing by at all times.
5. At the request of the White House, the kitchen of Air Force
   One is always prepared to serve pizza.

2. Intransitive verbs

Intransitive verbs (Vi) do not need a direct object since the action of an
intransitive verb is complete in and of itself.

→ When she saw the helicopter approaching too close, the pilot
  shouted.
    Vi

➜ The plane swerved.
            Vi

3. Transitive verbs

Transitive verbs (Vt) describe an action that is directly received by a direct object (DO), which is needed to complete the action and the meaning of the verb. A direct object answers one of these questions: Whom? What?

➜ When a president uses a Coast Guard plane, the call sign for
                   Vt   DO
the plane is Coast Guard One.

Note in the above sentence that the direct object receives the action of the transitive verb directly. **What** does a president use? A Coast Guard plane.

Transitive verbs can also trigger the use of an indirect object, which receives the action of the verb in an indirect manner. An indirect object (IO) answers one of these questions: To whom? To what? For whom? For what?

➜ Because of her quick thinking during a disaster, the President
  gave the pilot a medal.
  Vt   IO   DO

To whom did the President give the medal? The pilot. (the indirect object)

What did the President give? A medal. (the direct object)

EXERCISE 2

Directions: Underline the transitive verbs, and circle the direct objects in the following sentences.

Example: The pilot <u>canceled</u> (the flight.)

1. With the new pilot at the controls, Air Force One left the runway.

2. After landing, the Secret Service agents guided the President off the plane and into the hangar.

3. The committee had requested a secret meeting before the convention.

4. Although the President's advisors opposed the idea, the President agreed.

5. While the meeting occurred, the new pilot told himself that he had a great job.

6b   Auxiliary verbs and modals

Helping verbs and modals are types of auxiliary verbs and can be used to mark main verbs for tense (present, past, future), voice (active, passive), and aspect (perfect, progressive). A helping verb or a modal, if used, always occurs before the main verb.

Helping verb➜ The pilot **is celebrating** tonight.
Aux   MainV

Modal➜ Tomorrow, we **may encounter** another problem.
Aux   MainV

Auxiliary verbs and modals

Forms of *to be*➜ is, am, are, was, were, be, being, been

Forms of *to do*➜ did, do, does

Forms of *to have*➜ has, have, had

Modals➜ can, could, may, might, must, shall, should, will, would

---

6c   Verbals

Verbals are derived from verbs but function as other parts of speech, including nouns and adjectives. Verbals may take objects or modifiers, just as a verb may. The three types of verbals include gerunds, infinitives, and participles.

1. Gerunds

Gerunds are verbs that end in *-ing* and function as nouns.

As subject➔ Flying is difficult.
            Gerund

As subject➔ Flying **a plane** is sometimes difficult.
            Gerund DO

As object➔ One difficult part of flying is knowing about
weather conditions.   Obj of Prep

As subject complement➔ My favorite activity is flying.
                                Subj Comp

2. Infinitives

Infinitives are *to* plus the base form of verbs.

Infinitives ➔ to fly, to see, to know, to sign

As subject➔ To fly is difficult.

As subject➔ To fly a plane is sometimes difficult.

As direct object➔ When I go on vacation, I want to swim.

3. Participles

Present participles are verb forms that end in *–ing*, and past participles end in suffixes such as *–ed*, *–en*, *–d*, *–n*, or *–t*. Regular verbs take the *–ed* suffix, and irregular verbs can take a variety of endings.

Regular verbs ➔ signed, talked, walked

Irregular verbs ➔ flown, hid, run, burst

Participles, whether present or past, function as adjectives, and as such, usually appear before or after the noun they are modifying.

Before noun➔ The ear-piercing plane left the hangar early.

Before noun➔ The reconstructed plane left the hangar early.
               Adj

After noun➔ The pilot, show-ing his anxiety, was taken to his plane.

After noun➔ The pilot, shown
               Adj Phrase
to his plane, was anxious to take off.

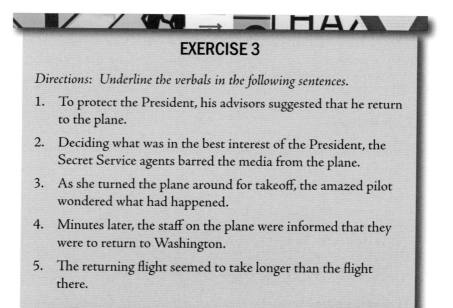

EXERCISE 3

Directions: *Underline the verbals in the following sentences.*

1. To protect the President, his advisors suggested that he return to the plane.

2. Deciding what was in the best interest of the President, the Secret Service agents barred the media from the plane.

3. As she turned the plane around for takeoff, the amazed pilot wondered what had happened.

4. Minutes later, the staff on the plane were informed that they were to return to Washington.

5. The returning flight seemed to take longer than the flight there.

6d   Regular and irregular verbs

All English verbs, except for the verb *be*, have six basic forms: the base form, the infinitive, the third person singular, the past tense, the present participle, and the past participle. The present participle will always appear with a form of the helping verb/auxiliary *be* in front of it, and the past participle will always appear with a form of the helping verb/auxiliary *have* in front of it.

Base➜ sign

Infinitive➜ to sign

3rd person singular➜ signs

Past tense➜ signed

Present participle➜ is signing

Past participle➜ has signed

Sign is a regular verb; that is, it takes regular endings for the past tense (*–ed*) and past participle (*–d* or *–ed*). Past tense verbs that do not end with *–d* or *–ed* are called irregular verbs. An irregular verb can take on a variety of endings, including what is called a null or zero ending. Here are a few examples of some irregular endings. A full list is provided for you starting on page 38.

Base➜ cost, forget, say

Infinitive➜ to cost, to forget, to say

3rd person singular➜ costs, forgets, says

Past tense➜ cost, forgot, said

Present participle➜ is costing, is forgetting, is saying

Past participle➜ has cost, has forgotten, has said

Did You Know?

What's with the "irregular" verbs? *Swim, swam, swum. Drive, drove, driven. Sing, sang, sung.* Verbs whose internal vowels change for past tense (rather than simply adding an *–ed*, as in *walk, walked*) are called "strong verbs" and date back to Old English. Though these are some of the oldest verbs in our language, there aren't many left. Most have become weak verbs as English has evolved and simplified. For example, *oke* has become *ached*, *clew* has become *clawed*, and *stope* has become *stepped*.

Common irregular verbs

Base	Past tense	Past participle
arise	arose	arisen
awake	awoke, awaked	awaked, awoke
be	was, were	been
beat	beat	beaten, beat
become	became	become
begin	began	begun
bend	bent	bent
bite	bit	bitten
blow	blew	blown
break	broke	broken
bring	brought	brought
build	built	built
burst	burst	burst
buy	bought	bought
catch	caught	caught
choose	chose	chosen
cling	clung	clung
come	came	come
cost	cost	cost
creep	crept	crept
deal	dealt	dealt
dive	dove, dived	dived
do	did	done
drag	dragged	dragged
draw	drew	drawn
dream	dreamed, dreamt	dreamed, dreamt
drink	drank	drunk
drive	drove	driven
drown	drowned	drowned
eat	ate	eaten

Common irregular verbs

Base	Past tense	Past participle
fall	fell	fallen
fight	fought	fought
flee	fled	fled
flow	flowed	flowed
fly	flew	flown
forbid	forbad, forbade	forbidden, forbid
forget	forgot	forgotten, forgot
forsake	forsook	forsaken
freeze	froze	frozen
get	got	gotten, got
give	gave	given
go	went	gone
grind	ground	ground
grow	grew	grown
hang (to execute)	hanged	hanged
hang (to suspend)	hanged	hung
have	had	had
hear	heard	heard
hide	hid	hidden, hid
hurt	hurt	hurt
keep	kept	kept
know	knew	known
lay (to put)	laid	laid
lead	led	led
lend	lent	lent
let	let	let
lie (to recline)	lay	lain
lie (to deceive)	lied	lied
lose	lost	lost
pay	paid	paid

Common irregular verbs

Base	Past tense	Past participle
put	put	put
raise	raised	raised
read	read	read
ride	rode	ridden
ring	rang	rung
rise	rose	risen
run	ran	run
say	said	said
see	saw	seen
seek	sought	sought
set (to place)	set	set
shake	shook	shaken
shine (to light)	shone	shone
shine (to polish)	shined	shined
shoot	shot	shot
show	showed	shown
shrink	shrank	shrunk
sing	sang, sung	sung
sink	sank, sunk	sunk
sit (to be seated)	sat	sat
slay	slew	slain
sleep	slept	slept
slide	slid	slid
speak	spoke	spoken
spin	spun	spun
spring	sprang, sprung	sprung
stand	stood	stood
steal	stole	stolen
stick	stuck	stuck
stink	stank/stunk	stunk

Common irregular verbs		
Base	**Past tense**	**Past participle**
stride	strode	stridden
strike	struck	struck, stricken
strive	strove	striven
swear	swore	sworn
swim	swam	swum
swing	swung	swung
take	took	taken
teach	taught	taught
tear	torn	torn
think	thought	thought
throw	threw	thrown
wake	waked, woke	waked, woken
wear	wore	worn
weave	wove	woven
wring	wrung	wrung
write	wrote	written

6e   Number and person of a verb

The number of a verb refers to whether it is singular or plural; this depends on whether the subject is singular or plural.

Singular➜ She **signs** the log each time she **flies**.

Plural➜ They **sign** the log each time they **fly**.

The person of a verb refers to whether it is first, second, or third person. The verb form changes only when the verb is in the present tense and is used with a third-person singular subject.

Conjugation of the regular verb *to sign* and the irregular verb *to fly*

	Regular	Irregular
1st person singular (I)	sign	fly
2nd person singular (you)	sign	fly
3rd person singular (he, she, it)	signs	flies
1st person plural (we)	sign	fly
2nd person plural (you)	sign	fly
3rd person plural (they)	sign	fly

6f Tense of a verb

Verb tense refers to when the action of the verb occurs in relation to when the action is being described. Although English has suffixes that mark present and past, we use modals, such as *will*, to mark future tense as well.

Simple present is used to describe actions occurring at the present time or on a regular basis.

→ She signs for her friend who understands only American Sign Language.

Simple past is used to describe actions that were completed in the past.

→ During class last week, she signed for her friend who understands only ASL.

A

Simple future is used to describe actions that will occur in the future.

→ During class next week, she will sign for her friend who understands only ASL.

EXERCISE 4

Directions: Specify the tense (present, past, or future) of the underlined verbs in the following sentences.

1. The price of oil <u>dropped</u> this year, but it is still expensive to fly.

2. Moreover, the airlines <u>will add</u> even more surcharges this year.

3. When I <u>went</u> to Jamaica last year, I thought there <u>were</u> already enough surcharges.

4. I <u>am</u> at home contemplating flying to Jamaica again, but those surcharges <u>may stop</u> me.

5. Staying at home, though, usually also <u>costs</u> a lot of gas money.

6g   Aspect of a verb

Markers that represent verb aspects (progressive and perfect) are used to describe actions that are more complex.

1. Progressive

Progressive aspect is used to describe actions in progress. The auxiliary *be* plus the suffix *–ing* together mark a verb for progressive aspect.

→ She **is** sig**ning** for a friend during class today.
  be + –ing

Remember that the auxiliary *be* has a variety of forms: *is, am, are, was, were, be, being, been.* All of the following sentences use progressive aspect. Note that the main verb (*sign*) is marked by both the auxiliary *be* and the suffix *–ing*.

→ I **am** sig**ning** for a friend during class today.
  be + –ing

→ They **are** sig**ning** for friends during class today.
    be + –ing

Progressive aspect can combine with past, present, or future tenses, as long as the action being described is in progress.

→ I **am** sign**ing** for a friend during class today.
   be   +   –ing

→ I **was** sign**ing** for a friend during class today.
   be   +   –ing

→ I **will be** sign**ing** for a friend during class today.
   be   +   –ing

2. Perfect

Perfect aspect is used to describe actions that were or will be completed before another action. The auxiliary *have* plus the past participle marker of the verb is used to mark perfect aspect.

→ I **have** sign**ed** for my friend in class before.
   have +   –ed

Remember that the auxiliary *have* has a variety of forms: *has, have, had*. All of the following sentences use perfect aspect. Note that the main verb (*sign*) is marked by both the auxiliary *have* and the past participle marker of –*ed* that is used for regular verbs.

→ She **has** sign**ed** for her friend in class before.
   have +   –ed

→ They **have** sign**ed** for their friends in class before.
   have +   –ed

Irregular verbs are also marked with the auxiliary *have* occurring before the verb; however, the past participle form can vary. See page 38 for a list of common irregular verbs.

→ She **has** fl**own** three times in Air Force One since last year.
   have +   –ed

Perfect aspect can combine with past, present, or future tenses, as long as the action being described is described in terms of another action.

→ I **have** sign**ed** for a friend during class today.
   have +   –ed

➔ I **had** sign**ed** for a friend during class yesterday.
  have + –ed

➔ By this time tomorrow, I **will have** sign**ed** for a friend during class.   *have + –ed*

Progressive aspect and perfect aspect can also occur together.

Present perfect progressive➔ She **has been** sign**ing** for her friend for three weeks now.

Note that the auxiliary *has* and the ending *–en* work together to give perfect aspect to the verb *sign* in the above sentence (in purple), and the auxiliary *be* and the ending *–ing* work together to give progressive aspect (in blue).

EXERCISE 5

Directions: Identify each underlined verb by its tense (present, past, future) and its aspect (perfect, progressive).

Example: I <u>have wanted</u> to fly to Jamaica for a long time. (present perfect)

1. Last year, I <u>was going</u> to Jamaica when I learned that I <u>had lost</u> my job.

2. Now that I have a new job, I <u>am going</u> on vacation soon.

3. However, even though I <u>had wanted</u> to go to Jamaica last year, I <u>am having</u> thoughts about going to the mountains now.

4. My company <u>is having</u> a contest, and the winner and three friends <u>will be going</u> to Aspen.

5. Having never won a contest before, I <u>am having</u> second thoughts about buying raffle tickets.

The whole of nature, as has been said, is a conjugation of the **verb** to eat, in the active and in the passive.
                                        –William Ralph Inge

6h Voice of a verb

The voice of a verb refers to the relationship the subject has with the verb. If the subject is doing the acting, active voice is used. If the subject of the sentence is receiving the action, passive voice is used.

1. Active voice

Active voice indicates that the subject is doing something now (present tense), in the past (past tense), or in the future (future tense).

Present➜ She **pilots** Air Force One for the president and his staff.

Past➜ She **piloted** Air Force One all last week without a break.

Future➜ She **will pilot** Air Force One all next week.

Active voice can be combined with both verb aspects—progressive and perfect.

Present progressive➜ She **is piloting** the plane today.

Future perfect➜ She **will have piloted** the plane for three years when her anniversary date arrives.

2. Passive voice

Passive voice indicates that the subject is being (present tense), has been (past tense), or will be (future tense) acted upon. Passive voice is marked by the auxiliary *be* plus the past participle form of the verb.

Present➜ The plane **is named** Air Force One (by the U.S. Government) because it is an Air Force aircraft.

Present➜ Commander John Stewart **is shocked** when the alarm goes off.

Past➜ The plane **was named** Air Force One because it is an Air Force aircraft.

Future➜ The newly commissioned plane **will be called** *The Enterprise.*

Note that the direct object takes subject position, and the actor/subject is placed in a *by* phrase. This *by* phrase can sometimes be deleted, and the verb is still passive.

Passive voice can be combined with both aspects—progressive and perfect.

> Present progressive passive➡ The pilot is being cautioned today for poor judgment.

> Past perfect passive➡ The plane had been flown for three hours when the alarm went off.

Use the passive voice accurately and sparingly in academic writing—its overuse is a pet peeve of many instructors and editors. However, passive voice is frequently used in writing about science and technology, when the direct object should be emphasized, or when the actual subject is anonymous or being hidden.

➡ The clouds were formed by noxious gas.

➡ Air Force One was flown to Israel.

➡ Your car was hit.

EXERCISE 6

Directions: In the following paragraph, change 10 verb phrases from the passive to the active.

Cultures all over the world have signs and symbols for good luck. Many people are familiar with four leaf clovers, but there are many more good luck charms than that! Crickets are considered lucky by European, Middle Eastern, Far Eastern, and Native American cultures. Ladybugs are similarly considered lucky, especially for the person on whom one lands, and scarabs were believed to be a sign of good fortune by Ancient Egyptians. Aside from insects, many animals are valued for being lucky. In Chinese culture, tigers are believed to be important symbols in astrology; elephants are associated with defeating death due to their long life spans. Pigs are included in a German expression that means, "Good luck is at hand." Even inanimate objects are regarded as auspicious: horseshoes, dream catchers, and pots of gold (found at the end of rainbows) are thought to bring luck to the possessors.

SUBJECT/VERB AGREEMENT

Subjects and verbs need to agree grammatically. This section highlights some of the most common problems writers have in making subjects and verbs agree.

7a   Check for simple subjects or head nouns

Knowing which word is the simple subject or the head noun can help you with subject-verb agreement, especially when there are post-modifiers that come between the head noun and the verb. In the following sentences, the complete subject is in blue, and the simple subject or head noun is underlined.

→ The <u>pilot</u> is ready to take off.

→ The call <u>sign</u> for the president's plane changes with different planes; <u>Air Force One</u> is maintained by the Air Force, Navy One by the Navy, and Coast Guard One by the Coast Guard.

7b   Check for prepositional phrases

A prepositional phrase can come between a subject and its verb and cause confusion.

→ <u>Each</u> of the pilots is ready to fly Air Force One.

In the sentence above, *each* is the simple subject or head noun, and it is this simple subject that needs to agree with the verb *is*. Except with a few indefinite pronouns (see 7d), you can ignore prepositional phrases when trying to determine what the simple subject is.

→ To fly in the clouds is a great way to escape everyday problems.

7c   Check for parenthetical statements or interjections

Parenthetical statements or interjections that interrupt the sentence should not be considered when determining subject-verb agreement. These types of interrupters are easy to spot if punctuated correctly with commas.

→ The pilot, in addition to the co-pilot, was unable to fly the plane.

→ Scott Johnson, though, was able to take control in the cockpit.

7d   Check for indefinite pronouns as subjects

Most indefinite pronouns when used as subjects take singular verbs. See 3g for a list of indefinite pronouns.

→ Something is wrong with the cockpit door today. Is that a sign of trouble?

Some indefinite pronouns when used as subjects take plural verbs. These include *both, few, many, others,* and *several.*

→ Both Sally and John are pilots.

→ Both are pilots.

Some indefinite pronouns when used as subjects can take either singular or plural verbs. These include *all, any, enough, more, most, none,* and *some.* The noun that the indefinite pronoun refers to determines whether the subject is considered singular or plural.

➜ Some of the <u>pilots</u> are unhappy about the coming tests.

➜ Some of the <u>ice</u> is melting.

7e   Check for compound subjects

In compound subjects, there will be more than one head or simple subject.

When the compound subject is joined by *and*, use a plural verb form.

➜ <u>She</u> and <u>he</u> are able to fly the plane.

➜ <u>Sally</u> and <u>John</u> always leave when the situation gets uncomfortable.

➜ The <u>pilot</u> and the <u>co-pilot</u> always leave the controls unattended.

When the compound subject is joined by *or*, use a singular verb form.

➜ <u>She</u> or <u>he</u> is able to fly the plane.

➜ <u>Sally</u> or <u>John</u> leaves when the situation gets uncomfortable.

➜ When <u>the pilot</u> or <u>co-pilot</u> leaves the controls unattended, a buzzer sounds in the cockpit.

When the indefinite pronouns *every* and *each* are used before compound subjects, look only at the indefinite pronoun and use a singular verb for subject-verb agreement.

➜ <u>Every</u> pilot and co-pilot learns how to land in dangerous situations.

When the correlative conjunctions *either…or*/*neither…nor* are used to join compound subjects, the verb should agree with the subject that is closest to the verb.

Singular➜ Neither John nor <u>Sally</u> is here today to fly the plane.

Plural➜ Neither John nor the other <u>pilots</u> are here today to fly the plane.

EXERCISE 1

Directions: Change thirteen verbs in the following paragraph that do not agree with their subjects.

Evil omens and signs of bad luck is known throughout the world. Western cultures believes walking under a ladder or having a black cat crosses your path will ensure a disaster of some kind. Spilling salt are also bad luck; the only remedy is to throw some salt over your right shoulder. Breaking a mirror cause seven years of bad luck, and you might as well stay in bed on Friday the 13th, because nothing good happen on this day. In fact, the number 13 should just be avoided altogether. In Russian culture, people who whistle indoors will loses all their money. Also, two people is never supposed to shake hands or talk across a threshold, and, if you forgets an item at home, don't go back for it: bad luck come to anyone who return home for a forgotten item. Never forgets that superstitious signs is around every corner.

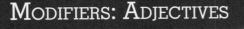

MODIFIERS: ADJECTIVES

Don't tell me the moon is shining; show me the glint of light on broken glass.
— Anton Chekhov

8a   Forms

Adjectives have three forms: base (or positive), comparative, and superlative. The base form is used when describing one thing without comparing it to anything else.

→ Breaking a mirror can be bad luck, but if so, I will probably have bad luck for a hundred years.

The comparative form of an adjective compares one thing to another and uses the suffix *-er* or the words *more* or *less* to make the comparison. Usually, you will use *more* or *less* for adjectives with three or more syllables. Consult a dictionary if you are not sure.

→ My walk to school was longer today because I had to avoid three black cats.

→ It took more concentration to get to school today because I had to avoid three black cats.

The superlative form of an adjective compares three or more things and uses the suffix *−est* or the words *most* or *least* to make the comparison. Usually, you will use *most* or *least* for adjectives with three or more syllables. Consult a dictionary if you are not sure.

➜ Out of my three outings this week, the one to school took the longest time.

➜ My trip to school this week was the most annoying trip ever.

Some adjectives have irregular comparative and superlative forms.

➜ I had the worst time getting to school today because of three black cats.

➜ I would feel better if I were not so superstitious.

Irregular adjectives		
Base	**Comparative**	**Superlative**
good	better	best
bad	worse	worst
little	less	least
many	more	most
much	more	most
some	more	most

8b   Types

Adjectives usually occur before the noun they modify; however, they can also occur in subject complement position when they follow a linking verb (see **6a1**).

Before the noun➜ When I was cooking spaghetti, I spilled salt, so I was sure to throw it over my left shoulder.

Subject complement➜ The salt was messy, but I did not care at that point.

If two or more words function as an adjective before a noun, use hyphens to join the words together.

→ One of my well-known recipes calls for a lot of salt.

If the two or more words come after the verb, do not hyphenate.

→ One of my salty recipes is well known.

Adjectives can be part of larger adjective phrases. When an adjective has a pre-modifier or a post-modifier, these modifiers are part of the adjective phrase. This is important to know because you would never want to separate an adjective from its modifier with a comma or another type of punctuation. Adverbs (such as *very, so, quite, rather, hardly, frequently*) can pre-modify adjectives, and infinitives (such as *to go, to sell, to feel*) and relative clauses (such as *who will go* or *that shares my values*) can post-modify adjectives.

Adjective as single word→ The salt was messy.

Adjective phrase with pre-modifier→ The salt was very messy.

Adjective phrase with post-modifier→ The salt was gritty to the touch.

Adjective phrase with pre-modifier and post-modifier→ The salt was so messy that I had to stop cooking and clean it up.

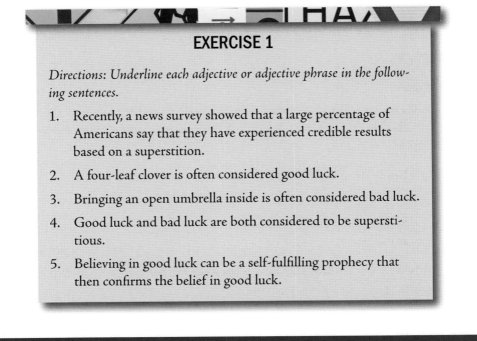

EXERCISE 1

Directions: Underline each adjective or adjective phrase in the following sentences.

1. Recently, a news survey showed that a large percentage of Americans say that they have experienced credible results based on a superstition.
2. A four-leaf clover is often considered good luck.
3. Bringing an open umbrella inside is often considered bad luck.
4. Good luck and bad luck are both considered to be superstitious.
5. Believing in good luck can be a self-fulfilling prophecy that then confirms the belief in good luck.

8c   Functions

Adjectives describe, quantify, or identify a pronoun, noun, or noun phrase.

> Describes➜ If you are superstitious, a black cat crossing in front of you is a sign of bad luck.

> Quantifies➜ Do you have more bad luck if several black cats cross your path?

> Identifies➜ I have watched that cat cross my path three times now.

Pronouns, articles, and numbers can also be used as adjectives to help quantify or identify.

> Quantifies➜ I walked under four ladders on my way to work.

> Identifies➜ It was the cat walking under the ladder with me on Friday the 13th that really scared me.

Chapter 9

Modifiers: Adverbs

9a   Forms

Adverbs have three forms: base (or positive), comparative, and superlative. Use the base form when describing one thing without comparing it to anything else.

→   The band Sign's cover of an Iron Maiden song pleased the crowd *immensely*.

The comparative form of an adverb compares one thing to another and uses the suffix *–er* or the words *more* or *less* to make the comparison. Usually, you will use *more* or *less* for adverbs with three or more syllables. Consult a dictionary if you are not sure.

→   The bass pounded *more heavily* than in the original song.

The superlative form of an adverb compares three or more things and uses the suffix *–est* or the words *most* or *least* to make the comparison. Usually, you will use *most* or *least* for adverbs with three or more syllables. Consult a dictionary if you are not sure.

→   Out of all the concerts I have seen this year, the audience in Iceland reacted the *most enthusiastically* of all.

Some adverbs have irregular comparative and superlative forms.

→   We thought their cover of the song was performed *better* than the original.

Irregular adverbs		
Base	**Comparative**	**Superlative**
well	better	best
badly	worse	worst
far (distance)	farther	farthest
far	further	furthest
much	more	most

9b   Types

Adverbs can be single words, but they can also be part of larger adverbial phrases. When they occur inside a larger phrase, they can be pre-modified by other adverbs (such as *quite, rather, very, so*), and they can also be post-modified by a prepositional phrase (such as *for her*).

Single adverb➔ During their performance, they sing force-fully.

Adverb with pre-modifier➔ During their performance, they sing quite forcefully.

Adverb with post-modifier➔ During their performance, they sing forcefully to the audience.

Adverb with pre-modifier and post-modifier➔ During their performance, they sing quite forcefully to the audience.

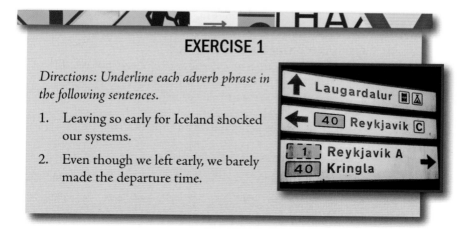

EXERCISE 1

Directions: Underline each adverb phrase in the following sentences.

1. Leaving so early for Iceland shocked our systems.

2. Even though we left early, we barely made the departure time.

3. Sally moved quite quickly for her, but she still was rather slow.

4. We all slept on the plane; consequently, we went straight to the concert.

5. To see Sign in Iceland was frankly one of the highlights of my life.

9c Functions

Adverb functions include those that modify verbs, adjectives, other adverbs, and entire clauses. An adverb's main function is to describe how, when, where, why, how frequently, and how much.

When (modifying the verb)➔ We **left** immediately for
                V

Iceland when we discovered the band Sign was having a free concert.

Where (modifying the verb)➔ I **would like to**
               V

travel there for the music and the adventure.

Why (modifying a clause)➔ I **have wanted to see**
               Ind. Clause

the band because of their music.

How frequently (modifying an adjective)➔ Seeing the band in concert was more **exciting** than any of us had imagined.
               Adj

How much (modifying another adverb)➔ I yelled more **frequently** at the concert than at any other I have ever attended.
  Adv

How (modifying an entire clause)➔ Seriously, **I have never had a better time on a trip.**
Ind. Clause

Adverbs, in the form of adverbial conjunctions (also called conjunctive adverbs or transitions), can connect two sentences together. See **15f** for more information on what punctuation can be used to join two sentences together with transitions.

Adverbial conjunction➔ I wanted to see the band; however, I was late for the plane.

Common adverbial conjunctions	
accordingly	nevertheless
certainly	nonetheless
consequently	otherwise
furthermore	similarly
hence	thereafter
however	therefore
indeed	thus
instead	undoubtedly
moreover	

Modifiers: Prepositions

A preposition is a word that gives information about the relationship between the object of the preposition and the word or phrase the preposition is modifying. A preposition occurs in a prepositional phrase that consists of a preposition + noun phrase.

10a   Forms

There are three forms of prepositions: simple, compound, and phrasal.

Some simple prepositions ➔ at, in, on, near, to

➔ We ran **to** the arena when we heard the music.

Some compound prepositions ➔ nearby, outside, throughout, underneath

➔ Our seats were **underneath** the biggest speakers I have ever seen.

Some phrasal prepositions ➔ by means of, in front of, on account of, subsequent to, due to the

➔ **On account of** the loud music, I ended up with a headache for three days.

10b Types

Prepositions are always part of prepositional phrases that include the preposition and the object of the preposition. The object of a preposition can be a pronoun, noun, noun phrase, noun clause or another word class functioning as a noun.

➔ **to them**
   Prep Pronoun

➔ **to the arena**
   Prep   NP

➔ underneath **the biggest speakers I have ever seen**
   Prep   NP

➔ on account of **the loud music**
   Prep   NP

➔ subsequent to **leaving the arena**
   Prep   Gerund

➔ on **what I saw that day**
   Prep   Noun Clause

Prepositional phrases are recursive, meaning that they can appear within other prepositional phrases.

➔ I got lost in the middle <u>of the arena</u>.

EXERCISE 1

Directions: Underline each prepositional phrase, and circle each preposition. If a prepositional phrase is within another prepositional phrase, underline it twice.

1. When you think of prepositions, think of three boxes and all the spatial relationships that can occur between those three boxes.

2. You can be among the boxes or between two boxes.

3. In the middle of two boxes, you can find another box.

4. You can be above one box while being below another one.

5. At 3:00 p.m. every day, you could take a piece of candy out of one of the boxes.

Did You Know?

In English, prepositions occur before nouns (as the *pre-* implies) and show a relationship between two things (e.g., *The dog* in *the car*). However, not all languages have prepositions. Some languages, like Japanese, Turkish, and Hindi, have postpositions, which follow the noun instead.

10c Functions

Prepositional phrases function in many important ways in sentences. They can be adverbials, post-modifiers of nouns, adverbial complements, indirect objects, objects of adjectives, or objects of adverbs.

Prepositional phrases that function as adverbials—giving information about how, when, why—can usually move to various positions in the sentence.

→ In the spring, I will go see the band again.

→ I will go see the band again in the spring.

→ I will, in the spring, go see the band again.

Prepositional phrases can function as post-modifiers of nouns or noun phrases, but the prepositional phrase cannot move away from the noun it modifies.

→ The band in the arena, not the band in the street, was my favorite.

In the above sentence, if you moved *in the arena* to the front of the sentence, the sentence meaning would change.

Prepositional phrases can also function as adverbial complements when they follow a linking verb.

→ I would like to be in Iceland.

In the sentence above, if you moved *in Iceland* to the front of the sentence, the sentence would then become incomplete.

Another function that prepositional phrases can perform is that of an indirect object, usually with the prepositions *to* or *for*.

→ For three hundred dollars, the ticket office **would send tickets**
   to me.   V   DO
    IO

Prepositional phrases can also function as the complement or object of an adjective or adverb.

→ I used to be **afraid** of any hard rock band.
              Adj   Obj of Adj

→ **Fortunately** for me, I outgrew that sentiment.
   Adv   Obj of Adv

List of prepositions

aboard	down from	opposite of
about	due to	out
above	during	out of
according to	except	outside
across	except for	outside of
across from	excepting	over
after	for	over to
against	from	owing to
along	from among	past
alongside	from between	prior to
alongside of	from under	regarding
amid	in	round
among	in addition to	round about
apart from	in back of	save
around	in behalf of	save for
as	in front of	since
aside from	in place of	subsequent to
as well as	in regard to	together with
at	in regards to	through
away from	inside	throughout
because of	inside of	till
before	in spite of	to
behind	instead of	toward
below	into	under
beneath	like	underneath
beside	near	until
besides	near to	unto
between	next to	up
beyond	of	up to
by	off	upon
by means of	on	with
by way of	on account of	within
concerning	on behalf of	without
considering	onto	with regard to
despite	on top of	
down	opposite	

Section II Word Level: Basic Usage and Style

11 **Appropriate Word Choice**

12 **Commonly Confused or Misspelled Words**

13 **Using the Dictionary**

14 **Using and Overusing the Thesaurus**

APPROPRIATE WORD CHOICE

11a   Check for exactness and clarity

1. Be precise

Make every word and phrase count by making your point in the fewest possible words.

Wordy:

→ In point of fact, in language, a code is a
sign or rule that allows you to change a
piece of information into another sign,
form, or representation, and this new
sign, form, or representation does not
necessarily have to be of the same system.

Concise:

→ A code is a sign that changes information into another sign,
sometimes not in the same system.

2. Use specific, concrete words

Student writers often are asked to give their opinions about literature,
films, or music. Using vague descriptors such as *good, bad, great, best,
greatest,* and *worst* weakens writing. Make descriptions stronger by using
specific, concrete words.

Vague:

→ *The Old Man and the Sea* is the best novel.

Specific:

→ In *The Old Man and the Sea*, Ernest Hemingway depicts the accurate and heart-wrenching life of a fisherman.

In addition, be sure to use concrete words, instead of vague or abstract ones, to make a description the strongest it can be. This would be a good time to check a thesaurus (see Chapter 14).

Using specific, concrete words	
Instead of this...	**Try this...**
blue	azure, cobalt, navy, sea blue, turquoise
car	Ford Escort, Toyota Camry, Volkswagen Beetle
friend	school acquaintance, close friend, movie pal
house	home, abode, igloo, apartment, student dormitories
hungry	famished, ravenous, starving
piece of literature	short story, poem, novel, play
river	Danube, Mississippi, Nile
the city	Austin, Los Angeles, Nashville, New York

When searching for a more specific or concrete word, be careful not to just let your computer thesaurus make an automatic replacement. For instance, if you just automatically substitute a more specific word for *blue*, you might end up with a problematic sentence, as shown below.

→ I wanted to buy the blue car.

Automatic substitute from thesaurus → I wanted to buy the depressed car.

Effective substitute from thesaurus → I wanted to buy the navy car.

3. Delete empty words and phrases

It is not the number of words you use, but the exactness of the words that demonstrates writing maturity. Using empty phrases or expletives, such as *there/it + be*, may be grammatically correct, but you can be more concise by just dropping them.

Wordy:

➔ There were only three sailors on *The Enterprise* who knew semaphore signs.

Concise:

➔ Only three sailors on *The Enterprise* knew semaphore signs.

If your instructor assigns a first-person essay, be sure that you do not overuse the empty phrases that can sometimes go along with this type of writing. Some instructors call these empty phrases "weasel words" because they can make your writing sound non-authoritative. By dropping these empty phrases or weasel words, you can present your views with more authority.

Wordy:

➔ In my opinion, I think that learning Morse code is difficult.

Concise:

➔ Learning Morse code is difficult.

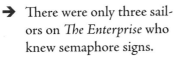

Weasel words	
I am sure (that)	In my opinion
I believe (that)	It is my opinion (that)
I know (that)	It is true (that)
I think (that)	To my knowledge
I think the facts reveal (that)	

4. Replace wordy prepositional phrases with more concise adverbs

Wordy descriptions sometimes fill up a lot of space but do not say anything important or necessary. This type of wordiness usually includes unnecessary prepositional phrases that can be deleted without changing any real meaning.

Wordy:

➔ In this day and age in the event that a boat has trouble in the water, semaphores or Morse code can be used to signal for help.

Concise:

➔ When in trouble, boaters can use semaphores or Morse code to signal for help.

Using adverbs for conciseness

Replace these prepositional phrases	with these adverbs
at all times	always
at that point in time	then
at the present time	now, today
at this moment	now, today
beyond a shadow of a doubt	certainly, surely
due to the fact that	because
for the purpose of	for
in order to	to
in point of fact	undoubtedly, clearly
in spite of the fact that	although
in the event that	if, when
in the final analysis	finally
in this day and age	today
in view of the fact that	because
it is clear that	clearly
it is obvious that	obviously

it is my opinion that	(drop completely)
there is no question that	unquestionably, certainly
without a doubt	undoubtedly

5. Describe exactly who, what, when, where, why, and how

Vague descriptions or empty words contribute nothing to the meaning of the sentence or the description you are trying to give. Rephrase these vague descriptions into specific words. Once you have identified the specifics (who, what, when, where, why, how), do not repeat the same information.

Wordy:

→ When on the water and not in close contact with other boats, boaters can use Morse code, but when on the water and in eye view of another boat, boaters can use semaphores.

Concise:

→ Boaters can use semaphores when close to another boat and Morse code when farther than eye view.

MORSE CODE

	American	International
A	● ▬	● ▬
Á		● ▬ ● ▬
Ä		● ▬ ● ▬ ●
Å		● ▬ ▬ ● ▬
B	▬ ● ● ●	▬ ● ● ●
C	● ● ●	▬ ● ▬ ●
CH		▬ ▬ ▬ ▬
D	▬ ● ●	▬ ● ●
E	●	●
É		● ● ▬ ● ●
F	● ▬ ●	● ● ▬ ●
G	▬ ▬ ●	▬ ▬ ●
H	● ● ● ●	● ● ● ●
I	● ●	● ●
J	▬ ● ▬ ●	● ▬ ▬ ▬
K	▬ ● ▬	▬ ● ▬
L	▬	● ▬ ● ●
M	▬ ▬	▬ ▬
N	▬ ●	▬ ●
Ñ		▬ ▬ ● ▬ ▬

6. Use figurative language when appropriate

Using words in an imaginative or creative way, rather than in the literal sense, is figurative language. The most common figures of speech are metaphors (a comparison of dissimilar things) and similes (a comparison of dissimilar things using *like* or *as*).

Simile→ The boat glided on the water like a pelican in flight.

Metaphor→ Morse code is the Model T of communication.

However, be careful about being too flowery with descriptions. Flowery language is writing that often contains too many adjectives, adverbs, or words that you have looked up in a thesaurus and used incorrectly.

Flowery:

→ The old faded scarlet dinghy sashayed on the cool, fresh, and blue water like a storm-tossed pelican in dangerous flight.

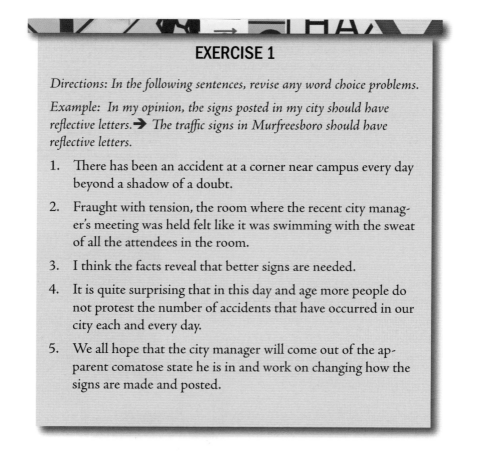

Concise:

→ The old red dinghy bounced on the water.

EXERCISE 1

Directions: In the following sentences, revise any word choice problems.

Example: In my opinion, the signs posted in my city should have reflective letters.→ *The traffic signs in Murfreesboro should have reflective letters.*

1. There has been an accident at a corner near campus every day beyond a shadow of a doubt.

2. Fraught with tension, the room where the recent city manager's meeting was held felt like it was swimming with the sweat of all the attendees in the room.

3. I think the facts reveal that better signs are needed.

4. It is quite surprising that in this day and age more people do not protest the number of accidents that have occurred in our city each and every day.

5. We all hope that the city manager will come out of the apparent comatose state he is in and work on changing how the signs are made and posted.

11b Check for completeness

The words we use in conversations often have clear references in the environment or context around us. However, in academic and professional writing, some conversational words need to be replaced for full clarity and transparency.

Deictic or pointing words, such as *here, there, this,* and *that,* that are frequently used in spoken language need clear antecedents or full descriptions in writing.

Unclear reference:

➔ When traveling by sea, be sure to take that manual.

Clear reference:

➔ When traveling by sea, be sure to take the semaphore manual.

Intensifiers, such as *so, such,* and *too,* that are used in speech to mean "very" or "exceptionally" usually need an extra phrase or clause to describe **why** something is being intensified.

Unclear reference:

➔ Morse code is so out of date.

Clear reference:

➔ Morse code, which was created in the early 1840s, is so out of date that it is rarely used anymore.

When comparing two or more things in academic writing, be sure to provide both parts of the comparison.

Unclear reference:

➔ Semaphore codes are even older.

Clear and full reference:

➔ Semaphore codes, created in the early 1800s, are even older than Morse code, which was first used in the 1840s.

11c   Check for tired, stale, or unnatural language

Descriptive language that is innovative can quickly capture the reader's attention and interest. Note the difference between the following two sentences.

Simple➜ The boat floated out to sea.

Descriptive➜ The rowboat drifted two miles off shore.

However, as writers, we need to be careful not to get so caught up in our description that we borrow the overused expressions of others. As a rule, it is best to stay away from clichés and idioms that have lost their original innovativeness.

Some clichés to avoid	
after all is said and done	easier said than done
beat around the bush	face the music
believe it or not	fish out of water
best foot forward	flat as a pancake
better late than never	food for thought
calm before the storm	grin and bear it
cart before the horse	in a nutshell
chalk up a victory	in one ear and out the other
come through with flying colors	in the nick of time
crying shame	last but not least
don't rock the boat	more than meets the eye
drop in the bucket	raining cats and dogs

Overused idiom/cliché:

➜   I felt like I was *out to sea* as I learned Morse code.

Straightforward description:

➜   Morse code was difficult to learn.

If you are asked as a writer to be creative and innovative in your expressions, such as when you write a narrative or descriptive essay, stay away from clichés, and use some creativity of your own.

Innovative/creative description:

→ Morse code was as difficult to learn as snowboarding on a mountain of Jell-O.

Jargon, the language used by a particular profession or a group of people, is usually too technical to be natural for an academic essay. Reword techno-speak into more straightforward descriptions.

Jargon:

→ Morse code is a type of character encoding that uses rhythmic language and telegraphic information to transmit a given communication.

Straightforward description:

→ Morse code uses dots and dashes to send out messages.

Did You Know?

William Shakespeare is credited with the first usage of around 2,000 words in the English language. He is also responsible for some of the most well-known idioms, some of which are now clichés: *neither rhyme nor reason, in my mind's eye, I must be cruel only to be kind, dead as a door-nail, it was Greek to me, love is blind, pomp and circumstance, a good riddance,* and *I have been in such a pickle.*

11d   Check for appropriate levels of formality

What is Academic English? For some instructors, this term refers to good grammar and formal style. For others, it refers to having students be constructive critics and clear writers. Whatever it means, most instructors will expect you to use a style that is more formal than your conversational English but not to the point where your writing sounds stilted and pretentious. Remember that formality depends on the audience and purpose of the writing assignment; if you are unsure about what is expected of you, ask your instructor.

Informal language, in the form of slang or colloquial language, is usually not part of academic writing, unless you are writing a narrative that uses dialogue. Even though some slang words (such as *jazz* or *mob*) can become part of the broader standard language, most slang is considered too localized and too informal for academic writing.

Slang description:

→ That boat was too cool.

→ That boat was wicked.

→ That boat was tight.

→ That boat was dope.

Academic description:

→ *The Enterprise*, a new addition to the fleet, has innovative engines that are less harmful to the environment.

Colloquial language, relaxed or casual speech used across many speakers, is also not usually part of academic writing. Words or expressions such as *a lot, gonna,* and *wanna* are too informal for essay writing.

Colloquial description:

→ The boaters wanna learn how to use semaphores in case of emergency.

Academic description:

→ The boaters want to learn how to use semaphores in case of emergency.

Doublespeak or doubletalk is words or expressions that are used to hide or distort the truth, such as using *protective custody* instead of *imprisonment* or *pre-hostility* instead of *peace*. In argumentative essays, using doublespeak can sound cagey or shifty.

Doublespeak description:

→ State employees now have job flexibility.

Academic description:

→ State employees now have a lack of job security because they are only employed week to week.

Be careful that when you are more formal in your writing, you do not go too far and sound pretentious, sometimes referred to as writing *gobbledygook*. This can happen if you use a thesaurus without considering the context or formality of the essay or letter you are writing. Also, be sure to use American English spelling, rather than British English.

Pretentious:

→ When I finalized my perusal of the optimal methodology to acquire the semaphore signals, I ascertained that it was more effortless to gain knowledge of Morse code.

Academic:

→ Learning Morse code was easier than learning semaphore signs.

Pretentious words

Instead of...	Try...
aficionado	fan
ascertain	find out
commence	begin
conviviality	friendliness
desist	stop
imbroglio	mess
instantiate	support
finalize	finish, complete
impact	affect
jejune	boring, childish
lugubrious	gloomy
methodology	method
nadir	lowest point
optimal	best
peruse	look at, read
potentiate	improve effectiveness
utilize	use

Did You Know?

British and American English, though mutually intelligible, have a number of distinct differences. Aside from pronunciation and vocabulary, spelling is often very different. We can thank Noah Webster (writer of the eponymous dictionary) for standardizing many American spellings, such as dropping the *u* from words like *colour* and *labour*, ending words with –*er* instead of –*re* (*center/centre*), and replacing –*ce* endings with –*se* (*offense, suspense*) to name a few examples. Not all of Webster's spelling reforms were accepted, though—*medicin*, *soop*, and *tung* never caught on.

11e   Check for sexist and offensive language

Use language that gives equal value and respect for all people and places.

1. Use appropriate words for gender

Give equal treatment to each gender; do not privilege either. Also, be sure not to use the generic *he* for all writing occasions. Try rephrasing singular subjects to plural ones; this allows you to switch from the singular pronoun (she or he) to a plural one (they).

Possible sexist language:

→ The sailor learned Morse Code in his training.

Inclusive language:

→ Sailors learn Morse Code in training.

Do not assume that one gender cannot do a particular type of work or gender role, as in *the male nurse, the female astronaut, faculty wives,* and *both men and their wives.*

Sexist language:

→ The stewardess learned Morse code in training.

Inclusive language:

→ The flight attendant learned Morse code in training.

Sexist language:

→ The sailors brought their wives and kids to the dock party.

Inclusive language:

→ The sailors brought their families to the dock party.

Here are some substitutions that you might consider when writing about job titles.

Recommended terms for job titles	
Instead of...	Try...
barman, barmaid	bartender
businessman	businessperson, executive, manager, staff person
chairman	chair, presiding officer, moderator
congressman	member of Congress, representative, senator
comedienne	comedian
fireman	firefighter
mailman	letter carrier, mail carrier, postal worker
salesman	salesperson, sales representative
sculptress	sculptor
steward, stewardess	flight attendant
usherette	usher
waiter, waitress	server

2. Use appropriate words for age

In academic writing, use non-offensive terms when referring to the age of a person.

Recommended terms for age	
Instead of...	Try...
kids (to age 18)	children
kids (college students)	students, young adults, adults, men, women
elderly, old man, old woman	senior citizens, older adults

3. Use appropriate words for ethnicity or race

Be sure to use terms that are non-discriminatory and non-offensive when referring to the ethnic backgrounds or races of people. If unsure, you can check for acceptable general or specific terms in a current dictionary.

Acceptable terms for ethnicity or race

General Terms for People in the United States	Specific Terms for People in the United States
African American, Black	
American Indian, Native American	Alaska Native, Cherokee, Hopi, Navajo
Anglo-American, White American, White	French American, Irish American, Polish American
Arab American	Egyptian American, Lebanese American
Asian American	Chinese American, Japanese American, Korean American, Thai American
Hispanic, Hispanic American, Latino/a	Mexican American, Puerto Rican
Pacific Islander American, Native Hawaiian	

4. Use appropriate words for disability or illness

The current preference in referring to people with disabilities or illnesses is to put the *person* first. For example, refer to *a person with disabilities* or *a person who is differently abled* rather than *a disabled person*.

Recommended terms for disability or illness

Instead of this...	Try this...
AIDS victim	a person with AIDS
blind person, visually impaired person	a person with a visual impairment
deaf person	a person with a hearing impairment
dumb person	a person with speech impairment
handicapped person, disabled person	a person with disabilities
neurotic person	a person with a psychological disability
quadriplegics	a person who is quadriplegic

5. Use appropriate words for geographical areas

Because social and political boundaries may change, you can use *a person from (place name)* when referring to someone and her place of origin or residence and rarely be wrong. Definitely, stay away from any derogatory terms for a person's origin. The terms that are most frequently seen as problematic include the following.

Recommended terms for geographical areas	
Instead of...	**Try this...**
American	person from the United States, U.S. citizen
Arab	Egyptian, Iraqi, Saudi Arabian, Yemeni
English, Irish (from Northern Ireland), Welsh	British, person from the United Kingdom, U.K. citizen
Oriental	Asian, Asian American, Japanese, Korean, Chinese
Polish	Pole, person from Poland

EXERCISE 2

Directions: The following summary of a news event contains 12 words that are not appropriate for the more standardized language used for summarizing. Change these words to more appropriately reflect the summary writing you might do in a writing course.

Two kids have been taken into custody by the cops in connection with a recent string of vandalism in the area. The kids are accused of vandalizing stop signs in commemoration of the latest volume of the Harry Potter film franchise, *Harry Potter and the Half-Blood Prince*, by writing the name of evil wizard Voldemort on dozens of stop signs. Fanatics of the series might appreciate the vandals' urging to "STOP Voldemort," but the authorities were less entertained by the trick, which will cost the county $50 per devastated sign. The cops gave a statement warning would-be vandals that vandalism will not be tolerated, no matter how harmless or humorous vandalism may seem.

http://www.wisn.com/news/20061083/detail.html

Chapter 12

COMMONLY CONFUSED OR MISSPELLED WORDS

We can trace why words become commonly confused back to one thing—spelling. English spelling comes from a set of conventions or rules that have been agreed upon by dictionary editors. Since English has been a language for around 1600 years, how some words are spelled has changed many times. Regardless of these historic changes and how they often make it difficult to figure out a standardized alphabetic form for many sounds, most English words now have fixed spellings that can be looked up in dictionaries at any time.

Since using good spelling is usually considered a sign that a writer is educated, it is a good idea to work on improving your spelling, no matter how good you are at it. One way to improve your spelling is to read more, keeping a spelling list or journal in which you write down and practice new words. Another way is to own your own college dictionary, using it to look up the spellings and definitions of words you have trouble spelling. Since computerized dictionaries often lead you to use words you may not understand, be sure not only to use the dictionary provided with your word processor, but to use print dictionaries as well. For more specific help in using your dictionary, see Chapter 13.

Did You Know?

Ever wonder why English spelling is so unpredictable? English has a long history of foreign influence, which not only accounts for many of the unusual spellings, but also often indicates the origin of the word. For example, the words *doubt* and *debt* originally entered English from French influence, but misguided linguists added the silent *b* hundreds of years ago to both words to reflect the words' Latin origins (*dubitare* and *debitum*, respectively). While these alterations might make spelling and pronunciation frustrating (especially for non-native speakers), they reveal the rich history of English.

12a   Check for words that are always separate

A common spelling error is to run together words that should be written as two. The following phrases should always be written as separate words.

→ a lot, all right, even if, even though, going to, in fact, just as, no one, of course

12b   Check for words that can be written together or apart

The spelling of some words depends on the meaning you intend. For example, *already* means "previously" and *all ready* means "prepared." First, decide upon the meaning, and then choose the correct form by consulting your dictionary.

Different spacing, different meaning

One word	Two words
already	all ready
altogether	all together
always	all ways
anybody	any body
anyone	any one
anyway	any way
awhile	a while
everybody	every body
everyday	every day
everyone	every one
however	how ever
into	in to
maybe	may be
nobody	no body
somebody	some body
someone	some one
whatever	what ever
whoever	who ever

12c Check for words that are pronounced the same or similarly

In English, we have many homophones—words that are pronounced the same but have different meanings. Homophones use different spellings, and since this is what distinguishes the meaning, you need to use your dictionary to find the correct word. Here is a list of the most commonly misspelled homophones.

Most commonly misspelled homophones

it's (it is or it has)	its (possessive)
you're (you are)	your (possessive)
they're (they are)	their (possessive), there (place)
who's (who is or who has)	whose (possessive)

sweet???
try one of these
cookies or rice
crispy treats!!!
Their delicious

What's the problem with this sign
at a bake sale?

Here are some other commonly confused or misspelled words.
Learning these will help you become a proficient speller and editor.

Other commonly confused words

A	A
a	an
*alot (ungrammatical)	a lot
accept	except
access	excess
adapt	adopt
adverse	averse
advice	advise
affect	effect
agree to	agree with

aisle	isle
allude	elude
allusion	illusion
already	all ready
alright	all right
altar	alter
altogether	all together
among	amongst between
amoral	immoral
amount	number
and/or	and or
angry at	angry with
annual	biannual semiannual biennial perennial
ant	aunt
ante-	anti-
anybody	any body
anyone	any one
anymore	any more
anyway	anyways
assistance	assistants
assure	ensure insure
ate	eight
awhile	a while
B	**B**
backup	back up
bad	badly poorly
bare	bear

base	bass
be	bee
beach	beech
because of	due to
being as	being that
berry	bury
berth	birth
beside	besides
between	among amongst
blew	blue
board	bored
brake	break
bring	take
breadth	breath
breath	breathe
business	busyness
by	bye buy
C	**C**
can	may
canvas	canvass
capital	capitol
cell	sell
censor	censure
cent	sent scent
cereal	serial
chord	cord
chose	choose
climactic	climatic
coarse	course
compare to	compare with
complement	compliment

conscience	conscious
consequently	subsequently
continual	continuous
could have	could of
counsel	council
criteria	criterion
D	**D**
dairy	diary
data	datum
dear	deer
decent	descent
desert	dessert
device	devise
dew	due
die	dye
different from	different than
disinterred	uninterested
discreet	discrete
do not	don't
dual	duel
due to	because of
dying	dyeing
E	**E**
effect	affect
elicit	illicit
elude	allude
emigrate from	immigrate to
eminent	imminent
ensure	insure
everyone	every one
except	accept
explicit	implicit

F	F
faint	feint
fair	fare
farther	further
fewer	less
firstly	first
flour	flower
for	fore four
former	latter
formally	formerly
further	farther
G	**G**
good	well
gorilla	guerilla
grate	great
H	**H**
hair	hare
hanged	hung
he/she	he or she
heal	heel
healthful	healthy
hear	here
heard	herd
higher	hire
his/her	his or her
hole	whole
hostel	hostile
hung	hanged
I	**I**
idle	idol
if	whether
illusion	allusion

immigrate	emigrate
immoral	amoral
implicit	explicit
imply	infer
in	into
ingenious	ingenuous
insure	assure ensure
in regard to	in regards to
*irregardless (ungrammatical)	regardless
it's	its
K	**K**
knew	new
know	no
L	**L**
later	latter
lay	lie
lead	led
learn	teach
leave	let
led	lead
lend	borrow loan
less	fewer
lie	lay
like	as as if
literally	figuratively
loose	lose loss
lots	lots of
M	**M**
made	maid

mail	male
main	mane
may	can
maybe	may be
maze	maize
meat	meet
medal	metal, meddle
media	medium
miner	minor
moral	morale
N	**N**
number	amount
O	**O**
oar	ore
of	off
OK	O.K. okay
off	off of
one	won
P	**P**
pain	pane
pair	pear, pare
passed	past
patients	patience
peace	piece
peak	peek, pique
peer	pier
percent	per cent percentage
personal	personnel
phenomena	phenomenon
plain	plane

pore	pour
	poor
precede	proceed
pretty	rather
	quite
principal	principle
proceed	precede
Q	**Q**
quiet	quite
quote	quotation
R	**R**
rain	reign, rein
raise	rays
real	very
	really
respectfully	respectively
right	write
	wright
	rite
rise	raise
role	roll
S	**S**
sail	sale
scene	seen
scent	sent, cent
seed	cede
seem	seam
set	sit
shall	will
should of	should have
sight	cite
	site
should have	should of
sit	set

site	cite
	sight
sole	soul
some	sum
somebody	some body
someone	some one
sometime	some time
	sometimes
so	very
stationary	stationery
steal	steel
suppose to	supposed to
sure	surely
T	**T**
take	bring
taught	taut
team	teem
than	then
that	which
their	there
	they're
*theirselves (ungrammatical)	themselves
there	their
	they're
thorough	through
threw	through
tide	tied
to	too
	two
toward	towards
U	**U**
*most unique (ungrammatical)	unique
*use to (ungrammatical)	used to

V	V
vain	vane
	vein

W	W
waist	waste
wait	weight
wait for	wait on
wander	wonder
ware	wear
	where
way	weigh
way	ways
weather	whether
well	good
were	where, wear
which	that
	who
while	whereas
who	which
	that
who	whom
who's	whose
wood	would
would have	would of

Y	Y
your	you're

EXERCISE 1

Directions: Correct any problems with commonly confused or misspelled words.

Who would of thought that a simple hike threw the woods would result in a classic emblem of Americana? Beginning in the mid 19th century, people from all over started coming too Lookout Mountain near Chattanooga, Tennessee too see "Rock City" and experience it's natural rock formations. In the 1920s, a businessman named Garnet Carter began developing Lookout Mountain into a residential neighborhood called Fairyland, but his wife had other plans. Freida Carter began exploring Rock City—now her property—and turning it into an elaborate rock garden. Recognizing the potential profit of his wife's ornate garden, Garnet opened Rock City to the public in 1932. Business was slow, however, so Garnet had to find a way to entice visitors to there garden with more advertising then they currently had. Garnet hired Clark Byers to paint farmers' barns for free as long as the phrase "See Rock City" was added. Farmers from Michigan to Texas excepted the offer, and the iconic black and white signs on red barns became part of are American landscape. The advertisements had—and continue to have—a significant effect on the Carters' business; every year, over half a million people see the sites of Rock City, likely having past many of the famous signs on there way to Lookout Mountain.

http://www.seerockcity.com/pages/Our-Story/

USING THE DICTIONARY

> Language is not an abstract construction of the learned, or of dictionary makers, but is something arising out of the work, needs, ties, joys, affections, tastes, of long generations of humanity, and has its bases broad and low, close to the ground.
>
> – Noah Webster

Dictionaries are invaluable tools for writers, in that they provide the correct spellings of words, give guidance about accurate meanings, and offer other information essential for effective writing. Every writer should have a personal copy of a collegiate or abridged dictionary, such as *Merriam-Webster's Collegiate Dictionary*, at hand for help with content development and editing. In your school or local library, you will find unabridged dictionaries, such as *The Oxford English Dictionary* or *Webster's Third New International Dictionary of the English Language* (available in print, on CD-ROM, or through your university library's portal), which give complete coverage of English words, including sample sentences and interesting information about word origins. When using dictionaries online, be sure to use one that is reputable, such as the Merriam-Webster online dictionary or American Heritage online dictionary.

Merriam-Webster   http://www.merriam-webster.com

American Heritage   http://dictionary.reference.com

When you are writing on a specialized topic, such as idioms or literature, you can also find specialized dictionaries in your local or school library that focus exclusively on that topic. Visit the OWL (Online Writing

Lab) at Purdue University for more information on how to choose and evaluate dictionaries.

Online Writing Lab
http://owl.english.purdue.edu/owl/resource/738/02/

Helpful hint

The spell-checker in your word-processing program may be helpful to a certain extent when you are concerned about the spelling of a word; however, a dictionary not only will help you with spelling, it will also help you expand those 50,000 or so words that you are now using.

Did You Know?

The *Oxford English Dictionary* (OED) is considered by many to be the greatest dictionary of the English language. Since its inception in 1857, the OED has attempted to record the meaning and origin of every word in the English language by including the quotation where the word first appeared. Originally published in installments, the first edition took over 70 years to complete. The second edition, published in 1989, is 20 volumes, spanning 21,730 pages and including 291,500 entries. It would take 60 years for one person to proofread the text.

What's the problem with this sign?

Sign
Spelling

Pronunciation

[sahyn] —noun
Part of speech

1. a token; indication.
2. any object, action, event, pattern, etc., that conveys a meaning.
3. a conventional *Definitions* mark, figure, or symbol used as an abbreviation for the word or words it represents.
4. a motion or gesture used to express or convey an idea, command, decision, etc.: *Her nod was a sign that it was time to leave.*
5. an omen; portent: *a sign of approaching decadence.*
6. sign of the zodiac.
Sample sentence
7. sign language def. 1 .
8. Usually, signs. traces, as footprints, of a wild animal.

—verb *(used with object)*
Entry for sign used as a transitive verb
9. to affix a signature to: *to sign a letter.*
10. to write as a signature: *to sign one's name.* *Out-of-date usage*
11. to engage by written agreement: *to sign a new player.*
12. *Obsolete .* to direct or appoint by a sign.

—verb *(used without object)*
Entry for sign used as an intransitive verb
13. to write one's signature, as a token of agreement, obligation, receipt, etc.: *to sign for a package.*
14. to make a sign or signal: *He signed to her to go away.*

—verb phrases
Entry for sign used in phrases
15. sign in, to record or authorize one's arrival (or departure) by signing a register. Also, sign out.
16. sign up, to enlist, as in an organization or group; to register or subscribe: *to sign up for the navy; to sign up for class.*

Origin:
Date of first occurrence
1175–1225; (n.) ME *signe* < OF < L *signum* mark, sign, ensign, signal, image; (v.) ME *signen* to mark with a sign, esp. the sign of the cross < OF *signer* < L *signāre* to mark with a sign, inscribe, affix a seal to, deriv. of *signum* *Origin*

—Related forms
Check for related forms
signless, *adjective*
signlike, *adjective*
post·sign, *verb (used with object)*
un·signed, *adjective*

—Synonyms
Synonyms with examples
1. trace, hint, suggestion. 1, 4. signal. 5. indication, hint, augury.
SIGN, OMEN, PORTENT name that which gives evidence of a future event. SIGN is a general word for whatever gives evidence of an event—past, present, or future: *Dark clouds are a sign of rain or snow.*

EXERCISE 1

Directions: Use your dictionary to correct any misspelled words in this paragraph.

The song "The Sign" by Ace of Base tells the storey of a woman's realization that she must end an unhealthy, dificult relationship with a loser in order to live a better life. Though the listner does not know what specificly "the sign" is, the singer makes it clear that her new life, unrecognizible to her ex ("you would hardly recognize me") is infinately better than it was in that relationship. With her epifany, the singer realized that not only was her ex "not the one for [her]," but her ex was definately not going to change for the good. "No one's going to drag you up to get into the light where you belong," she says, suggesting that although she sees potential in her ex, no one is willing—or capable—to make him live in "the light."

However, she questions whether or not potential for good even exists: "But where do you belong?" she asks, unsure of this person's ability to live a signifcant existence. She knows, though, that her ex was unable to "bring [her] joy." Whatever the sign was that she recieved, she makes it clear that she is "happy now" having "left [her ex] all alone."

Chapter 14

USING AND OVERUSING THE THESAURUS

When you use a dictionary, you usually know at least a little bit about the word you are looking up. With a thesaurus, you usually know a general definition but need to find a specific word that will fit the topic and context about which you are writing. Be sure to review all the synonyms that are offered as a substitute for the word you look up; you need to consider the synonyms in the context of your essay or writing, and then choose the one that fits.

Helpful hint

The thesaurus that came with your word processor may be helpful, but just clicking on the first synonym it offers may harm, rather than help, your writing. Use a thesaurus in conjunction with a dictionary, and you will be able to correctly choose the appropriate word for the context.

Sign

When using a thesaurus, find the ENTRY and DEFINITION before you look at the synonyms. On this page, there are two noun entries.

Main Entry   sign

Part of speech

Part of Speech: noun

Definition: indication, evidence   **Definition**

Synonyms: assurance, augury, auspice, badge, beacon, bell, caution, clue, divination, flag, foreknowledge, foreshadowing, forewarning, gesture, giveaway, handwriting on wall, herald, hint, light, manifestation, mark, nod, note, omen, precursor, prediction, premonition, presage, proof, signal, suggestion, symbol, symptom, token, trace, vestige, warning, wave, whistle, wink

Use synonyms that are already familiar to you, or be sure to look them up in a dictionary to use them appropriately.

Main Entry   sign

Part of Speech: noun

Noun usage with a different definition

Definition: document with information; symbol

Synonyms: badge, board, character, cipher, crest, device, emblem, ensign, guidepost, insignia, logo, mark, notice, placard, proof, representation, signboard, signpost

Part of Speech: verb   **Verb usage**

Definition: write name

Synonyms: acknowledge, authorize, autograph, confirm, endorse, initial, ink, inscribe, put John Hancock on, put John Henry on, set one's hand to, signature, witness

Phrasal synonyms

Part of Speech: verb

Definition: motion to another

Synonyms: beckon, express, flag, gesticulate, gesture, indicate, motion, signal, signalize, signify, use sign language, wave

Be sure to know the full definition and appropriate context for an unfamiliar word before using it

Part of Speech: noun, verb

Related Adjectives: armorial, characteristic, connotative, curiological, demonstrative, diagnostic, emblematic, indelible, indicated, indicating, indicative, indicatory, individual, jolloped, known by, marked, pantomimic, pathognomonic, pointed, recognizable by, representative, symbolic, symptomatic, typical

EXERCISE 1

Directions: This student apparently overused the thesaurus as he was writing this letter to his instructor. See if you can help him out by replacing inappropriate words with more appropriate ones.

Dear Professor Walker,

I'm very sorry that I was absent for the eighth time this semester. As I was driving back to school yesterday (I'm from out of state), I missed my egress off the interstate because a tempest had blown down several road signs, including the one directing me to university grounds. Since I'm novel to the area, I didn't apprehend that I had missed anything until I had driven three hours out of my way. By the time I figured out that something was erroneous, it was late at night and I was too weary to continue driving. I called home to ask what I should do, and my patriarch told me to discontinue for the night and find my way back in the morning, causing me to miss your 8:00 a.m. Monday class. I'm sure you'll concur that my safety was much more momentous than your English class, so I'll assume that you will not castigate me for another absence. Also, I was hoping I might have an extension on the essay that was due on Monday; I was planning to write it Sunday night when I got back to my dorm, but obviously I was at the hotel and stressed out. I did, however, inscribe a letter to the Tennessee Department of Transportation expressing my frustration over their neglect to replace the missing signs, which I'll be happy to show you as attestation of the incident. Thank you for understanding, and I promise I'll be in class for the residual ten weeks of the semester.

Sincerely,

Dan Johnson

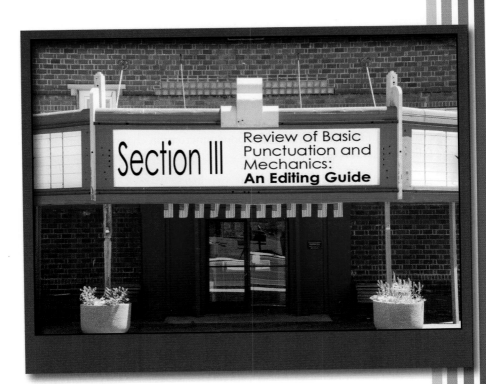

Section III

Review of Basic Punctuation and Mechanics: **An Editing Guide**

15 The Comma

16 The Semicolon

17 The Colon

18 The Period, Exclamation Point, and Question Mark

19 The Apostrophe

20 Quotation Marks

21 The Hyphen

22 The Dash

23 Parentheses

24 Brackets

25 The Slash

26 Ellipses

27 Capitalization

28 Italics

Basic punctuation principles exist in written English and other languages to provide general guidelines on how to present different types of phrases and clauses. Learning these basic rules can help you present your writing in a way that is consistent across the papers you write for your college courses and other types of writing you may do in the future.

Punctuation is a set of rules generally agreed upon by editors and academics although some variety in the application of rules may occur across different types of college disciplines or businesses. The punctuation and mechanics you use can do more than just highlight sentence beginnings and endings; it can also carry or change meaning. For example, consider how punctuation changes the meaning in the following sentences.

> The rock is over Fred.
>
> It is over Fred.
>
> It is over, Fred.
>
> It is over, Fred!

In the first sentence, someone is describing a falling rock over Fred's head. In the second sentence, someone is describing where the rock is. However, in the third sentence, with the addition of the comma, the meaning changes to someone telling Fred that his life is over, possibly due to the falling rock over his head. The period indicates that this is a declaration and not an exclamation and that there is probably no way out of the situation. However, add an exclamation mark, and the sentence turns into an exclamation—a warning to Fred to watch out for the rock.

The basic principles presented in this section can guide you when you have questions about how to use appropriate punctuation and mechanics at the word or sentence level. This way, you can understand and use the conventions of written English or even change the meanings of sentences as you present them to your reader.

THE COMMA

Commas are one of the most frequently used punctuation marks. Unfortunately, commas are also the most frequently misused punctuation mark. Having a reference tool available is always a good idea when you are not sure about how a comma rule applies to your sentence, but the abundance of comma rules can sometimes be frustrating. In this chapter, you will learn to use commas more effectively.

In this section, comma rules are presented in the order of frequently used sentence-level comma rules followed by less frequently used rules. In addition to this useful set-up, you will also find a laminated one-page QUICK EDITING ROADMAP inside your copy of this handbook. Using up-to-date research on college writing, I have developed this guide as a quick reference to the sentence-level rules that confuse writers the most. Half of the rules included on the QUICK EDITING ROADMAP are comma rules.

15a Set off introductory words, phrases, and clauses

1. Set off introductory words and phrases

Commas are often used to set off introductory words and phrases. If the word
or phrase includes a verb, a comma should
always be used to separate the word or
phrase from the main sentence.

→ Shocked, Alex put out his cigarette when he saw the new No Smoking sign.

→ Frustrated by the new sign, Alex put out his cigarette.

If the introductory word is a single preposition or adverb, you may omit the comma.

→ Yesterday the guests grumbled about the new sign.

If the introductory prepositional phrase is short (usually viewed as being five words or fewer), you may also omit the comma.

→ Below the stage the guests grumbled about the new sign.

Helpful hint

If you are unsure about punctuating an introductory word, phrase, or clause, use a comma. The presence of a comma, rather than its absence, is always a good choice.

→ Yesterday, the guests grumbled about the new sign.

→ Below the stage, the guests grumbled about the new sign.

2. Set off introductory clauses

Always use a comma after an introductory clause. The use of a verb in any kind of introductory word, phrase, or clause is the clue to always using a comma.

→ Since he had recently quit smoking, Alex was happy to see the new No Smoking sign.

→ Although Chris was unhappy about the new sign, Alex was quite content.

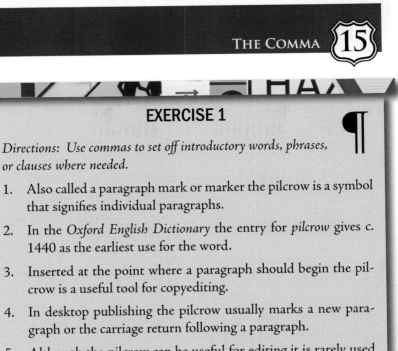

EXERCISE 1

Directions: Use commas to set off introductory words, phrases, or clauses where needed.

1. Also called a paragraph mark or marker the pilcrow is a symbol that signifies individual paragraphs.

2. In the *Oxford English Dictionary* the entry for *pilcrow* gives c. 1440 as the earliest use for the word.

3. Inserted at the point where a paragraph should begin the pilcrow is a useful tool for copyediting.

4. In desktop publishing the pilcrow usually marks a new paragraph or the carriage return following a paragraph.

5. Although the pilcrow can be useful for editing it is rarely used when documenting sources.

15b   Combine independent clauses in compound sentences

A comma is used between two independent clauses that are joined by a coordinating conjunction, such as any of the FANBOYS—*for, and, nor, but, or, yet, so.*

> Independent clause/simple sentence➔Chris was unhappy about the new sign.

> Independent clause/simple sentence➔Alex was quite content about the new sign.

> Compound sentence➔ Chris was unhappy about the new sign, **but** Alex was quite content.

Be sure that the clauses on each side of the comma + conjunction are independent. A comma is never used between conjoined noun phrases or conjoined verb phrases.

Misused comma➡ Chris, and Alex had a terrible argument outside the building.

OK➡Chris and Alex had a terrible argument outside the building.

Misused comma➡Chris was unhappy about the sign, and left campus early.

OK➡ Chris was unhappy about the sign and left campus early.

You can sometimes omit the comma when the two clauses are short—this is not always acceptable to all instructors or editors, though. You will always be correct if you include the comma.

➡   Chris was unhappy and he left.

➡   Chris was unhappy, and he left.

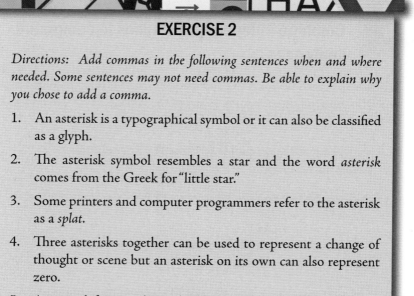

EXERCISE 2

Directions: Add commas in the following sentences when and where needed. Some sentences may not need commas. Be able to explain why you chose to add a comma.

1. An asterisk is a typographical symbol or it can also be classified as a glyph.

2. The asterisk symbol resembles a star and the word *asterisk* comes from the Greek for "little star."

3. Some printers and computer programmers refer to the asterisk as a *splat*.

4. Three asterisks together can be used to represent a change of thought or scene but an asterisk on its own can also represent zero.

5. A great defensive play in baseball can be noted on a baseball trading card with an asterisk.

15c   Separate items in a series

Commas are used to separate words, phrases, or clauses in a series. A series contains at least three items that are parallel with each other (e.g., three nouns or three phrases).

→ **Chris, Alex, and Max** spent three hours arguing about the new signs around campus.

→ I saw the three musketeers—**Chris, Alex, and Max**—outside the building.

→ Chris **talked, cajoled, and yelled** as he tried to convince the administrators.

→ As I left the building, Max was **taking down the sign, yelling at some strangers, and jumping up and down.**

If the items in a series that you are connecting already have commas, use semicolons to separate them.

→ When the campus police arrived, they wanted to ticket Chris, who began the argument; Alex, who escalated the argument; and Max, who threw the first punch.

15d   Set off non-essential elements

Commas can be used to enclose non-essential information that is included in a sentence. To be non-essential, the information needs to be unnecessary for a reader to understand the central meaning of the sentence.

1. Relative clauses

Relative clauses can be essential or non-essential when it comes to understanding the main meaning of the full sentence. Relative clauses that are not necessary are non-restrictive and need to be set off by commas.

→ Chris and Alex, **who were in my English class**, were arguing violently.

In the above sentence, the information about which class Chris and Alex were in is non-essential to the meaning of the independent clause.

If a relative clause is essential to the full meaning of the sentence, it is restrictive and should not have any commas around it.

→ The audience that was closest to Chris and Alex was getting violent as well.

In the sentence above, the relative clause ("that was closest to Chris and Alex") is essential information. It was just the audience closest to Chris and Alex who were getting violent, not those in the audience farther away.

Using *that* for non-essential relative clauses and a comma plus a relative pronoun, such as *which* or *who*, for essential relative clauses is a way that some editors and writers help distinguish between non-essential and essential sentence elements. If you are required to follow MLA (Modern Language Association) or APA (American Psychological Association) guidelines, follow this convention. However, even MLA acknowledges that some writers do not follow this convention, so it's a good idea to check with your instructor about this grammar rule that is in flux.

Remember, though, that punctuation works together with meaning. Two sentences that look almost the same can use different punctuation due to the meaning the writer has in mind.

Non-restrictive relative clause→ Tennessee, which is a beautiful state, has all the signs of a bad economy.

Restrictive relative clause→ I like the Tennessee that is a beautiful state and not the one that has signs of a bad economy.

In the first sentence above, the main idea of the sentence can be understood without the relative clause *which is a beautiful state*. This makes the relative clause non-essential, requiring commas. In the second sentence, the main idea of the sentence can only be understood with the two relative clauses *that is a beautiful state* and *that has signs of a bad economy* included. This makes the two relative clauses essential, thus requiring no commas.

2. Participial phrases

Participial phrases are verb phrases that describe nouns. They take commas wherever they occur—at the beginning of the sentence, in the middle of the sentence, or at the end of the sentence.

Sentence with participial phrase➜
The Hollywood sign, first built in
1923, was restored in 1978 with
money from Gene Autry, Alice Cooper, and others.

Sentence with participial phrase➜ The Hollywood sign,
located in Griffith Park and not Hollywood, was restored in
1978 with money from Gene Autry, Alice Cooper, and others.

3. Appositives

Appositives are nouns, noun phrases, and noun clauses that rename
nouns. The same restrictive/non-restrictive comma rule that applies to
relative clauses applies to appositives (see 15d for more information on
restrictive and non-restrictive elements).

Sentence with non-restrictive appositive➜ The Hollywood
sign, a national monument, was restored in 1978 with money
from Gene Autry, Alice Cooper, and others.

Sentence with restrictive appositive➜ The musician Alice
Cooper helped fund the restoration of the Hollywood sign.

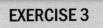

EXERCISE 3 &

*Directions: Add commas where needed to set off non-essential
clauses, phrases, and appositives. Not all sentences will need a comma.*

1. The ampersand is a symbol that represents the word *and*.

2. The ampersand is rarely used in academic writing which is
   more formal than personal writing.

3. However, if an ampersand is part of the name of a business
   such as in Jacoby & Meyers, then a writer should use the ampersand.

4. In APA documentation style, the ampersand representing the
   word *and* is used.

5. Stephen Fry now a prolific author and Hugh Laurie now television's Dr. House performed a skit about ampersands on their
   television show.

15e   Separate coordinate adjectives

A comma is used to separate coordinate adjectives. Adjectives are considered coordinate when they directly and equally modify a noun phrase. One test to see whether you are using coordinate adjectives is to reverse their order—if the original modification relationship exists, you have coordinate adjectives. Another test to see whether you are using co-ordinate adjectives is to place an *and* between the two adjectives—once again, if the original meaning exists, you have coordinate adjectives.

→   Sam and Alex saw the dull, unappealing billboard for the movie and changed their minds about seeing it.

→   Sam and Alex saw the unappealing, dull billboard for the movie and changed their minds about seeing it.

Did You Know?

"Put a comma where you pause." Have you ever been told to punctuate based upon how a sentence is spoken? While you'll get in trouble if you follow this advice too much, it's not entirely misguided. Punctuation marks were originally intended to aid orators when reading a text aloud, and only in the past 100 or so years has punctuation become standardized. The comma can be traced back to the 3rd century BCE when Aristophanes of Byzantium invented a system of dots to separate verse; different groupings of dots represented different types of breaths needed to complete the reading of part of a text. Although the word comma comes from the Greek *komma* ("something cut off"), the shape of today's comma was standardized in the 16th century when the original comma—the diagonal slash (/)—dropped to the bottom of the line and curved.

15f Set off interrupters

1. Transitions

When an adverbial conjunction (also called a conjunctive adverb) appears in the middle of a sentence, it is separated off from the main sentence with commas.

→ The Hollywood sign, moreover, does not include any of the original letters.

→ Alice Cooper, however, donated money for the renovation in honor of Groucho Marx.

Adverbial conjunctions can also be used to connect two independent clauses when the adverbial conjunction is enclosed by a semicolon and a comma. Since adverbial conjunctions function as both transitions and as compound sentence connectors, it is wise to always double check the punctuation that you use with an adverbial conjunction.

Adverbial conjunctions

Addition → moreover, furthermore, likewise, finally, additionally, also, incidentally

Contrast → however, nevertheless, in contrast, on the contrary, nonetheless, otherwise, on the other hand, in comparison, conversely, instead

Comparison → similarly, likewise

Exemplification → for example, for instance

Intensification → indeed, in fact, moreover, still, certainly

Result → therefore, thus, consequently, as a result, finally, then, accordingly, hence, subsequently, undoubtedly

Time → meanwhile, then, next, finally, still, now

2. Interjections

A comma is used to mark or enclose a weak exclamation or interjection, separating it from the rest of the sentence. An interjection can come at the beginning, in the middle, or at the end of a sentence.

→ For goodness sake, the instruction book about traffic signs is over 20 pages long.

→ The instruction book about traffic signs is over 20 pages long, for goodness sake.

→ I do not understand, for goodness sake, why that book about traffic signs is so long.

3. Direct address

A comma is used to mark or enclose a noun phrase that is used as a direct address. When you use a noun phrase that names the person or persons being spoken to, you are using the form of a direct address.

→ "Sam, did you see the billboard for *Terminator: Salvation?*"

→ "Did you see the billboard for *Terminator: Salvation*, Sam?"

→ "I thought the billboard for *Jumper* was good, Sam, but did you see the one for *Terminator: Salvation?*"

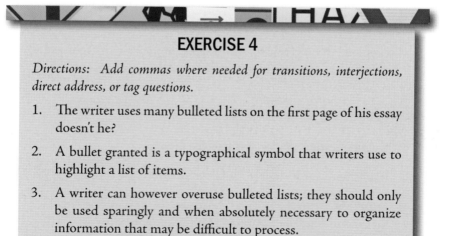

EXERCISE 4

Directions: Add commas where needed for transitions, interjections, direct address, or tag questions.

1. The writer uses many bulleted lists on the first page of his essay doesn't he?

2. A bullet granted is a typographical symbol that writers use to highlight a list of items.

3. A writer can however overuse bulleted lists; they should only be used sparingly and when absolutely necessary to organize information that may be difficult to process.

4. Bullets come in many shapes and sizes and are common in academic writing.

5. Chris do you use a lot of bullets in your essay writing?

4. Tag questions

Commas are also used to mark tags, which are added to the end of a sentence to question whether the statement that precedes the tag is accurate or not.

→ The poster for *Sherlock Holmes* made the main character look somewhat dastardly, didn't it?

→ It has been a long time since we have had a modern Sherlock Holmes, hasn't it?

15g   Set off quotations or dialogue

Commas are used to set off a speaker's exact words from the rest of the sentence.

→ Chris complained, "That book is over 20 pages long."

→ "That book is over 20 pages long," Chris complained.

→ "That book," Chris complained, "is over 20 pages long."

Commas are not used with indirect quotations.

→ Chris complained that the book was too long.

Commas are not used after an exclamation point or question mark.

→ "That book is too long!" complained Chris.

→ "How long is that book on traffic signs?" asked Chris with a frown on his face.

15h   Set off geographic locations

Commas are used to set off items in an address or in the name of a place.

→ Please send any comments about the new sign to Department of Signage, Box 50, Fairbanks, Alaska 99701.

→ Murfreesboro, Tennessee, is near Nashville.

→ Be sure to check out the new sign at The Stone's River Mall, Murfreesboro, Tennessee.

A comma is never used between the name of a state and a ZIP Code.

→ You should send your card and return postage to the Department of Signage, Box 50, Fairbanks, AK 99701.

15i   Set off dates

Commas are used to set off items in a date. Use commas between the day and month, the date and year, and the year and the rest of the sentence.

→ The smoking signs were changed on Monday, January 1, 2010, when the new law took effect.

A comma is never used between the date and month or the month and year when the date is written in inverted order.

→ The smoking signs were changed on Monday, 1 January 2010, when the new law took effect.

A comma is never used when only the month and year are given.

→ The smoking signs were changed in January 2010.

15j   Set off titles

A comma is used to set off a person's title or degree.

→ Dr. Watson had a sign outside his front door that said John H. Watson, M.D.

→ Juliet Freestone, PhD, noted expert on Sherlock Holmes, will speak at the library today.

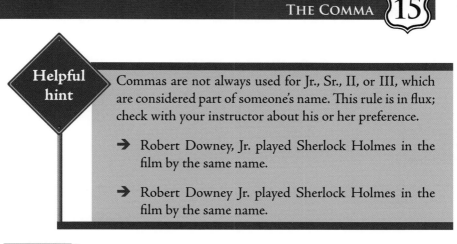

Helpful hint

Commas are not always used for Jr., Sr., II, or III, which are considered part of someone's name. This rule is in flux; check with your instructor about his or her preference.

➔ Robert Downey, Jr. played Sherlock Holmes in the film by the same name.

➔ Robert Downey Jr. played Sherlock Holmes in the film by the same name.

15k   Set off numbers

When numbers are longer than four digits, use commas to separate them, placing a comma every three digits starting from the right.

➔ 1,000

➔ 1,000,000

➔ 1,000,000,000

Do not use commas in the above way when writing years, telephone numbers, street addresses, or zip codes.

15l   Prevent confusion

Most grammar handbooks will tell you to use commas to prevent confusion or for clarity. These might be the kinds of examples shared with you.

➔ What Chris did, did affect all of us.

➔ It was the sign she had waited for, for years.

However, if you find yourself needing to use a comma to avoid confusion, you probably need to revise the entire sentence.

➔ What Chris did that day affected all of us.

➔ She had waited for years for the sign.

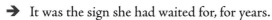

THE SEMICOLON

A semicolon connects phrases or clauses that are closely linked in meaning. Using a semicolon is limited to three situations.

16a Connect independent clauses

Semicolons can connect two independent clauses (or simple sentences) to form a compound sentence.

Simple sentence/independent clause➔ The Chinese zodiac uses twelve animals to represent human qualities.

Simple sentence/independent clause➔ The Chinese zodiac runs on a twelve-year cycle.

Compound sentence➔ The Chinese zodiac uses twelve animals to represent human qualities; it also runs on a twelve-year cycle.

16b Use with adverbial conjunctions or transitional phrases to connect clauses

Two simple sentences can be connected with an adverbial conjunction (also known as a conjunctive adverb) when a semicolon is used to the left of the adverbial conjunction and a comma to the right of it. See **15f** for a list of adverbial conjunctions.

Transitional phrases

after all	in contrast
as a matter of fact	in fact
as a result	in like manner
at any rate	in other words
at the same time	in the meantime
equally important	on one hand
even so	on the contrary
for example	on the other hand
for instance	to illustrate
in addition	while this may be true
in conclusion	

→ The Chinese zodiac uses twelve animals to represent human qualities; furthermore, it runs on a twelve-year cycle.

→ The Chinese zodiac uses twelve animals to represent human qualities; in fact, it runs on a twelve-year cycle.

16c Separate groups that contain commas

If the items in a series that you are connecting already have commas, use semicolons to separate them.

→ The Chinese zodiac uses twelve animals, such as the boar and the snake, to represent human qualities; runs on a twelve-year cycle; and is widely used throughout Asia, not just in China.

Chinese zodiac

EXERCISE 1

Directions: Revise these sentences, adding semicolons where needed. Not all sentences will need semicolons.

1. Bob Berner first introduced the backslash to computer programming in the 1960s it is sometimes called a *slosh*.

2. The backslash is a typographical mark furthermore it is an ASCII character.

3. The backslash is also used to separate the directory and file parts of a website address.

4. The backslash, a typographical mark, is used in computing to indicate that whatever follows should be treated differently or specially it is used in mathematics to indicate a set difference and it is used with the forward slash in linguistics to indicate phonemes.

5. Asian programmers can use other characters that are treated exactly the same as the backslash consequently this can cause some confusion.

Chapter 17

THE COLON

The colon has a variety of uses, but its overall function is to connect elements while still keeping them slightly separated from each other.

MLA guidelines suggest using one space after a colon; however, the MLA also allows for two spaces if this strategy is used consistently. APA guidelines require one space after a colon.

According to the MLA, the first letter of the word that follows a colon should be in lower case, unless that word is one that is normally capitalized or is part of a rule, principle, or quotation. However, according to the APA, the first letter of the sentence following a colon should be in upper case if the sentence is an independent clause. Since the rule for using capitalization with a colon can change across documentation styles, it is a good idea to ask your instructor for clarification about which style she or he prefers.

17a   Connect independent clauses

A colon is used to connect two independent clauses (or simple sentences) when the clause to the left of the colon is of a general or abstract nature and the clause to the right gives more specific information.

→ The Chinese zodiac uses twelve animals and runs on a twelve-year cycle: the animals represent different qualities of human nature, such as calmness or righteousness.

17b Add emphasis

Colons can be used to emphasize words, phrases, or clauses.

→ When I first studied the Chinese zodiac, I could not believe my sign: the pig.

17c Introduce a series or list

A colon is used to introduce a list or a series of words or phrases. As you can see in the sentence below, on the left side of the colon is an independent clause.

→ The Chinese zodiac also describes its animal signs with four elements: fire, metal, water, and wood.

Colons should not follow phrases like *such as, for example, includes,* or *including.* In fact, no punctuation should be used after these phrases when giving a list.

Okay→ The Chinese zodiac has signs such as roosters, snakes, and boars.

17d Introduce a quotation or saying

A colon should be used to introduce a quotation or saying when it is a complete sentence.

→ I have a Chinese proverb by which I live: "When you only have two pennies left in the world, buy a loaf of bread with one and a lily with the other."

17e Use for salutations in formal letters

In a formal business letter, the colon is commonly used in the salutation. A comma can be used for personal letters.

→ Dear Judge Smith:

17f   Connect numbers

Colons are used for connecting numbers in a variety of ways.

1. Connect ratios

➔ The ratio of sunny days to snow days is 45:1.

2. Connect chapters and verses of holy texts

➔ Ezra 6:18

➔ Job 29:4

➔ Qur'an 3:3

➔ Vedanta-sutra 4:1:12

3. Connect hours, minutes, and seconds

➔ 11:05:01

➔ 3:13 a.m.

➔ 7:03 p.m.

17g   Connect titles and subtitles

➔ *The Chinese Zodiac: Twelve Personalities Represented by Animals*

17h   Separate geographical location and publisher name in bibliographic entries

➔ Southlake, TX: Fountainhead, 2010.

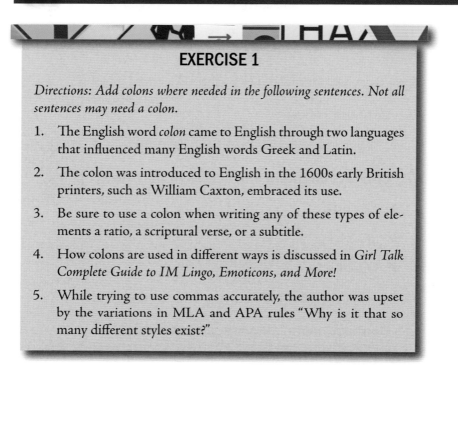

EXERCISE 1

Directions: Add colons where needed in the following sentences. Not all sentences may need a colon.

1. The English word *colon* came to English through two languages that influenced many English words Greek and Latin.

2. The colon was introduced to English in the 1600s early British printers, such as William Caxton, embraced its use.

3. Be sure to use a colon when writing any of these types of elements a ratio, a scriptural verse, or a subtitle.

4. How colons are used in different ways is discussed in *Girl Talk Complete Guide to IM Lingo, Emoticons, and More!*

5. While trying to use commas accurately, the author was upset by the variations in MLA and APA rules "Why is it that so many different styles exist?"

Chapter 18

THE PERIOD, EXCLAMATION POINT, AND QUESTION MARK

Choosing end punctuation is easy if you know the type and function of the sentence you are writing. Writers use declarative sentences to give information, imperative sentences to give instructions or commands, interrogative sentences to obtain information, and exclamatory sentences to express emotion.

Declarative sentence or statement➔ The Chinese zodiac has four elements.

Imperative sentence or command➔Tell me which zodiac sign I am.

Interrogative sentence or question➔How many Chinese zodiac signs are there?

Exclamatory sentence or exclamation➔ You're a Boar! Really!

18a   Use a period to end a sentence or separate initials or abbreviations

No iron can pierce the heart with such force as a period put just at the right place.

−Isaac Babel

1. End a sentence

A period ends a declarative sentence that gives information, makes a statement, or gives a mild command.

> Gives information➔ In the Chinese zodiac, different animals not only rule each year, different ones rule each day.

> Makes a statement➔ The Chinese zodiac is fascinating, especially when it is compared to our Western zodiac.

> Gives a mild command➔Learn the animals and elements of the Chinese zodiac for the quiz tomorrow.

2. Separate initials or abbreviations

Periods are placed after an initial or an abbreviation.

> ➔ Ms. Smith, Mr. Smith, Mrs. Smith, Dr. Allison D. Smith, Adam D. Smith, Jr., Sen. Thomas P. Smith, Prof. Adam Smith, Rev. Smith

Using periods for the above list is always correct. Some other initials or abbreviations can take a period or not. This is something you will need to check with your instructor or with the specific style guidelines you are using, such as Modern Language Association (MLA) or American Psychological Association (APA). For instance, both MLA and APA suggest not using periods or spaces in abbreviations composed only of capital letters, but some instructors prefer that students use periods.

The following abbreviations can appear with or without periods.

> ➔ BA, BS, MA, PhD

> ➔ GP, LPN, MBA, MD, RN

> ➔ BC, BCE, AD, CE, AM, PM

States can often be abbreviated in a variety of ways, including some forms that take periods. For instance, *PA* or *Penn.* can be used for the state of Pennsylvania. However, in formal writing, it is not commonly accepted for states to be abbreviated.

18b   Emphasize with an exclamation point

An exclamation mark is used at the end of an exclamatory sentence to express a strong feeling or to give emphasis.

→ This is the last time I will comment. Stop asking me!

→ Imagine! The foundation of astrology goes back thousands of years.

> Cut out all those exclamation marks. An exclamation mark is like laughing at your own jokes.
> —F. Scott Fitzgerald

18c   End a direct question, show uncertainty, or embed a short question with a question mark

1. End a direct question

A question mark is used at the end of a direct question or interrogative.

→ Are there any similarities between the Chinese zodiac and Western astrology?

Helpful hint

A question mark is never used for an indirect question.

→ Molly asked why I used Chinese zodiac examples.

2. Show uncertainty

A question mark can also be used to show uncertainty about a fact or piece of information. When used this way, the question mark should be placed within parentheses.

→ Western astrology began in the 2nd century AD (?).

Western zodiac

3.   Embed a short question within a sentence

A short question can be embedded within a longer sentence in three ways: within parentheses, enclosed by dashes, or just within the sentence itself.

➜   Western astrology began in the 2nd century AD (is this similar to Chinese astrology?) and has twelve signs.

➜   Western astrology began in the 2nd century AD—is this similar to Chinese astrology?—and has twelve signs.

➜   When she asked the question, why are Western and Chinese zodiacs so similar? at the lecture, the speaker gave her a point-by-point answer.

Helpful hint

Although embedding questions within longer sentences is grammatical, it is rarely done and often questioned. A writer might want to revise these types of sentences into something that is more common.

EXERCISE 1

Directions: Fill in the blanks with the correct punctuation mark: period (.), exclamation point (!), or question mark (?).

1.   Have you ever gotten lost reading something that is poorly written___

2.   Punctuation marks are like tiny road signs for the reader___

3.   Also referred to as a full stop, the period tells the reader that a complete thought, or sentence, has come to an end___

4.   Although periods are the most common way to end a sentence, did you know that there are two other ways to do this___

5.   The exclamation point is sometimes overused by excited students___ Be careful___

Chapter 19

THE APOSTROPHE

The apostrophe is used in a variety of situations and is one of the most complicated punctuation marks to use. Unless you know for sure that the way you use it is always correct, it is a good idea to double check its use during your editing sessions or revise your sentence to avoid it.

19a Mark omissions when parts of words are removed

An apostrophe is used to show that one or more letters have been omitted. For instance, use an apostrophe to show in *I'm* that the *a* has been deleted.

1. Mark contractions when parts of words are removed

→ I'm, you're, he's, she's, it's, they're, we're

→ I hadn't, you haven't

→ I can't, I couldn't, you won't, you wouldn't, they'll, they shouldn't

2. Mark numbers when parts of numbers are removed

→ in the year '95

3. Mark words used to represent oral language

When using unusual or informal spellings to represent oral language, you can use apostrophes to mark contractions.

→ a-walkin', trekin', y'all

Did You Know?

You ain't gonna believe this! *Ain't* is, in fact, a word. This "improper" word is a contraction of *am* (from the verb *to be*) and *not*—similar in construction to *isn't* and *aren't*. Grammatically, it should follow a first person pronoun (*I*), but it is often used in informal speech following any noun. But watch out! *Ain't* ain't acceptable in formal English.

19b   Form plurals

The MLA recommends that an apostrophe along with an −*s* be used to create the plural of abbreviations that include lowercase letters, uppercase letters, or both.

→ A's, B's, C's, D's, E's

→ PhD's, Mind your P's and Q's!

However, many instructors prefer that no apostrophe be used at all.

→ As, Bs, Cs, Ds, Es

→ PhDs, Mind your Ps and Qs

Some instructors may prefer that you italicize the letter and use regular font style for the −*s* ending.

→ *A*s, *B*s, *C*s, *D*s, *E*s

It is best to check with your instructor on how he or she wants you to format letters.

> **Helpful hint**
>
> Apostrophes, in general, should not be used to form the plurals of numbers, abbreviations or acronyms that include all uppercase letters, and phrases that refer to words.
>
> → 1980s, the 60s
>
> → TAs, CEOs, IOUs
>
> → She uses many *ands* but not enough other conjunctions in her writing.

How would you edit this sign?

19c Form possessives

An apostrophe is used in various ways to form possessives. Knowing the difference between singular nouns, indefinite pronouns, and plural nouns will help you use the apostrophe correctly.

1. Form singular possessives

A. Singular nouns

An apostrophe and *—s* can be added to most singular nouns and acronyms to form the possessive.

→ Sam's book, the student's pen, the new sign's message

→ the CEO's email, MLA's style guide

Helpful hint

In the past, several apostrophe rules were dependent on what letter ended the singular noun. However, *The MLA Handbook for Writers of Research Papers* now recommends always using an apostrophe and −*s* at the end of any singular noun. If your instructor wants you to use another style guide for your research and writing, you will need to check how this rule is handled in that system.

→ Giles's plan, the boss's idea, Ms. Jones's books

B. PERSONAL PRONOUNS

Possessive pronouns and possessive adjectives do not take an apostrophe since they already show possession.

→ my, your, yours, his, her, hers, its, our, ours, their, theirs

C. INDEFINITE PRONOUNS

An apostrophe and an −*s* is used at the end of an indefinite pronoun to show possession.

→ anyone's, anybody's, everyone's, everybody's, someone's, somebody's

2. Mark plural possessives

Plural nouns that do not end in −*s* take only the apostrophe plus an −*s* to form the possessive. Plural nouns that end in −*s* only take the apostrophe.

→ the children's song, the geese's honk, the data's collection

→ the cats' meows, the judges' decision, the zodiacs' signs, the Smiths' house , the Joneses' cat

3. Form possessive compound nouns

When a sentence includes conjoined nouns, the type of ownership or possession determines how to use the apostrophe. If each noun has separate ownership, each noun is marked by the possessive. If the nouns have ownership together, only the last noun is made possessive by using the apostrophe.

Separate ownership➔Sam's and Alex's zodiac signs are not compatible.

Joint ownership ➔Jack and Jill's pail fell down the hill.

19d   Form compounds

An apostrophe and −s is placed at the end of a compound word when signaling possession.

➔   my mother-in-law's sign, mother-of-pearl's color

An apostrophe and −s can be placed at the end of a plural compound word, or the possession can be signaled with an *of* phrase.

➔   my brothers-in-law's zodiac signs

➔   the zodiac signs of my brothers-in-law

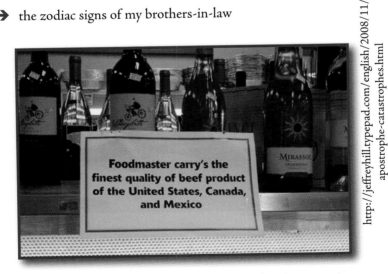

http://jeffreyhill.typepad.com/english/2008/11/apostrophe-catastrophes.html

What is wrong with the sign in this picture?

EXERCISE 1

Directions: Add the missing apostrophes to the following paragraph.

I cant believe how lucky I was to land the latest client for my advertising company. Its not that I doubted my abilities, but this client has been particularly picky in choosing an advertising firm to represent it. Since its such an established company, the boards decision to reinvent themselves with a new logo could launch them into future success or signal the end of their heyday. Its a delicate situation to be sure, and Im excited for the challenge. I already have an idea in mind, and its success could land me a significant promotion if all goes to plan. Though I cant disclose specific details, Ill just say that the clients former business focus was on an outdated technology. Now that theyve adapted to modern technological advances, my job is to bring their image up to date as well. Ive handled similar situations with other outdated companies images with success, so Im confident that I'll be able to pull this off. I cant wait to see my familys reaction when I tell them about this great news!

QUOTATION MARKS

Quotation marks are used in a variety of situations as described below. Generally, when a quotation mark falls at the end of a clause or sentence, place periods and commas inside the quotation mark.

→ My instructor assigned us a new story entitled "Signs and Symbols."

→ When I read "Signs and Symbols," I was reminded of a story from my childhood.

When you use MLA style for in-text citations, the period follows the citation in parentheses.

→ Margaret Jones, in her essay on sign language, says that "anyone who really wants to learn sign language can do so relatively easily" (101).

20a   Signal titles of short works

Quotation marks are used to enclose the titles of short works, including poems, short stories, lectures, book chapters, song titles, magazine articles, newspaper articles, encyclopedia entries, and television/radio episodes.

→ "Pedestrians Not Permitted on this Highway" – a poem by Jackson H. Day

→ "Signs and Symbols" – a short story by Vladimir Nabokov

→ "The Signs of Life" – a lecture by Augustus D. Waller, MD

→ "Signs Inconjunct" – a book chapter by Ptolemy

→ "Signs" – a song by Five Man Electrical Band

→ "Swine Flu Myth: The Symptoms Are Like Regular Flu" – a magazine article

→ "CDC: Swine Flu Outbreak Signs Encouraging" – a newspaper article

→ "Sign Language (Communications)" – an encyclopedia entry

→ "Born Under a Bad Sign" – episode from television's *Supernatural*

Helpful hint
To highlight the title of a larger or longer work, use italics. Thus, you should italicize the titles of poetry collections, short story collections, anthologies, books, albums/CDs, magazines, newspapers, encyclopedias, television series, and radio series.

20b Set off a direct quotation

Quotation marks are also used to set off direct quotations.

→ "The thunderstorm last night was the first sign of spring," said the ABC weatherman.

→ Albert Einstein said, "The true sign of intelligence is not knowledge but imagination."

20c Set off dialogue in prose

Quotation marks are used to set off dialogue. Be sure to use a separate paragraph for each speaker, and use quotation marks around everything each person says.

→ from *Signs* (2002 film):
"What kind of a machine bends a stalk of corn without breaking it?" asked Officer Caroline.

Graham responded, "It can't be by hand; it's too perfect."

Did You Know?

Quotation marks were first used in printing during the middle of the 16th century. Up to the 18th century, some printers would repeat the quotation mark at the beginning of every line in a long quotation. When printers stopped this repetition of the quotation mark at the beginning of every line, the empty left margin was left behind, giving the modern form of the indented block quotation.

20d   Share a few lines of poetry

Quotation marks are used when quoting four or fewer lines of poetry. Be sure to enclose all material from the poem in quotation marks, and use a slash—with a space on each side of the slash—to show where the original line was divided. When quoting material from a source, be sure to give the documentation information.

→ I cannot help but compare my visit to the lines of one of my favorite poems by Jackson H. Day called "Wesley Theological Seminary: No Thoroughfare": "O you who see this sign, pray it may go/And all it represents; and later, lo/This path can be the broadest thoroughfare" (II.4-6).

20e   Share personal thoughts

→ During the visit, I could not help but compare my reception to the metaphor of a favorite poem: "I wish these people would think about how they could create the broadest of thoroughfares."

20f   Signal something being discussed, defined, or used in an unusual or ironic manner

→ I never thought there were so many sentences with the word "sign" in them.

→ Joe has been "signing off" to his girlfriend lately, meaning that he has been showing off.

→ At the bar, when Joe said his "sign" meant he was open for business, I had to laugh.

Helpful hint

When you want to place a quotation within a quotation, use single quotation marks within double quotation marks.

→ "What would you suggest I do when I'm feeling frustrated at being left out of things?" Mark asked his friend, the 60s fan.

→ His friend replied, "I'd go and listen to 'Signs' by the Five Man Electrical Band."

What's wrong with this sign?

EXERCISE 1

Directions: Add quotation marks and capital letters where needed.

1. What does a red sky mean? asked my friend John.

2. I asked when did you see the red sky? The time of day can influence the meaning of red sky.

3. Shakespeare has a quotation in his play *Venus and Adonis* about a red morn.

4. An old adage about sailing during a red sky says red sky at night, sailor's delight. red sky in morning, sailor's warning.

5. Malcolm Coleman even wrote a poem entitled red sky.

THE HYPHEN

Helpful hint

A hyphen is not a dash; a hyphen is one keyboard stroke. A dash equals two hyphens, without spacing before or after. See Chapter 22 for when to use a dash.

21a   Join words to make compound adjectives

A hyphen is used to join two adjectives into a compound adjective before a noun. Do not use a hyphen between the two adjectives when they follow a verb and are not in front of a noun to describe it.

→ freeze-dried coffee, red-light district, well-lighted sign, carry-on luggage

→ She can't tolerate coffee that is freeze dried.

21b   Connect prefixes and suffixes to root words

1. Join certain prefixes (*all-*, *ex-*, *half-*, and *self-*) to a root word

→ all-inclusive, ex-husband, halfback, self-starter

2. Link a single letter to a noun or participle

A hyphen can also be used to join single letters to a noun or participle.

→ X-ray, y-axis, U-turn, G-rated

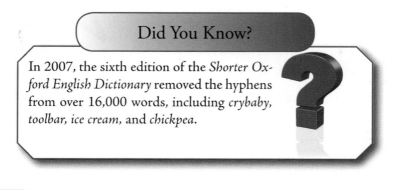

Did You Know?

In 2007, the sixth edition of the *Shorter Oxford English Dictionary* removed the hyphens from over 16,000 words, including *crybaby, toolbar, ice cream,* and *chickpea.*

21c   Join words to make compound numbers

A hyphen is used to join compound numbers from *twenty-one* to *ninety-nine.*

→ twenty-one, thirty-two, forty-three, forty-four

Attention Dog Guardians:
Dogs are restricted from Main Areas, Beaches & must be leashed on trails. Please pick up after your dogs. Thank-you.

Attention Dogs:
Grrrr, Bark, Woof
Good Dog.

Storrs Pond Recreation Area Management

What's wrong with this sign?

21d   Join numbers

Hyphens are used to join the numerator and denominator in a fraction. They are also used to give a person's life span or a score.

→ one-fourth, two-thirds, four-fifths

→ Edward Minor Gallaudet (1837-1917) was the founder and first president of a university for the deaf.

→ In last night's bowling championship, Smith beat Jones 222-219.

21e   Prevent confusion

A hyphen should be used to avoid awkward spelling or confusion when using a prefix or suffix.

→ pre-eminent, re-educate, anti-infective

→ The football player will re-sign. vs. The football player will resign.

EXERCISE 1

Directions: Add a hyphen where necessary.

1. My motherinlaw's Xray was the first sign of her health crisis.
2. The recreation or remodeling of a piece of art can cause controversy.
3. *Signs* is a hairraising film from beginning to end, even though the audience does not know what is truly happening until halfway through.
4. Although M. Night Shyamalan is best known for *The Sixth Sense*, *Signs* is also a well known film.
5. Both *The Sixth Sense* and *Signs* are truly all American films.

Photo from: crackdmuskegonnewz.blogspot.com: "Hyphen-Nation."

THE DASH

A dash is two strokes of the hyphen key without spacing before, after, or between them. Dashes are used in a variety of ways as seen below. Be sure, though, that you need to use a dash and not a hyphen. See Chapter 21 for rules on hyphen use.

22a Highlight introductory material

A dash can be used to highlight introductory material. Usually, the clause that follows the dash will give further explanation about the introductory material.

→ A pig or a boar—those are the two names for my Chinese zodiac sign.

22b Set off parenthetical, explanatory, or contrasted material

→ I cannot accept either name—a pig or boar—for my Chinese zodiac sign.

→ Chinese zodiac signs—based on animals and natural elements—describe general qualities of a person's nature.

→ I'd much rather be a dragon—not a pig—for my Chinese zodiac sign.

22c   Add emphasis

Dashes can be used instead of commas when you want to add emphasis to something.

→   I still can't believe what my Chinese zodiac sign is—a pig or boar!

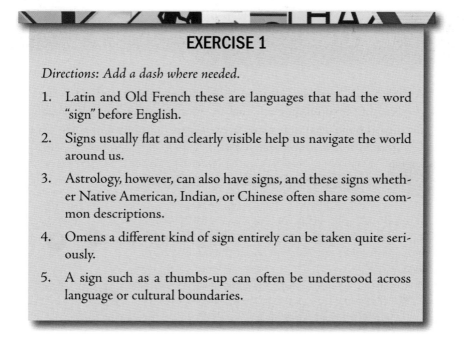

EXERCISE 1

Directions: Add a dash where needed.

1.   Latin and Old French these are languages that had the word "sign" before English.

2.   Signs usually flat and clearly visible help us navigate the world around us.

3.   Astrology, however, can also have signs, and these signs whether Native American, Indian, or Chinese often share some common descriptions.

4.   Omens a different kind of sign entirely can be taken quite seriously.

5.   A sign such as a thumbs-up can often be understood across language or cultural boundaries.

PARENTHESES

A parenthesis (the singular form of "parentheses") is a type of bracket. A dash is more commonly used nowadays in formal writing although parentheses and dashes basically have the same function.

23a Enclose explanatory, minor, or secondary information

Parentheses are used to add material that might interrupt the flow of the sentence. The added information is considered secondary or minor to the main idea of the sentence.

→ In the Chinese zodiac, a person with the boar (pig) sign is honest, sociable, and hard-working.

23b Enclose in-text citations

Parentheses are also used to enclose in-text citations when you need to document your source(s).

MLA in-text citation→ Williams theorizes that the overlap in different systems of astrology is due to "the inherent relationship between travel and storytelling" (234).

APA in-text citation→ Although astrology systems around the world may differ, some overlap is possible due to how stories and travel go together (Williams, 234).

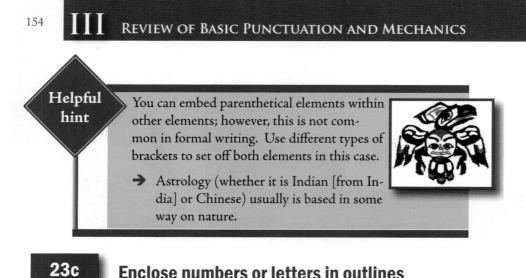

Helpful hint

You can embed parenthetical elements within other elements; however, this is not common in formal writing. Use different types of brackets to set off both elements in this case.

→ Astrology (whether it is Indian [from India] or Chinese) usually is based in some way on nature.

23c   **Enclose numbers or letters in outlines**

Parentheses can be used at different levels of outlines to enclose numbers or letters.

→ I.

    A.

    B.

        1.

            a.

            b.

                (1)

                (2)

            c.

                (1)

                    (a)

                    (b)

                (2)

BRACKETS

Use square brackets to signal corrections or errors

1. Signal editorial correction

Square brackets are usually used to signal that an editorial correction or clarification has been made within a quotation.

→ "The inherent relationship between [the Chinese and Western] systems of astrology is due to exploration and storytelling" (Williams 234).

2. Signal editorial error

Square brackets that are placed around the word *sic* ("as such" in Latin) signal that an editorial error was made by the original writer or speaker.

→ "The inherent relationship between [*sic*] the three systems of astrology is due to exploration and storytelling" (Williams 234).

> **Helpful hint**
>
> You can avoid using square brackets by being selective in choosing what you use as quoted material. If you can summarize or paraphrase, instead of quoting, a section that lacks clarity or has a typographical error, do so.

24b   Use angle brackets to signal Web addresses

Angle brackets (< >) are used to signal Web addresses and separate them unmistakably from the rest of the sentence.

Angle brackets also allow for the end punctuation to fall outside the brackets, thus not creating any confusion about whether the end punctuation is part of the Web address.

→   To learn more about Chinese astrology, visit <http://chinesezodiac.com>.

Chapter 25

THE SLASH

The slash (/) is often called the forward slash to distinguish it from the backslash (\) used in Web addresses. It is also sometimes called the diagonal or the oblique.

25a Quote lines of poetry

When quoting more than one line of poetry, use a slash (or diagonal) is used to show where each line of poetry ends. Be sure to place a space on each side of the slash.

→ I cannot help but compare my visit to the lines of a favorite poem by Jackson H. Day called "Wesley Theological Seminary: No Thoroughfare": "O you who see this sign, pray it may go / And all it represents; and later, lo / This path can be the broadest thoroughfare" (II.4-6).

25b Show a choice

A slash can also be used between two words to show that either choice is available or acceptable.

→ the in/out door, the up/down button

Chapter 26

ELLIPSES

26a　Signal omissions

Ellipses (or ellipsis points) consist of three periods that are spaced equally apart. They are used in quotations to indicate that words have been omitted. If the omission occurs at the end of a sentence, put the ellipses after the period that is at the end of the sentence.

> Original➜ "My attitude towards punctuation is that it ought to be as conventional as possible. The game of golf would lose a good deal if croquet mallets and billiard cues were allowed on the putting green. You ought to be able to show that you can do it a good deal better than anyone else with the regular tools before you have a license to bring in your own improvements."
>
> –Ernest Hemingway

> Quotation➜ "My attitude towards punctuation is that it ought to be as conventional as possible. . . . You ought to be able to show that you can do it a good deal better than anyone else . . . before you have a license to bring in your own improvements."

When quoting poetry, use a line of ellipsis points to signal that you have dropped a line or more of the poem.

GIVE ME A SIGN

By Linda R. O'Connell
2008

Give me a sign
of any kind
at all.

That tells me we share
the same soul.

. . .

And walk with me
forever.

Until the moonlight is not required.

For this love
within our hearts,

Would light the world
on fire.

26b ## Signal a pause or hesitation

Ellipses can also be used to signal a pause or hesitation.

➔ I wish . . . that punctuation was as conventional as possible, just as Hemingway describes it.

CAPITALIZATION

27a   Indicate the first word

1. Indicate the first word in a sentence

Capitalization is used for the first word in every sentence.

→ Traffic signs are sometimes difficult to understand.

2. Indicate the first word in a quotation

Capitalization is also used to indicate the first word in a quotation.

→ My brother told the police officer, "But the sign was covered by a tree branch."

3. Indicate the first word inside parentheses

Capitalization is used when a full sentence is placed within parentheses. If the parenthetical statement is inserted into another sentence, do not capitalize.

→ My brother told the officer that the sign was covered by a tree branch. (However, it wasn't.)

→ My brother told the officer (from our father's precinct) that the sign was covered by a tree branch.

→ My brother told the officer (the officer was from our father's precinct) that the sign was covered by a tree branch.

4. Indicate the first word in a sentence following a colon

Capitalization after a colon is optional; however, capitalize the first word after a colon if you want to emphasize the sentence.

➔ My brother has had several tickets: he has been caught driving with a broken headlight, driving too fast in a school zone, and not stopping for a pedestrian in the crosswalk.

➔ The police officer voided the ticket: He was from our father's precinct.

27b   Indicate proper nouns and proper adjectives

Capitalization is used to indicate proper nouns and proper adjectives.

1. Indicate proper nouns

Proper nouns name specific people, places, things, or ideas. For more information on proper nouns, see 2b.

People➔Abigail Breslin, Joaquin Phoenix, Aunt Joan, Uncle Ralph, Senator Jones, Reverend Smith, Dr. Black, Chief Johnson, Professor White

Places➔ Europe, Australia, Alaska, Washington, D.C., the South, the Northeast, the Mississippi River, the Grand Canyon, New York City, United States

Organizations, governmental institutions, and academic institutions➔Federal Bureau of Investigation, Department of Labor, the United Nations, Long Beach City College, Harvard University

Abbreviations of titles and organizations➔ AAA, FBI, MD, MLA, PhD, UN, UCLA

Monuments and buildings➔ the Washington Monument, the Willis Tower, the Taj Mahal, the Eiffel Tower

Languages➔ Chinese, English, Arabic, Swahili, Spanish, French, Japanese, Russian, Mandarin, American Sign Language

Races➔ American Indian, Alaskan Native, Pacific Islander, African American, Black, White, Asian

Nationalities➔Spanish, Ethiopian, Arabic, Chinese, South African, Greek, American

Religions and religious terms➔ Buddhism, Islam, Christianity, Judaism, Shinto, Protestant, Catholic, Baptist, Buddha, Mohammed, God, Jesus, Moses, Talmud, Bible, Koran, Allah, Jehovah, Genesis

Course titles➔ English 101, Biology 1001, French 300, English Composition 101, Modern War Ethics, An Introduction to Computer History

Days and months➔ January, March, May, Sunday, Tuesday, Thursday

2. Indicate proper adjectives

Capitalization is also used for proper adjectives, which are usually derived from proper nouns and can be found inside a proper noun phrase.

➔ Chinese food, English language, Spanish eyes

27c   Indicate titles and subtitles

Capitalization is used for titles of books, stories, plays, poems, songs, articles, films, newspapers, magazines, works of art, musical compositions, and photographs. Always capitalize the first word in the title, no matter the type of word. Also, if using MLA (Modern Language Association) style, capitalize all other words in the title or subtitle except for articles (*a, an, the*), conjunctions (*for, and, nor, but, or, yet, so*), and short prepositions (*in, on, for, to*). If using another style, such as from the APA (American Psychological Association), be sure to check specific guidelines.

Books➔ *The World According to Garp*

Books with subtitles➔*Chinese Astrology: Exploring the Eastern Zodiac*

Short stories➜ "Everyday Use"

Plays➜ *Hamlet*

Poems➜ "Casey at the Bat"

Songs➜ "Rudolph, the Red-Nosed Reindeer"

Articles➜ "Fifty Ways to Avoid the Flu"

Films➜ *Moulin Rouge*

Newspapers➜ *The New York Times*

Magazines and journals➜ *Vogue, English Journal*

Works of art➜ *Starry Night*

Musical compositions➜ *Romeo et Juliette*

Photographs➜ *The Kiss*

Vessels➜ *Spruce Goose, Queen Mary*

VJ Day, The Kiss, New York 1945
Gelatin Silver by Alfred Eisenstaedt
© Time Inc.

27d   Indicate acronyms

Acronyms are made up of the first letter of each word in a phrase. For instance, *FBI* is the acronym for "Federal Bureau of Investigation." Acronyms are usually capitalized except for those that have become regular words such as *scuba*, *laser*, and *radar*.

Acronyms ➜CBS, CEO, CIA, FAQ, SAT, USA, WGN

Did You Know?

The official name for the Roman Empire, long before the Christian era, was SPQR, an acronym that means *Senatus Populusque Romanus* or "the Senate and the People of Rome."

EXERCISE 1

Directions: Capitalize where needed.

1. when I visited china and the great wall, I had two books in my backpack: *the signs of life in the universe* and *life after school.*

2. i learned quite quickly that I should have been carrying a chinese-english dictionary.

3. people often asked me on my asian trip whether i was canadian, australian, or american.

4. while visiting monasteries, my brother alex and i learned about buddha and buddhism (and also lao tse and taoism).

5. we also learned that the people's republic of china (the prc) and the republic of china (roc) are considered two different countries (china and taiwan, respectively) by all countries except for the prc.

ITALICS

Italics are used to emphasize special words, phrases, or clauses. If you are writing by hand or are unable to use italics, you can underline the items that should be in italics.

28a Highlight titles

1. Highlight titles of longer works

To highlight the title of a larger or longer work, use italics. Thus, you should italicize the titles of poetry or short story collections, anthologies, books, albums/CDs, magazines, newspapers, encyclopedias, television series, and radio series.

→ *Signs of Life: A Book of Visual Poetry* by John Ecko

→ *Vital Signs: International Short Stories on Aging* by Dorothy Sennett and Anne Czarniecki

→ *The Signs of Language Revisited: An Anthology in Honor of Ursula Bellugi and Edward Klima* – edited by Karen Emmorey and Harlan L. Lane

→ *Lonely Planet Signspotting* – a book by Doug Lansky

→ *The Sign* – a CD by Ace of Base

→ *Vital Signs* – a magazine

→ *Encyclopedia Britannica* – an encyclopedia

→ *Sign of the Times* – a television series

→ *The Bob and Tom Radio Show* – a radio series

> **Helpful hint**
>
> Quotation marks are used to enclose the titles of short works, including poems, short stories, lectures, book chapters, song titles, magazine articles, newspaper articles, encyclopedia entries, and television/radio episodes.
>
> → "Signs and Wonder" is episode 7.9 of *The X-Files*.
>
> For information on using quotation marks, see Chapter 20.

2. Highlight legal cases

Italics are used to highlight the titles of legal cases.

> → *Roe v. Wade, Brown v. Board of Education of Topeka, State v. Scopes*

3. Identify naval and air ships

Italics are used to identify naval crafts, aircraft, and spacecraft.

> → *Nimitz, Titanic, Queen Mary*
> → *Spruce Goose, Spirit of St. Louis, Lockheed Vega, Air Force One*
> → *Challenger, Atlantis, Enterprise, Sputnik, Explorer*

28b   Highlight special letters, words, phrases, or clauses

Italics are used to highlight special letters, words, phrases, and clauses.

1. Highlight non-English words

Italics are used when you write a non-English word or phrase. If the word or phrase is used multiple times, use italics only the first time it is used.

French phrase for "joy of living" ➜ Every time I see Karen, I drink in her *joie de vivre*.

Japanese word for "special singing and dancing" ➜ My favorite part of Japanese night was the *kabuki* theater.

Arabic phrase for "have a safe journey" ➜ As he left me on the trail, the guide wished me, *"Bissalama."*

The English language has borrowed heavily from other languages for centuries, and some of these words are now considered part of English. For these types of everyday words, you do not use italics.

➜ soy (Japanese), glasnost (Russian), banana (Wolof), Kwanzaa (Swahili), cider (Hebrew)

Did You Know?

In 1973, a survey (by Thomas Finkenstaedt and Dieter Wolff) of about 80,000 words found in the *Shorter Oxford Dictionary* (3rd edition) showed that 28.3% of the English words were borrowed from French, 28.24% from Latin, 25% from Germanic languages (including Old and Middle English), and 5.32% from Greek. All other languages contributed less than 1% of the borrowed words (with 3.28% deriving from proper names and 4.03% of the word origins being unknown).

2. Highlight referenced or discussed letters, words, phrases, and clauses

You also use italics to highlight words that you are discussing, defining, or using in a special way.

➜ Words with the letters *SK* at the beginning are usually of Scandinavian origin.

➜ I had no idea that the word *banana* came from the African language Wolof.

→ *Leviathan* had the original meaning of "sea monster" but now refers to anything of an unusually large size.

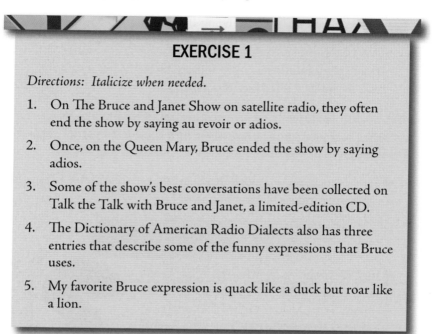

EXERCISE 1

Directions: Italicize when needed.

1. On The Bruce and Janet Show on satellite radio, they often end the show by saying au revoir or adios.

2. Once, on the Queen Mary, Bruce ended the show by saying adios.

3. Some of the show's best conversations have been collected on Talk the Talk with Bruce and Janet, a limited-edition CD.

4. The Dictionary of American Radio Dialects also has three entries that describe some of the funny expressions that Bruce uses.

5. My favorite Bruce expression is quack like a duck but roar like a lion.

Section IV Sentence Level: Basic Grammar

29 **The Simple Sentence**
30 **The Compound Sentence**
31 **The Complex Sentence**
32 **The Compound-Complex Sentence**

THE SIMPLE SENTENCE

29a   The simple sentence

A simple sentence contains a subject and main verb combination, either or both of which may be conjoined. There are two kinds of clauses: independent and dependent. An independent clause, sometimes called a main clause, can stand alone as a simple, but complete, sentence. A dependent clause—with its own subject and verb—can never stand alone and is never part of a simple sentence.

> Independent clause/simple sentence➜ Sam saw the stop sign.
>
> Conjoined noun phrase➜ Sam and Chris saw the stop sign.
>
> Conjoined verb phrase➜ Sam saw the stop sign and braked the car at the same time.

An independent clause can be modified in a variety of ways and still be a simple sentence. Most often, simple sentences are modified with either participial verb phrases, which are verb phrases that do not include an auxiliary, or prepositional phrases (see 6c3).

> ➜ Driving down Elm Street,
>   Participial VP
>   **Sam saw the stop sign.**
>   Independent Clause

→ Stopped at the corner, **Sam saw the stop sign.**
    Participial Phrase   Independent Clause

→ **Sam saw the stop sign** at the corner.
    Independent Clause   Prep Phrase

Simple sentences can be modified by participial phrases and prepositional phrases at the same time.

→ Driving down Elm Street,
    Participial Phrase
Sam saw the stop sign at the corner.
Independent Clause   Prep Phrase

Multiple prepositional phrases can also be used in the same simple sentence.

→ **Sam saw the stop sign** at the corner of Elm and Sixth.
    Independent Clause   Prep Phrase   Prep Phrase

As you may have already noticed, participial phrases that appear at the beginning of the sentence always have a comma that separates the phrase from the independent clause. In fact, all phrases or clauses that contain a verb and occur at the beginning of a sentence should be separated from the main clause by a comma.

When you write a sentence that has a prepositional phrase at the beginning, you have the option of including a comma or not; however, if the introductory prepositional phrase is five words or longer, it usually takes a comma.

OK→ In spring the stop sign at Elm and Sixth is covered with a tree branch.

OK→ In spring, the stop sign at Elm and Sixth is covered with a tree branch.

OK→ At the corner of Elm and Sixth, the stop sign is covered with a tree branch.

29b   Check for common errors with the simple sentence

1. Check for overuse of simple sentences

Simple sentences are often used for effect or emphasis and should be used sparingly. Be sure that you do not overuse simple sentences, so when you are ready to use them for emphasis, they can stand out from the more complex sentences around them. See how the addition of a simple sentence in the combination below stands out against the more complex sentence that precedes it.

➜   Our city manager says that there are no funds available to cut the overgrown tree branch on Elm and Sixth; however, there were enough funds for her recent junket to Las Vegas. She needs to stop irrelevant spending now.

2. Check for fragments

Be sure that simple sentences have both a subject and predicate. If one or the other is missing, you have created a common sentence error—the fragment.

Fragment (missing a subject)➜ Leaving the party with his friends in the blue car.

OK➜ Sam left the party with his friends in the blue car.

OK➜ Leaving the party early, Sam went with his friends in the blue car.

Fragment (missing a predicate)➜ My neighbor Sam and his friends, along with many of the people at the party.

OK➜ My neighbor Sam and his friends, along with many of the people at the party, were in the backyard.

Sentences that give directions or a command have an understood subject (*you*), so even though a subject may not appear explicitly in the sentence, the implied subject makes the sentence an independent clause and not a fragment.

➜   (You should) Go east on Elm, and then turn on Sixth.

3. Check for parallelism

When conjoining multiple instances of the same type of word class or phrase, be sure that they are in parallel form.

> Not parallel→ Sam ran quickly to the sign at the corner, returned just as quickly, and singing all the while.

> OK→ Sam ran quickly to the sign at the corner, returned just as quickly, and sang all the while.

EXERCISE 1

Directions: Revise any fragments below into full sentences.

Example: Many people have had accidents at the tree-covered stop sign. For instance, my neighbor John.→ Many people, including my neighbor John, have had accidents at the tree-covered stop sign.

1. Nothing has been done to fix the problem. No tree work. No sign moving.

2. I like to visit my friends on Elm Street. Who have a pool and a hot tub.

3. My friends' daughter had an accident at the stop sign at Sixth and Elm. Not seeing the sign.

4. The city manager needs to take the accidents seriously. Along with other city officials losing more funds due to court cases.

5. Running for office to fix the small problems of our city, including the overgrown trees that are blocking traffic signs.

Chapter 30

THE COMPOUND SENTENCE

30a   The compound sentence

One way to add variety to your writing is to use coordination to join some of your simple sentences together. When you coordinate or combine together two simple sentences (also known as two independent clauses), you create a compound sentence.

→ The signs for American Sign Language were originally based

Independent Clause

on French, and the signs for Signed English were originally

Independent Clause

based on English.

You can choose from four options to create compound sentences, and the option you choose determines the punctuation you will use.

Helpful hint

The compound sentence includes the combination of two full sentences, not two subjects, two verbs, or two verb phrases. For instance, the following sentences are not compound sentences, just simple sentences.

Compound subjects→ Mary and the new professor left the classroom early.

Compound verbs→ Mary laughed and cried at the same time.

Compound verb phrases→ Mary laughed at the joke and cried at the picture at the same time.

30b Use appropriate punctuation for the compound sentence

1. Punctuating a compound sentence—Option 1: Using a comma + conjunction

Notice that the two independent clauses on the previous page are joined together with a comma and a conjunction (*and*). Independent clauses can be joined in a variety of acceptable ways, and using a comma plus a coordinating conjunction is one of the most popular.

The conjunctions that you can use to join together two independent clauses can be remembered by using the mnemonic device FANBOYS, in which each letter represents one conjunction.

	F A N B O Y S
	for and nor but or yet so
F	American Sign Language is difficult for me, for I studied Signed English.
A	Some students learn American Sign Language, and they also learn Signed English.
N	I cannot use American Sign Language, nor can I use Signed English.
B	I learned some signs in school, but I want to learn more American Sign Language.
O	Maybe I will attend an American Sign Language class, or I will attend a special summer camp to learn this interesting language.
Y	Some students know American Sign Language, yet it is difficult for them to communicate in countries other than the United States with deaf students from other cultures.
S	In some colleges, American Sign Language is the only signing method used by the faculty, so those students who only use Signed English will be at a disadvantage.

2. Punctuating a compound sentence—Option 2: Using a semicolon

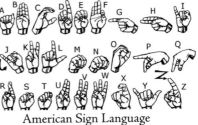

A semicolon can be used to connect two independent clauses. When you use a semicolon in this way, you suggest to the reader that the two connected clauses are related in some way.

American Sign Language

→ Some students learn American Sign Language; **they can also**
        Independent Clause
learn Signed English.
Independent Clause

3. Punctuating a compound sentence—Option 3: Using a semicolon + adverbial conjunction

Another way to connect two independent clauses is with a semicolon plus an adverbial conjunction (sometimes called a conjunctive adverb). Note that a comma follows the adverbial conjunction.

→ Some students attend a school that requires American Sign
        Independent Clause
Language; therefore, **knowing Signed English is not enough.**
                Independent Clause

You can use the acronym THIN TIC to help you remember some common adverbial conjunctions.

T   therefore

H   however

I   in fact

N   nevertheless

T   thus

I   indeed

C   consequently

Adverbial conjunctions signify relationships such as result, cause, contrast, or condition. Be sure to signal the appropriate relationship with the adverbial conjunction you use.

> Result ➜ I learned Signed English in elementary school; therefore, I had problems understanding some American Sign Language signs later on.

> Contrast ➜ American Sign Language is popular at Gallaudet University; however, English is used alongside ASL.

> Intensification ➜ American Sign Language and English are popular at Gallaudet University; indeed, many students use both.

Other than the common THIN TIC adverbial conjunctions, there are other adverbial conjunctions that can be used to connect two independent clauses and signify particular relationships. Here is a list to help you make appropriate choices.

> Addition ➜ moreover, furthermore, likewise, finally, additionally, also, incidentally, further, similarly, in addition

> Contrast ➜ however, nevertheless, in contrast, on the contrary, nonetheless, otherwise, on the other hand, in comparison, conversely, instead

> Comparison ➜ similarly, likewise, at the same time, comparatively

> Exemplification ➜ for example, for instance, namely, that is

> Intensification ➜ indeed, in fact, moreover, still, certainly, notably, undoubtedly

> Result ➜therefore, thus, consequently, as a result, finally, hence, then, accordingly, henceforth, subsequently, undoubtedly, in fact

> Time ➜ meanwhile, then, next, finally, still, now, thereafter

This image of a note placed on an information desk shows a compound sentence that has an error in punctuation. How could you fix the punctuation problem?

4. Punctuating a compound sentence—Option 4: Using a colon

Although not as common as the first three methods of joining two independent clauses together, you can also use a colon if the clause following the colon defines or elaborates the clause before the colon.

→ American Sign Language and Signed English are different in
                Independent Clause
one important way: many linguists consider American Sign
                Independent Clause
Language a full and complete language and Signed English not.

Since both independent clauses are connected in meaning and since the second independent clause elaborates on the first, giving more information about why, a colon can be used.

Image from www.laermer.com/category/the-language-of-life/

The above sign is missing the appropriate punctuation—how ironic! How would you edit this sign to make it grammatically correct?

30c   Common sentence errors with the compound sentence

1. Use a variety of punctuation, conjunctions, and adverbial conjunctions

Be careful when you decide how to join compound sentences. Combining sentences in the same way each time or in a way that creates an obviously consistent pattern will negatively impact your writing. It is best to use a variety of punctuation, conjunctions, and adverbial conjunctions.

2. Check for comma splices

Mistakenly joining two independent clauses together with only a comma creates a comma splice, one of the most frequent sentence errors that writers make. You can fix a comma splice by using one of the four options given above.

Comma splice➜ Some American students learn Signed English as children, they learn American Sign Language as adults.

OK➜ Some American students learn Signed English as children, and they learn American Sign Language as adults.

OK➜ Some American students learn Signed English as children; they then learn American Sign Language as adults.

OK➜ Some American students learn Signed English as children; then, they learn American Sign Language as adults.

3. Check for run-on or fused sentences

If you fail to join two independent clauses together with the appropriate punctuation, you can create another common sentence problem—the run-on or fused sentence.

Run-on/fused sentence➜ My third-grade teacher taught us some signs they were Signed English.

OK➜ My third-grade teacher taught us some signs, yet I don't know many now.

OK➜ My third-grade teacher taught us some signs; they were Signed English.

EXERCISE 1

Directions: The following paragraph contains five comma splices. Correct the errors by turning the comma splices into compound sentences.

I've never been one for believing in astrological signs, I couldn't really even tell you what my sign, Scorpio, actually means. But every now and then, I'll run across a daily horoscope chart, curiosity gets the better of me. One day in particular, my horoscope said to be careful in business dealings and avoid conflict. I had been having a disagreement with one of my clients, who was threatening to give her business to our biggest competitor, immediately that situation came to mind as I read the horoscope over my morning breakfast. I walked into the office later that morning, my secretary informed me that the client was waiting on me—and not happy. I quickly made up an excuse and left the office, remembering what was in store for Scorpios that day. Come to find out, the client's anger was not directed at me, but because she wasted her time coming to the office that morning, she decided to take her business elsewhere. My decision to avoid the conflict altogether resulted in my losing this client and significant income for my company, needless to say, I try to avoid horoscopes now.

Citation = http://news.bbc.co.uk/2/hi/uk_news/magazine/7292252.stm

EXERCISE 2

Directions: The following paragraph contains five run-on sentences. Correct them by adding the appropriate punctuation.

Who would have guessed that a simple piece of fruit would become synonymous with innovative technology well this is exactly what has happened with the symbol for Apple, Inc. With the increasing international popularity of the iPhone, Apple's logo is becoming one of the most recognizable symbols in business and technology today. The trademark silhouette of an apple missing a bite has been around practically since the company's inception although the company's earliest logo features a sketch of Isaac Newton sitting under the apple tree. Apple co-founder Steve Jobs hired Rob Janoff in 1976 to redesign the company's logo and the iconic rainbow apple design was born this version of Apple's apple remained in use until a redesign of the Macintosh operating system and computer hardware in 1998 warranted a monochrome makeover. Two more versions of the symbol would follow: an aqua theme in 2001 and the current glass theme unveiled in 2003, both of which gave the trademark a three dimensional, textured appearance though it's already an internationally recognized symbol, the Apple logo will only become even more common as the company continues to expand.

Chapter 31

THE COMPLEX SENTENCE

31a   The complex sentence

Another way to add variety to your writing is to use subordination and modification to create complex sentences. A complex sentence consists of a simple sentence (also known as an independent clause) plus one or more dependent clauses.

Dependent clauses, like independent clauses, contain a subject and predicate; however, whereas independent clauses can stand alone, dependent clauses are dependent or subordinate to an independent clause and must be attached to that independent clause to form a complete sentence. You can track most dependent clauses back to their independent counterparts, as in the set of sentences below.

Independent clause➜ Each letter in our alphabet is a sign.

Independent clause➜ Each letter in our alphabet gives us information about our language's history and sound system.

Complex sentence➜ Because each letter in our alphabet is a
                              Dependent Clause
sign, it gives us information about our language's history and
sound system.   Independent Clause

Note that the dependent clause above includes the subordinator "because" at the beginning of the clause. A dependent clause usually begins with a subordinator—also called a subordinating conjunction—or a relative pronoun. A subordinator or relative pronoun gives information about the relationship between the independent and dependent clause.

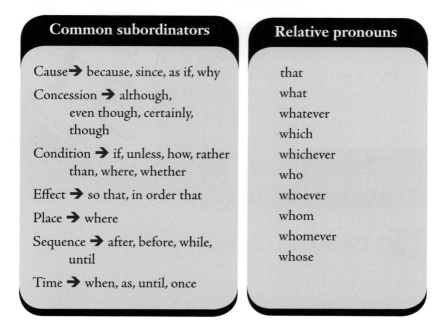

Common subordinators	Relative pronouns
Cause➜ because, since, as if, why	that
Concession ➜ although, even though, certainly, though	what whatever which
Condition ➜ if, unless, how, rather than, where, whether	whichever who
Effect ➜ so that, in order that	whoever
Place ➜ where	whom
Sequence ➜ after, before, while, until	whomever
Time ➜ when, as, until, once	whose

31b   Dependent clauses

Dependent clauses can be nominal (used like nouns), adjectival (used like adjectives), or adverbial (used like adverbs). This means that dependent clauses can be used as subjects, objects, or modifiers. Although it is sometimes difficult to distinguish which type of dependent clause is being used, it is a good idea to learn the different clause types because your choice of punctuation depends on how a clause is being used.

31c   Noun (or nominal) clauses

Dependent noun clauses can function as subjects, direct objects, subject complements, objects of prepositions, or appositives. Since these types of clauses are dependent or subordinate, they are always attached to an independent clause or a critical part of an independent clause. Noun clauses usually begin with a relative pronoun or with one of these subordinators: when, where, how, why or whether. There are two types of noun clauses: nominal relative clauses and appositive clauses.

1. Nominal relative clauses

Nominal relative clauses take the place of a subject, direct object, or an object of a preposition. A good way to see whether you are using a nominal relative clause is to see if you can substitute a pronoun (*it, she, he*) for the clause in question.

> In place of a subject ➔ What sound a letter makes is complicated.
> Dependent Clause/
> Noun Clause

> In place of a direct object ➔ For new language learners, it is sometimes difficult to know which letter represents a particular sound.
> Dependent Clause/
> Nominal Relative Clause

> In place of a subject complement ➔ This alphabet disconnection is why many linguists suggest changing our alphabet.
> Dependent Clause/Nominal Relative Clause

> In place of an object of the preposition ➔ Many linguists theorize about when the alphabet will become more transparent.
> Dependent Clause/Nominal Relative Clause

2. Appositive noun clauses

Appositive noun clauses follow nouns that are general or abstract in nature, such as a theory, reason, fact, or story. The appositive clause begins with a "that" and provides more information about the abstract noun.

> The alphabet disconnection theory that letters do not clearly
> Dependent Clause/
> match sounds is widely known by linguists.
> Appositive Noun Clause

It is important to be able to distinguish these dependent clauses as noun clauses because neither one of these dependent noun clauses requires a comma. Putting a comma around these clauses to highlight them or separate them in some way from the independent clause is a comma error.

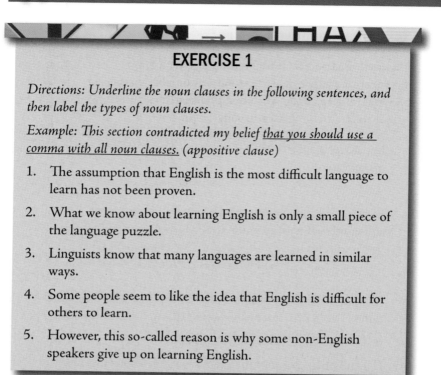

EXERCISE 1

Directions: Underline the noun clauses in the following sentences, and then label the types of noun clauses.

Example: This section contradicted my belief <u>that you should use a comma with all noun clauses.</u> (appositive clause)

1. The assumption that English is the most difficult language to learn has not been proven.

2. What we know about learning English is only a small piece of the language puzzle.

3. Linguists know that many languages are learned in similar ways.

4. Some people seem to like the idea that English is difficult for others to learn.

5. However, this so-called reason is why some non-English speakers give up on learning English.

31d Adjective (or adjectival) clauses

Adjective clauses, another type of dependent or subordinate clause, modify noun phrases, which can be made up of either nouns or pronouns. There are two types of adjective clauses: the comparative clause and the relative clause.

1. Comparative clauses

Comparative clauses compare two noun phrases and use the phrase *as XXX as* to make the comparison, where *XXX* is filled in with an adjective. The clause to the left of the *as XXX as* phrase is the beginning of the independent clause, and the clause to the right of the *as XXX as* phrase is the dependent clause.

→ That sign is **as uninformative as the one I saw at the zoo last week.**
                               Dependent Clause

→ She is **as tall as the sign is.**
        Dependent Clause

2. Relative clauses

Relative clauses, the most common type of dependent clause, are used to modify or give more information about the noun phrase to the clause's left. These clauses usually begin with a relative pronoun, such as that, which, who, whom, or whose.

→ Highway signs that are funny often defeat the purpose of their warning.   Relative Clause

→ The student who is signing for the deaf audience is obviously
                          Relative Clause
still learning American Sign Language.

→ The highway workers whose job it was to paint the new sign forgot the paint.   Relative Clause

Relative pronouns can sometimes be dropped if they can be understood to be part of the relative clause.

→ The signs [that] the highway workers need to paint are the
                          Relative Clause
ones [that] taggers have covered with graffiti.
                Relative Clause

Relative clauses can be essential or necessary for the full meaning of the sentence to be understood, or they can be non-essential. An essential relative clause is described as a restrictive relative clause. Restrictive relative clauses never take commas around the clause.

→ Highway signs that are covered in mud
              Restrictive Relative Clause
can cause accidents.

In the sentence above, not ALL highway signs cause accidents; only highway signs that are covered in mud can cause them. Thus, the relative clause is essential to understand the meaning of the full sentence.

➔   The architect who designed the building has a plaque with his
                    Restrictive Relative Clause
name on it near the front.

Likewise, in the sentence above, it is only the architect who designed the building who has a plaque, not just any architect. Therefore, this relative clause is also essential to the sentence.

A relative clause that is not essential to understand the full meaning of the sentence is described as a non-restrictive relative clause. Non-restrictive relative clauses always take commas around the clause.

➔   The signs along Route 66, which are often stolen, classify
                    Non-Restrictive Relative Clause
it as a national monument.

In the sentence above, the relative clause is not essential for us to understand the meaning of the main sentence. In the relative clause, we get extra or non-essential information. With or without the relative clause, we still understand that the signs along Route 66 label it as a national monument.

➔   The architect, who wore a seersucker suit to the ceremony, was
                    Non-Restrictive Relative Clause
awarded a plaque.

Likewise, in the above sentence, the relative clause is not essential. Whether he wore a seersucker or wool suit is not important; the architect would still have been awarded the plaque either way.

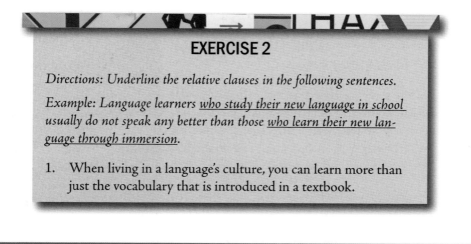

EXERCISE 2

Directions: Underline the relative clauses in the following sentences.

Example: Language learners who study their new language in school usually do not speak any better than those who learn their new language through immersion.

1.   When living in a language's culture, you can learn more than just the vocabulary that is introduced in a textbook.

2. Many language learners who live outside their native country find themselves learning new vocabulary from another language quickly.

3. The younger that a language learner is, the more chance she has of learning a new language.

4. Language textbooks, which are often published by a variety of publishers, can only get you so far into your new language.

5. It is a good idea to stay as long as you can in the country of the language that you are learning.

31e Adverb (or adverbial) clauses

Adverbial clauses begin with a subordinator (sometimes called a subordinating conjunction) and usually give information about cause/reason, concession, condition, effect, place, sequence, and time. The clauses do this by answering the questions *when? where? why? how? how frequently?* and *in what manner?* Adverbial clauses are always dependent or subordinate to the main or independent clause.

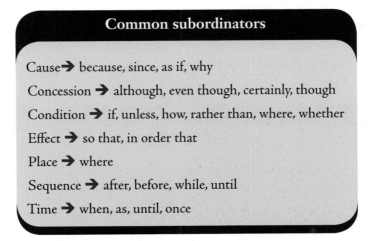

Common subordinators

Cause➔ because, since, as if, why

Concession ➔ although, even though, certainly, though

Condition ➔ if, unless, how, rather than, where, whether

Effect ➔ so that, in order that

Place ➔ where

Sequence ➔ after, before, while, until

Time ➔ when, as, until, once

➔ Because she was caught with the freeway sign in her car, she
             Adverbial (Dependent) Clause
was arrested for theft.

Notice that the adverbial clause above gives the reason why the woman was arrested, thus giving information about cause.

Adverbial clauses can function as adverbs, moving to various points in a sentence. When an adverbial clause is at the beginning of the sentence, use a comma to separate it off from the main or independent clause.

➔ Because the highway trooper was watching him
             Adverbial Clause
closely, the driver followed the detour sign.

When an adverbial clause appears in the middle of a sentence, you should also set it off by placing commas around the adverbial clause.

➔ The driver, because the highway trooper
             Adverbial Clause
watched him closely, followed the detour sign.

However, when an adverbial clause appears at the end of a sentence, it usually does not take a comma.

➔ The driver followed the detour sign because the highway
                          Adverbial Clause
trooper watched him closely.

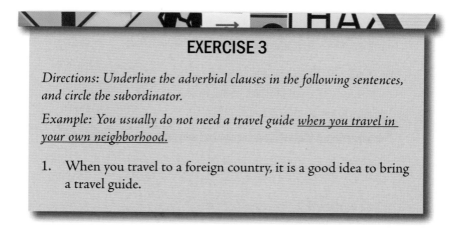

EXERCISE 3

Directions: Underline the adverbial clauses in the following sentences, and circle the subordinator.

Example: You usually do not need a travel guide <u>when you travel in your own neighborhood.</u>

1.   When you travel to a foreign country, it is a good idea to bring a travel guide.

2. Although travel guides can be helpful, they cannot get you out of complicated situations.

3. If you do find yourself with a serious problem in a foreign country, you should check if there is an embassy located near you.

4. Finding an embassy is a good idea, so that you feel more secure when dealing with the problem.

5. While embassy employees can usually help you with serious problems, they cannot provide a translator for you for everyday use.

31f   Common sentence errors with the complex sentence

1. Check for fragments

Dependent clauses do not express a complete thought, and they need to be attached to an independent clause to be grammatically complete. Because dependent clauses are clauses, they contain a subject and a full verb, a fact that sometimes leads a writer to use a dependent clause as a complete sentence. When dependent clauses are presented as a full sentence, they are fragments.

Fragment➜ Because the highway trooper watched him closely.
                          Dependent Clause

OK➜ The driver took the detour because the highway trooper watched him closely.   Dependent Clause

Fragment➜ When she saw the tornado.
                          Dependent Clause

OK➜ When she saw the tornado, she took it as a sign to take cover.   Dependent Clause

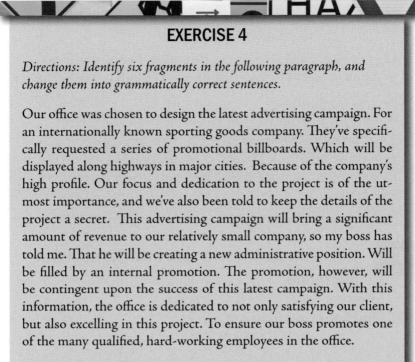

EXERCISE 4

Directions: Identify six fragments in the following paragraph, and change them into grammatically correct sentences.

Our office was chosen to design the latest advertising campaign. For an internationally known sporting goods company. They've specifically requested a series of promotional billboards. Which will be displayed along highways in major cities. Because of the company's high profile. Our focus and dedication to the project is of the utmost importance, and we've also been told to keep the details of the project a secret. This advertising campaign will bring a significant amount of revenue to our relatively small company, so my boss has told me. That he will be creating a new administrative position. Will be filled by an internal promotion. The promotion, however, will be contingent upon the success of this latest campaign. With this information, the office is dedicated to not only satisfying our client, but also excelling in this project. To ensure our boss promotes one of the many qualified, hard-working employees in the office.

Source= http://news.bbc.co.uk/2/hi/uk_news/magazine/7292252.stm

2. Check for unnecessary commas

A noun clause can replace a subject, direct object, subject complement, or object of a preposition. When using a noun clause to replace these items, avoid placing an unnecessary comma between the noun clause and the rest of the sentence.

Extra comma➜ What I like about Saturdays, is seeing all the
                            Dependent Noun Clause
yard sale signs in my neighborhood.

OK➜ What I like about Saturdays is seeing all the yard sale
                    Dependent Noun Clause
signs in my neighborhood.

3. Check for restrictive or non-restrictive punctuation

Be sure to use the correct punctuation for relative clauses. When they provide essential information, they are restrictive and should not have commas. When relative clauses provide non-essential or extra information, they are non-restrictive and should always be separated from the rest of the sentence with commas.

> Extra commas➜ The protester, who had the derogatory sign, was removed from the lecture.   Restrictive Relative Clause

> OK➜ The protester who had the derogatory sign was removed from the lecture.   Restrictive Relative Clause

In the above example, the relative clause gives necessary information—the reason the protester was removed from the lecture. Therefore, the relative clause is restrictive and does not take commas.

> Missing commas➜ M. Night Shyamalan who directed *Sixth*
>   Non-Restrictive
> *Sense* and *Signs* has not won an Academy Award.
> Relative Clause

> OK➜ M. Night Shyamalan, who directed *Sixth Sense* and
>   Non-Restrictive Relative Clause
> *Signs,* has not won an Academy Award.

In the example above, the information that Shyamalan directed the movies *Sixth Sense* and *Signs* is not essential to identify the noun being modified. Thus, the relative clause is non-restrictive and needs to have commas surrounding it.

4. Check for adverbial clause punctuation

When including an adverbial clause in your writing, be sure to use the appropriate punctuation. If the clause appears at the beginning of the sentence, use a comma between it and the independent clause. If the adverbial clause appears in the middle of the sentence, surround the clause with commas. And, finally, if the adverbial clause appears at the end of the sentence, do not use a comma to separate the dependent adverbial clause and the independent clause.

Missing comma➔ As I left the movie I saw a sign advertising
                        Dependent Clause
next week's feature.

OK➔ As I left the movie, I saw a sign advertising next week's
        Dependent Clause
feature.

Extra comma➔ I saw a sign advertising next week's feature, as I
left the movie.
Dependent Clause

OK➔ I saw a sign advertising next week's feature as I left the
movie.   Dependent
Clause

Chapter 32

THE COMPOUND-COMPLEX SENTENCE

32a   The compound-complex sentence

A compound-complex sentence is made up of two or more simple sentences or independent clauses (this is the compound part) and one or more subordinate or dependent clauses (this is the complex part).

→ **While she waited for a sign from the employees,** other shop-
            Dependent Clause
pers sneaked into the toy store, and **they were the ones fortu-**
        Independent Clause
nate enough to find the most popular toy for Christmas.
            Independent Clause

When you punctuate a compound-complex sentence, you use the rules for both compound and complex sentences. For instance, in the above sentence, the dependent adverbial clause appears at the beginning of the sentence; thus, it needs a comma between it and the independent clause. In addition, the combination of a comma and coordinating conjunction is used to join together the two independent clauses.

EXERCISE 1

Directions: Label the sentence type (simple, compound, complex, compound-complex) for each sentence in this paragraph.

_____It is often difficult to figure out where a language actually begins.

_____The problem is that historical records only date back only so far.

_____There are usually no recordings of early language; we can only guess at their initial sounds and words.

_____Historical documents that include symbols, characters, and drawings can help.

_____Language changes quickly, and that also complicates investigating the beginnings.

_____For instance, English dictionaries add and delete words during each publication period.

_____Words that may be slang today can be common words in a decade.

_____Languages rarely add new conjunctions, subordinators, or prepositions; however, they do add new nouns, verbs, and adjectives quite frequently.

_____It is a historical linguist's job to analyze the history of languages.

_____Even though this task can be frustrating at times, it can also be quite rewarding.

Did You Know?

How old is English? While this isn't an easy question to answer, Old English, a language that would look and sound foreign to modern English speakers, is thought to have been established when Germanic tribes, most notably the Anglo-Saxons, arrived to the British Isles in 449 CE. Not until the twelfth or thirteenth century had English evolved to the point that it would be intelligible to modern speakers.

32b Common sentence errors with the compound-complex sentence

Pay attention to the common sentence errors for both compound and complex sentences, and you will be successful in punctuating a compound-complex sentence.

1. Check for run-on or fused sentences

Run-on/fused sentence→ Students who use both American Sign Language and Signed English understand that some of the signs are the same and this makes it easier for them to learn both.

OK→ Students who use both American Sign Language and Signed English understand that some of the signs are the same, and this makes it easier for them to learn both.

2. Check for comma splices

Comma splice→ Students who use both American Sign Language and Signed English understand that some of the signs are the same, this makes it easier for them to learn both.

OK→ Students who use both American Sign Language and Signed English understand that some of the signs are the same, and this makes it easier for them to learn both.

3. Check for fragments

Fragment→ Students who use both American Sign Language and Signed English understand that some of the signs.

OK→Students who use both American Sign Language and Signed English understand that some of the signs are the same, and this makes it easier for them to learn both.

Section V — Sentence Level: Basic Usage and Style

33 **Sentence Focus**

34 **Sentence Functions**

35 **Sentence Order**

36 **Sentence Length**

Chapter 33

SENTENCE FOCUS

Be sure that all your sentences are focused on the main idea of your paragraph, essay, or document. In addition, check that the sentence style you use helps each idea flow from sentence to sentence.

33a   Use transitions

You can use a transition to establish a relationship between one sentence and the next, creating a flow of ideas that all support the main idea. Transitions can also help clarify meanings by highlighting relationships between words, phrases, or sentences. Writing without transitions often sounds disjointed and rambling, but be sure that the transitions you use fit the relationship you are trying to describe.

→ The Chinese zodiac has twelve signs, each representing a year in a 12-year cycle; likewise, Western astrology has twelve signs, each representing a month in a 12-month cycle.

→ As previously mentioned, I am frustrated that my Chinese zodiac sign is the boar.

Transitions

Addition→ moreover, furthermore, besides, likewise, also, too, finally, second, third, last, additionally

Cause→ since, because

Comparison→ similarly, likewise

Concession→ although, though, despite

Condition→ unless, provided that, if

Contrast→ but, yet, however, nevertheless, in contrast, on the contrary, nonetheless, whereas, even though, although, otherwise, on the other hand

Exception→ except

Exemplification→ for example, for instance

Intensification→ indeed, in fact

Place→ where, here, near, beyond

Purpose→ (in order) to, to this end

Repetition→ in other words, as I have said, as previously mentioned, as stated above

Result→ therefore, thus, consequently, as a result, hence

Summary→ in conclusion, in short, all in all, overall, finally

Time→ when, after, before, until, as long as, meanwhile, while, immediately, soon, afterward, then, henceforth

33b Emphasize key ideas

1. Use sentence order for emphasis

When you use a sentence that includes a list or series, be sure to use an order that is consistent. Listing items from most important to least important, or vice versa, will help you emphasize key ideas.

Poor order ➜ Before completing the sign project, we will need to check with these levels of government: city, national, regional, and county.

OK➜ Before completing the sign project, we will need to check with these levels of government: city, county, regional, and national.

2. Use end-focus for emphasis

In English, it is normal to arrange sentences so that the most important information comes at the end of the sentence. This end-focus allows you to organize general knowledge—information that is less obvious, less important, or already known—at the beginning of a sentence and lead up to the most important or emphasized information at the end.

End-focus➜ Before the sign project can be completed, we will need to get approval from the governor's office.

3. Use front-focus for emphasis

You can also place a sentence element in an abnormal position—usually at the front of the sentence—to make the element more emphatic. This type of front-focus is used effectively if you know the regular patterns of English sentences (see Chapter 35).

Front-focus➜ Red paint they used rarely for the signs, so using it at the governor's mansion allowed the signs to stand out.

4. Reorder negative adverbials for emphasis

Placing a negative adverbial at the beginning of a sentence places an emphasis on that part of the sentence.

Fronting a negative adverbial➜ Never have I seen such a paint color on a government sign!

5. Use parenthetical expressions

Parenthetical expressions, which are enclosed by punctuation, place an emphasis on the previous sentence element.

Parenthetic expression➜ At the governor's mansion, *for example*, they used red paint.

Parenthetic expression➜ Red paint, *of course*, will grab pedestrian attention.

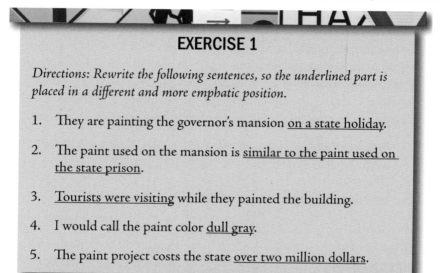

EXERCISE 1

Directions: Rewrite the following sentences, so the underlined part is placed in a different and more emphatic position.

1. They are painting the governor's mansion <u>on a state holiday</u>.

2. The paint used on the mansion is <u>similar to the paint used on the state prison</u>.

3. <u>Tourists were visiting</u> while they painted the building.

4. I would call the paint color <u>dull gray</u>.

5. The paint project costs the state <u>over two million dollars</u>.

33c   Be clear

1. Avoid tangents

To keep your sentence on topic, avoid tangents or irrelevant information.

Lack of focus ➜ I am frustrated that my Chinese zodiac sign is the boar, which by the way is also the sign for Arnold Schwarzenegger and Ronald Reagan, because I see myself more of a dragon.

OK➜ I am frustrated that my Chinese zodiac sign is the boar because I see myself more as a dragon.

2. Rephrase ambiguous expressions

Watch out for misplaced expressions that cause ambiguity. Place modifiers effectively in sentences, so the meaning you want to give is clear. Check out how the following ambiguous sentence can be rewritten to show its two different meanings.

> Ambiguous sentence➔ Writing clearly is important.
> Meaning #1➔ It is important to write clearly.
> Meaning #2➔ It is clear that writing is important.

Ambiguity can occur with conjoined noun phrases that have adjectives placed in an ambiguous position.

> Ambiguous sentence➔ The gray foyer and hallway were being painted next.
> Meaning #1➔ The gray foyer and gray hallway were being painted next.
> Meaning #2➔ The hallway (not gray) and the gray foyer were being painted next.

Be sure that any adjective that is used to describe the first noun in a conjoined noun phrase is placed in a position that allows for clear understanding.

3. Make sentence elements parallel

Make sure that your sentence meanings are clear by using parallel sentence elements. Combined or coordinated sentence elements should be similar in type. Notice the lack of parallelism in the sentence below. The *and* is used to join a full clause and a noun phrase. To fix the problem, you need to use either two full clauses or two noun phrases. The second sentence below is parallel and uses two full clauses.

> Lack of parallelism➔ They discontinued the painting because the results did not satisfy the governor and a lack of funding.
>   Independent Clause   NP

> Parallel➔ They discontinued the painting because the results did not satisfy the governor and there was a lack of funding.
>   Independent Clause   Independent Clause

33d   Show confidence

When you write, show that you know the topic well by using authority in your phrasing. Stay away from what some teachers and editors call *weasel words*, such as *I think, I believe, I know, I think I know.* See **11a** for more information on how not to "weasel."

Non-authoritative sentence➜ I think that I know why the Chinese zodiac has twelve signs and four elements.

OK➜ The Chinese zodiac has twelve signs, based on the months, and four elements, based on the seasons.

EXERCISE 2

Directions: Each of the following sentences has a clarity problem; rewrite them so their meanings are clear.

1. A letter requesting that the governor stop the painting of the mansion and choose another paint color was sent.

2. Although the governor only saw three letters, he knew there was a problem.

3. The color of the atrium, the color of the foyer, and the driveway concrete color did not match.

4. The angry governor and secretary both called the painters' office.

5. The governor wanted the painters, groundskeepers, and the painting supervisors to all be on the same page.

Chapter 34

SENTENCE FUNCTIONS

In English, there are four sentence functions that serve different purposes. Writers use declarative sentences to give information, imperative sentences to give instructions or commands, interrogative sentences to obtain information, and exclamatory sentences to express emotion. In academic writing, you will probably use more declarative sentences than any other type. However, if you are writing a narrative or descriptive essay or a piece of creative writing, you should use sentences with a variety of functions.

34a   Use declarative sentences to give information

Use declarative sentences that end with a period for statements that give information. Declarative sentences are the most common type of sentence function in English.

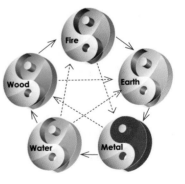

> Declarative sentence➔ The Chinese zodiac has five elements.

34b   Use imperative sentences to give commands

Imperative sentences usually do not have a subject; they are used to give instructions or commands.

> Imperative sentence➔ Tell me what zodiac sign I am.

> Imperative sentence➔ Do not tell me that you forgot the answer.

Imperatives can also take the form of *let* plus a subject.

Imperative sentence➔ Let's talk about the Chinese zodiac.

The imperative sentence can include *you* or a third person subject, but these types of subjects are not used very often.

Imperative sentence➔ You should tell me the answer now.

Imperative sentence➔ The guilty party should stand up now.

Imperative sentences can also add a noun phrase that directly addresses the subject of the sentence.

➔ You, tell me the answer now.

➔ Those students at the back, tell me the answer now.

34c   Use interrogative sentences to ask questions

To ask questions, use one of the six types of interrogative sentences, including yes/no questions, wh-questions, declarative questions, alternative questions, tag questions, and rhetorical questions.

A yes/no question begins with a verb and can be answered with a *yes* or *no* but can also be answered with other information as well.

Yes/No question➔ Should we mention that the Chinese zodiac is different from other zodiacs?

A wh-question starts with an interrogative word or phrase, usually *who, what, where, when, why,* or *how.*

Wh-question➔ How many Chinese zodiac signs are there?

A declarative question is in the form of a declarative sentence but asks a question. These types of questions take the declarative form but usually end with a question mark.

Declarative question➔ The Chinese zodiac has five elements?

Alternative questions give a choice or choices.

Alternative question➔ Do you prefer to be called a boar or a pig?

Tag questions can attach to declarative or interrogative sentences, making the sentences into questions. If the sentence part is negative, the tag will be positive, and vice versa.

Tag question➔ You're a boar, aren't you?

Tag question➔ Tell me your sign, won't you?

Rhetorical questions are basically equal to forceful declarative statements. Writers do not expect a reply to a rhetorical question.

Rhetorical question➔ Who could be happy being called a *pig*?

34d   Use exclamatory sentences to show surprise

Exclamatory sentences (sometimes called exclamatives) show surprise and end with an exclamation mark. They can begin with *what* or *how*.

Exclamatory sentence➔ What a strange name that is!

Exclamatory sentence➔ How strange that is!

These types of sentences can also look like a forceful declarative statement.

Exclamatory sentence➔ You're a Boar! Really!

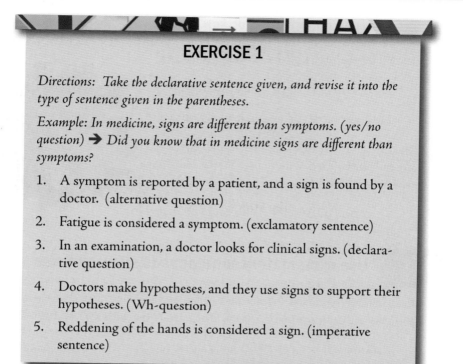

EXERCISE 1

Directions: Take the declarative sentence given, and revise it into the type of sentence given in the parentheses.

Example: In medicine, signs are different than symptoms. (yes/no question) ➔ *Did you know that in medicine signs are different than symptoms?*

1. A symptom is reported by a patient, and a sign is found by a doctor. (alternative question)

2. Fatigue is considered a symptom. (exclamatory sentence)

3. In an examination, a doctor looks for clinical signs. (declarative question)

4. Doctors make hypotheses, and they use signs to support their hypotheses. (Wh-question)

5. Reddening of the hands is considered a sign. (imperative sentence)

SENTENCE ORDER

35a Vary basic sentence order

In English, there are seven basic sentence orders for declarative sentences, influenced by different types of verbs and the elements that work with those verbs. Becoming familiar with these basic sentence orders will help you revise your writing if you find yourself frequently writing the same pattern or order. For more in-depth discussion of the word classes that form these patterns, see Section I.

1. Subject + intransitive verb

A sentence that includes an intransitive verb does not need anything to follow the verb for the sentence to be complete. However, the intransitive verb **can** be followed by an adverb or other optional elements, such as a prepositional phrase, and other optional elements can occur in other places in the sentence.

➜   Money talks.
     S   V

➜   Money talks loudly.

➜   Sometimes, money talks loudly.

➜   Sometimes, money talks loudly in a bad economy.

➜   Sometimes, in a bad economy, money talks loudly.

Notice that all of the sentences above have the same basic sentence order with the subject and intransitive verb at the center of the sentence. Even though these sentences might appear different, they have the same underlying pattern, and thus, if you write most of your sentences using this same pattern, your prose style will take on a monotonous rhythm.

2. Subject + transitive verb + direct object

A sentence that has a subject, transitive verb, and direct object is the most frequently used English sentence order. The transitive verb requires a noun or noun phrase as its direct object. A noun that comes after a direct object answers one of these questions: What? Whom? (What did the highway workers clean? Whom did John see?) Just like any other sentence pattern, this one can take optional elements, such as adverbs or prepositional phrases.

→ The highway workers **cleaned** the sign.
          S   V   DO

→ Yesterday, the highway workers cleaned the sign.

→ Yesterday, the highway workers cleaned the sign vigorously.

3. Subject + transitive verb + indirect object + direct object

Some transitive verbs require both a direct object and an indirect object. There is a simple way to tell the difference between an indirect object and a direct object. Direct objects answer one of these questions: What? or Whom? Indirect objects answer one of these questions: To what? To whom? For what? For whom?

→ The foreman **gave Chris** the work order.
          S   V   IO   DO

Gave what? the work order

To whom? Chris

You can also add optional elements to this type of sentence order.

→ At the beginning of the shift, the foreman gave Chris the lost work order.

4. Subject + transitive verb + direct object + object complement

A small number of transitive verbs—such as *declare, call, name*—require a direct object and object complement. The object complement is a necessary element in this type of sentence; it describes the direct object. Remember that a direct object answers one of these questions: Whom? What? An object complement can be either a noun phrase or an adjective phrase.

→ Sarah **called me a novice.**
  S   V   DO   NP

Whom did Sarah call a novice? me

→ Sarah **called me lazy.**
  S   V   DO Adj

Whom did Sarah call lazy? me

Just like with any other sentence pattern, you can add other optional elements, but you still have the same sentence pattern.

→ When I could not do the ASL sign for *water*, Sarah called me a novice.

5. Subject + transitive verb + direct object + adverbial complement

Some transitive verbs—such as *place, put*—require both a direct object and an adverbial complement. An adverbial complement is the name for a prepositional phrase that gives information about when, where, why, and how.

→ Alex **put the sign on the door.**
  S   V   DO   Adv

You can also lengthen this type of sentence pattern with optional elements.

→ Yesterday morning, Alex put the sign on the door with the red stripes.

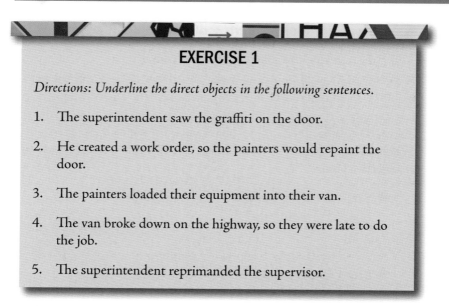

EXERCISE 1

Directions: Underline the direct objects in the following sentences.

1.   The superintendent saw the graffiti on the door.

2.   He created a work order, so the painters would repaint the door.

3.   The painters loaded their equipment into their van.

4.   The van broke down on the highway, so they were late to do the job.

5.   The superintendent reprimanded the supervisor.

6. Subject + linking verb + subject complement

A common sentence pattern includes a subject, linking verb, and subject complement. Linking verbs are verbs that describe a state of being: *be, appear, seem, taste, sound.* The linking verb, if you think in terms of math, functions as an equal sign, and the subject complement renames (noun phrase) or describes (adjective phrase).

> ➔ A changing traffic signal **is a sign.**
>   S   V NP

> ➔ A changing traffic signal **is frustrating.**
>   S   V Adj

Optional elements can also be added to this type of sentence.

> ➔ In the spring, a sound like a train engine is a sign.

> ➔ A sound like a train engine is scary, especially in the spring.

> ➔ A sound like a train engine is scary, especially when a tornado warning has sounded.

7. Subject + linking verb + adverbial complement

A linking verb can also take an adverbial complement. The adverbial complement—usually a prepositional phrase—is required for this type of sentence to be complete.

→ The warning signs **are on the back wall.**
      S   V   Prep Ph

Did You Know?

You might think that sentences in all languages are structured the same as many English sentences: begin with a subject, add a verb, and end with an object (e.g., *Sam drank the water*). But not all languages are subject-verb-object (SVO) languages. Many are SOV (e.g., *Sam the water drank*), including Japanese and Persian. There are even a few languages with VOS, OVS, and OSV word orders; Fijian, for example, has a VOS word order: *Drank the water Sam.*

35b   Vary sentence openings

You can vary sentence openings to help your writing not take on a dull or boring sentence rhythm.

1. Add introductory words, phrases, and clauses

Adding optional introductory words, phrases, or clauses can also lengthen your sentences, a sign of a more sophisticated and complex writing style.

Sample of dull or boring sentence rhythm→ The Hollywood sign is a national monument. The Hollywood sign is in Griffith Park in Los Angeles. The sign is 45 feet tall, and it has white letters. It was created as an advertisement in 1923.

Add a transitional/introductory word➔ The Hollywood sign is a national monument. However, it is located in Griffith Park and not Hollywood.

Add an introductory verb phrase➔ Located in Griffith Park, the Hollywood sign is a national monument.

Add an introductory prepositional phrase➔ In Griffith Park, the Hollywood sign is a national monument.

Add an introductory clause➔ Although the Hollywood sign was first created as an advertisement in 1923, it is now a national monument.

EXERCISE 2

Directions: Join the pairs of sentences together by using introductory words, phrases, or clauses.

Example: The Hollywood sign was created in 1923. The Hollywood sign is a national monument. ➔ Created in 1923, the Hollywood sign is a national monument.

1. The Welcome to Las Vegas sign is a historic landmark. The Welcome to Las Vegas sign is on the U.S. National Register of Historic Places.

2. The Welcome to Las Vegas sign is a historic landmark. It was funded and erected in May 1959.

3. The sign is in the town of Paradise. The sign is roughly four miles away from the city limits of Las Vegas.

4. In March 2009, Clark County council members nominated the sign to be

placed on the U.S. National Register of Historic Places. On May 1, 2009, the sign was placed on the U.S. National Register of Historic Places.

5. The sign is 25 feet tall. The sign is a classic roadside pole design.

2. Avoid *subject-itis*

When you keep using the same sentence pattern or order, your sentences can start to look like they all have the same beginning. Some teachers and editors call this *subject-itis*, labeling it as a sentence disease. Check out this group of sentences that all begin with a subject.

> The Hollywood sign is a national monument. The Hollywood sign is in Griffith Park in Los Angeles. The sign is 45 feet tall, and it has white letters. It was created as an advertisement in 1923.

One of the ways you can cure *subject-itis* is by using introductory words, phrases, or clauses. Another way is to do some sentence combining, joining some of the sentences together to form compound or complex sentences.

> Add an introductory participial phrase➔ Standing 45 feet tall with white letters, the Hollywood sign is a national monument located in Griffith Park in Los Angeles.

> Join sentences together➔ The Hollywood sign is a national monument located in Griffith Park in Los Angeles; its white letters stand 45 feet tall.

> Add an introductory participial phrase➔ Created as an advertisement in 1923, the Hollywood sign is a national monument located in Griffith Park; its white letters stand 45 feet tall.

35c   Fix misplaced modifiers

Modifiers can be used to add information to sentences, but they can sometimes cause problems as well if not placed in the correct position in the sentence.

1. Check for misleading or misplaced modifiers

If a modifier is misplaced, it can cause confusion or even give an unwanted meaning to a sentence. There are three main types of misleading or misplaced modifiers: squinting, limiting, and disruptive.

Squinting modifiers are words or phrases that can refer to more than one word or phrase in the sentence. Revise the sentence so the modifier is placed directly where it refers to only a single word or phrase.

> Squinting modifier➔ The girl in my English class is in the corner with the protest sign.

Is the girl in the corner? Is the protest sign in the corner? Are they both in the corner? Place the modifier where its meaning cannot be misleading.

> OK➔ The girl with the protest sign is in the corner; I know her from English class.

Limiting modifiers, such as *almost, even, just, merely,* and *only,* usually give information about how many or how often. Be careful where you place these modifiers since poor placement can cause ambiguity.

Limiting modifier poorly placed ➔ We **almost** had 30 signs painted by the end of the day.

How can you *almost have* something? The *almost* is modifying how many signs were done by the end of the day, so this limiting modifier needs to be next to the phrase it modifies.

OK➔ We had **almost** 30 signs painted by the end of the day.

Disruptive modifiers are any type of modifiers that come in the middle of a phrase or sentence, **and** their position allows them to disrupt that same phrase or sentence. Some disruptive modifiers can be grammatically correct and still be disruptive. Be sure that modifying phrases or clauses do not become long and winding paths that lead the reader off the main point.

Disruptive modifier ➔ We had 30 signs—**ten blue ones, five yellow ones, five red ones, three green ones, three purple ones, three orange ones, and one black one**—that needed to be painted by the end of the day.

OK➔ We had to paint 30 signs by the end of the day; they included **ten blue ones, five yellow ones, five red ones, three green ones, three purple ones, three orange ones, and one black one**.

Splitting a verb infinitive (*to* + *verb*) with a modifier is also disruptive. Although some instructors and editors accept split infinitives, many do not; it will always be fine to rework a split infinite.

Split infinitive➔ The foreman warned us to **carefully** place the signs in the truck.

OK➔ The foreman warned us to place the signs **carefully** in the truck.

Helpful hint

Some split infinitives are part of our culture; fixing them might cause confusion and comment.

➔ On *Star Trek*, the captain and crew want to **boldly** go where no one has gone before.

2. Check for dangling modifiers

Dangling modifiers are verbals (to + verb, verb + *–ing*, or verb + *–en/ –ed*) placed either at the beginning or end of the sentence and has the verbal modifying the wrong word.

> Dangling modifier ➜ Having been painted, we put the signs into the delivery truck.

The dangling modifier (*having been painted*) appears to modify *we*, but it should modify *the signs*. You can fix a dangling modifier in a variety of ways, including moving the word being modified into the correct position or rewording the entire sentence.

> OK➜ Having been painted, the signs were put into the delivery truck.

> OK➜ The painted signs were put into the truck.

> OK➜ We put the painted signs into the truck.

Participial phrases (phrases that start with with *–ing* [present] or *–ed* [past] participles) often become dangling modifiers.

> Dangling modifier ➜ Left on their own, the signs were put into the truck by the kids.

> OK➜ The kids, left on their own, put the signs into the truck.

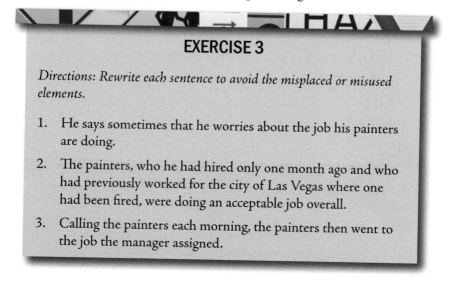

EXERCISE 3

Directions: Rewrite each sentence to avoid the misplaced or misused elements.

1. He says sometimes that he worries about the job his painters are doing.

2. The painters, who he had hired only one month ago and who had previously worked for the city of Las Vegas where one had been fired, were doing an acceptable job overall.

3. Calling the painters each morning, the painters then went to the job the manager assigned.

4. The painters sometimes left their equipment at the job site which sometimes included brushes and paint.

5. The manager wants his painting crew to only do good work.

35d Check direct v. indirect speech

Direct speech is highlighted with quotation marks. Indirect quotations or speech do not take quotation marks. When you use an indirect quotation or indirect speech, be sure to change the order of the sentence, if necessary, and use the correct punctuation.

Direct quotation➜ The manager said, "Put the signs in the truck."

Indirect quotation➜ The manager said to put the signs in the truck.

Direct question➜ Did you put the signs in the truck?

Indirect question➜ He asked if the signs had been put in the truck.

35e Check for empty phrases and clauses

Even though sentences that begin with *it* or *there* + *be* are grammatically correct, they use extra words or empty phrases that sometimes can be easily removed if the sentence is rephrased.

1. Check for empty *it*

Empty phrase ➜ It had taken three hours for the students to paint the signs.

OK➜ The students took three hours to paint the signs.

2. Check for empty *there*

Empty phrase ➜ There were three signs that the students forgot to paint.

OK➜ The students forgot to paint three signs.

SENTENCE LENGTH

A variety of sentences with a mixture of sentence lengths is a sign of a mature, sophisticated writing style. Becoming familiar with how to shorten or lengthen sentences will help you revise when your sentences are choppy, repetitive, or underdeveloped.

36a   Check for choppy sentences

Nothing is wrong with a short simple sentence every once in a while; however, many short simple sentences in a row can create a dull and repetitive rhythm that is uncomfortable for the reader. Consider the following sentences.

→ The Hollywood sign is a national monument. The Hollywood sign is in Griffith Park in Los Angeles. The sign is 45 feet tall. It has white letters. It was created as an advertisement in 1923.

What can you do to rephrase these short and choppy sentences that have the same simple-subject-predicate rhythm? You can join some of the sentences together by using coordinating conjunctions (*for, and, nor, but, or, yet, so*) and creating some compound sentences.

Compound sentences→ The Hollywood sign is a national monument, and it is located in Griffith Park in Los Angeles. The sign is 45 feet tall, and it has white letters. It was created as an advertisement in 1923.

What do you notice about the above sentences? Does compounding make that dull and repetitive rhythm disappear? Probably not enough.

Plus, it was difficult to join the last sentence to the rest of the description. To improve even more, you can try combining more of the sentences by using complex sentences.

> Complex sentences➔ The Hollywood sign, which is located in Griffith Park in Los Angeles, is 45 feet tall with white letters. It was created as an advertisement in 1923.

Combining sentences by creating complex sentences helped cut out words and made the first sentence flow much better. However, we are still left with the last simple sentence that was difficult to combine. To improve even more, you can combine all the sentences using both complex and compound strategies.

> Compound and complex➔ The Hollywood sign, which is located in Griffith Park in Los Angeles, is 45 feet tall with white letters; it was created as an advertisement in 1923.

For more information on using sentence combining to create compound, complex, and compound-complex sentences, see Section IV.

Helpful hint

You can check the grade level of your writing by looking at the Flesch-Kincaid index. You can pull this up in Microsoft Word under the grammar checker and spell checker menu.

36b   Check for excessive coordination

When you use compound sentences to bring some variety to your writing, you are using a combining strategy that we use quite often in oral language. Be careful, though, that you do not overuse it in your writing since doing so will make your writing sound too conversational for academic writing.

> Too conversational ➔ The Hollywood sign is located in Griffith Park in Los Angeles, and it is 45 feet tall and has white letters, and it was created as an advertisement in 1923.

Use compound sentences sparingly, and mix them with complex sentences or compound-complex sentences to bring more intricacy to your writing.

OK➜ The Hollywood sign, which is located in Griffith Park in Los Angeles, is 45 feet tall with white letters; it was created as an advertisement in 1923.

36c   Check for excessive subordination and modification

Complex sentences are created by using subordination, and adding this complexity to your writing gives a more sophisticated style. However, be careful that you do not overuse subordination and modification to the point where it is difficult for the reader to understand what you are joining or describing.

Too complex➜ The Hollywood sign, which was created as an advertisement in 1923 and which is located in Griffith Park, which is in Los Angeles, is 45 feet tall with white letters.

OK➜ The Hollywood sign, which is located in the Griffith Park of Los Angeles, is 45 feet tall with white letters; it was created as an advertisement in 1923.

EXERCISE 1

Directions: Revise these sentences that have excessive coordination, subordination, or modification.

1. The McDonald's sign that is in Pine Bluff, Arkansas, is the only surviving example of a single arch McDonald's sign in Arkansas; the sign was erected in 1962, and it remained in its original location until 2007, and it was added to the U.S. Register of Historic Places in 2006.

2. In 2007, the sign, which is in Pine Bluff, Arkansas, was moved to a new location, which was also in Pine Bluff, Arkansas.

3.   The Pine Bluff sign has many of the typical features of an
     early single arch McDonald's sign; it is back-lit; it has plastic
     panels in a metal frame; it has red advertising midway down
     the arch.

4.   No one knows how many single arch McDonald's signs still
     exist, but there is one in Biloxi, Mississippi, and there is one
     in Lancaster, Pennsylvania, and there is one in Green Bay,
     Wisconsin, and there is one in Huntsville, Alabama.

5.   The sign that is in Pine Bluff is the only single arch McDon-
     ald's sign that is on the U.S. Register of Historic Places, which
     is the United State's official list of buildings that are deemed
     worthy of preservation.

36d   Add descriptive words and phrases

You can enhance the descriptiveness of your sentences by adding
modifiers in different places in the sentence.

1. Add descriptive nouns and noun phrases

Develop more descriptive noun phrases by adding pre-modifiers, such
as adjectives, and post-modifiers, such as appositives, prepositional
phrases, or relative clauses. Doing so will lengthen your sentences and
show off your vocabulary.

Noun Phrase➔ the house

With pre-modifier➔ the **big blue**
house   Adj Adj

With pre-modifier and post-
modifier➔ the **big blue** house,
               Adj Adj
a Colonial, which is sitting on the corner of Sixth and Elm.
Appositive   Relative Clause

You can also lengthen your sentences and show off your vocabulary by replacing simple nouns with words that carry more than a simple description.

> Simple noun➜ house

> Possible variations➜ abode, adobe, Colonial, domicile, dwelling, habitat, igloo

2. Add descriptive verbs

Your sentences can become more descriptive by exchanging simple verbs for ones that fit the scene you are trying to set or describe. Remember, though, that your vocabulary should match the type of academic writing you are doing.

> Simple verb➜ go

> Possible variations➜ depart, exit, hit the road, make tracks, leave

3. Add descriptive adjectives

Adjectives can be used in three different ways to add more description to a sentence. Showing that you have the facility to use all three types demonstrates a more sophisticated writing style.

A. ADJECTIVES AS PRE-MODIFIERS

An adjective or adjective phrase can be used to modify the noun that follows it.

> Adjective➜ the wet sign

> Conjoined adjective phrase➜ the wet and moldy sign

> Adjective phrase with modifying adverb➜ the extremely wet and moldy sign

B. ADJECTIVES AS POST-MODIFIERS

An adjective or adjective phrase can modify the noun it follows.

> Adjective➜ That problem, undoable, was the only one I did not complete.

Conjoined adjective phrase➜ The sign, wet and moldy, needs to be replaced.

Adjective phrase with modifying adverb➜ The sign, quite wet and moldy, needs to be replaced.

C. Adjectives as complements

An adjective or adjective phrase can modify a subject as a subject complement, or it can modify a direct object as an object complement.

Subject complement/adjective➜ That problem is frustrating.

Subject complement/adjective phrase➜ That problem is quite frustrating.

Object complement/adjective➜ All the students called the problem undoable.

Object complement/adjective phrase➜ All the students called the problem frustratingly undoable.

4. Add descriptive adverbs

Adverbs or adverb phrases can be used to bring more description to your sentences by modifying verbs, adjectives, other adverbs, or even full sentences.

Modifying a verb➜ The Hollywood sign was created originally as an advertisement.

Modifying an adjective➜ The extremely tall Hollywood sign was created as an advertisement.

Modifying another adverb➜ The answer to the problem was quite frustratingly obvious after the teacher revealed it.

Modifying a sentence➜ The answer to the problem was frustrating; consequently, the students failed the test.

5. Add descriptive prepositional phrases

Prepositional phrases can be used to modify a variety of elements in a sentence. They can give optional adverbial-type information about time or place; they can add more detail to a noun phrase, adjective phrase, or adverbial phrase; or they can function as an adverbial complement.

Optional adverbial➔ In the spring, the Hollywood sign is cleaned.

Post-modifier to a noun➔ The Hollywood sign, in Griffith Park, is cleaned each spring.

Post-modifier to an adjective➔ Climbing to the Hollywood sign is supposed to be difficult for most people.

Post-modifier to an adverbial➔ The park ranger looked angrily at us when we started up the path to the Hollywood sign.

EXERCISE 2

Directions: Revise the following simple sentences by using the modifier type given in parentheses.

1. The Skipping Girl Vinegar sign is located on Victoria Street in Melbourne, Australia. (add descriptive adjective)

2. The sign is a painted metal structure. (add descriptive prepositional phrase)

3. The sign is also known as Little Audrey. (add descriptive noun phrase)

4. The sign was manufactured in 1936 to advertise vinegar. (add descriptive verb phrase)

5. The sign replicates the skipping girl on the original vinegar bottle. (add descriptive adjective)

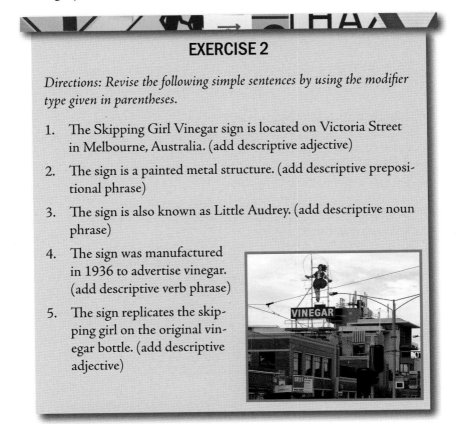

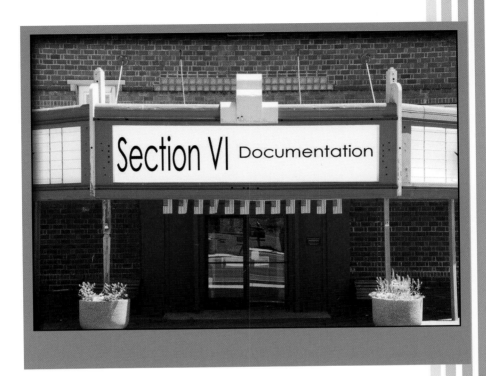

Section VI Documentation

37 **MLA Documentation**

38 **APA Documentation**

MLA Documentation

When you do research to find supporting evidence for your ideas or arguments, you need to credit your outside sources. Depending on what type of essay you are writing or which type of course you are writing for, you will need to choose a documentation style and continue with that style for the entire essay. Two of the most common styles, especially for freshman and sophomore students, are MLA (Modern Language Association) and APA (American Psychological Association).

If you write in composition, language, linguistics, and literature courses, you will often be asked to use documentation guidelines created by the MLA. The *MLA Handbook*, in its eighth edition, provides a full description of the conventions used by this particular community of writers; updates to the *MLA Handbook* can be found at www.style.mla.org.

MLA guidelines require that you give both an in-text citation and a Works Cited entry for any and all sources you use. Using accurate in-text citations helps guide your reader to the appropriate entry on the Works Cited page. For example, the in-text citation given below in parentheses directs the reader to the correct page of the book given in the Works Cited.

> In-text citation➔When a teenager sleeps more than 10 hours per night, it is time to question whether she is having significant problems (Jones 63).

> Entry in Works Cited➔

> Jones, Stephanie. *The Signs of Trouble*. Dilemma Publishing,

> 2010.

This chapter provides a general overview of MLA documentation style and an explanation of the most commonly used MLA documentation formats, including a few significant revisions since the previous edition.

Did You Know?

The Modern Language Association was founded in 1883 at The John Hopkins University as a group that discussed literature and modern languages, such as Spanish, French, Chinese, and English. The MLA, now with over 30,000 members in over 100 countries, is the primary professional association for literature and language scholars.

37a Using MLA in-text citations

In-text citations (also called *parenthetical citations*) point readers to where they can find more information about your researched supporting materials. When you use MLA documentation style, you need to indicate the author's last name and the location of the source material (page or paragraph number). Where this in-text information is placed depends on how you want to phrase the summarized, paraphrased, or quoted sentence. Be sure that the in-text citation guides the reader clearly to the source in the Works Cited, where complete information about the source is given.

The following are some of the most common examples of parenthetical citations.

1. Author's name in text

When using a parenthetical reference to a single source that is already named in the sentence, use this form: (Page number). Note that the period goes after the parentheses.

→ Stephanie Jones, author of *The Signs of Trouble*, describes "excessive sleeping, refraining from eating, and lying about simple things" as signs to look for when parents are concerned about their children (63).

2. Author's name in reference

When the author's name is not included in the preceding sentence, use this form for the parenthetical information at the end of the sentence: (Author's Last Name Page number). Note that there is no comma between the name and page in an MLA parenthetical reference, and also note that the period comes at the end of the sentence, after the parentheses.

→ When a teenager sleeps more than 10 hours per night, it is time to question whether she is having significant problems (Jones 63).

3. No author given

When a work has no credited author, use a clipped version of the work's title.

→ In a recent *Time* article, a list of 30 common signs of teenage trouble cites lack of sleep as the most common sign ("Thirty" 3).

4a. Two authors given

When you use a source that was written by two authors, use both authors' names in the text of the sentence or in the citation.

→ The idea that "complexity is a constant in biology" is not an innovative one (Sole and Goodwin 2).

4b. Three or more authors given

When you use a source written by three or more authors, include only the first author's name followed by *et al.* (Latin for "and others").

→ In Hong Kong, most signs are in Chinese and English; however, once you are in mainland China, English is rarely found on signs, except in tourist areas (Li, et al. 49).

5. Authors with the same last names

If your source material includes items by authors who have the same last name, use each author's first initial in the parentheses. If the two authors also share first initials, use one of the authors' full first names.

➜ When a teenager sleeps more than 10 hours per night, it is time to question whether she is having significant problems (S. Jones 63).

➜ Another sign of trouble can be when you do not see your child for meals (Sally Jones 114).

6. Encyclopedia or dictionary unsigned entry

When you use an encyclopedia or dictionary to look up a word or entry, be sure to include the word or entry title in the parenthetical entry.

➜ The word *thing* has more definitions than any other entry in the *Oxford English Dictionary* ("thing").

7. Lines of verse (plays, poetry or song lyrics)

When citing plays, give the act, scene, and line numbers of the material you use. Separate the act, scene, and line numbers with periods. For example, the quotation below comes from *Romeo and Juliet*, Act II, Scene 2, lines 43 and 44. MLA also advises using this method with biblical chapters and verses. Be sure, though, that the sequence goes from largest unit to smallest unit.

➜ Juliet grapples with how names can influence feelings as she questions, "What's in a name? That which we call a rose/By any other name would smell as sweet" (2.2.43-44).

Use a slash (/) to signify line breaks when you quote poetry or song lyrics, and put line numbers in the in-text citation instead of page numbers.

➜ An early song by Will Smith shows the frustration of children as he sings, "You know parents are the same/No matter time nor place/They don't understand that us kids/Are going to make some mistakes" (1-4).

8. Indirect quotation

When you use a quotation of a quotation—that is, a quotation that quotes from another source—use *qtd. in* to designate the source.

➜ Smith has said, "My parents really didn't understand me" (qtd. in Jones 8).

37b Using long or block quotations

Long or block quotations have special formatting requirements of their own.

1. Block quote of prose

If you quote a chunk of prose that is longer than four typed lines, you are using what is called a *block quotation*. Follow these MLA guidelines for block quotations:

1. If introducing the block quotation with a sentence, use a colon at the end of the sentence. If the introduction to your block quote is not a complete sentence, use whatever punctuation is appropriate to connect the introduction to the quote. If there is no grammatical need for punctuation, do not use any.

2. Begin the quotation on a new line.

3. Do not use quotation marks to enclose the block quote.

4. Indent the quote one half inch from the left margin.

5. Double space the entire quotation.

6. Put a period at the end of the quotation, and then add the parenthetical citation.

→ However, Lansky states:

> Despite the statement on www.signspotting.com that we don't accept signs with the intention of being funny, people like sending them in. I've opted not to use these as it could encourage people to start making them, sticking them up in their driveway, and snapping a picture. Plus, funny signs are so much more amusing when the humor is accidental. (72)

2. Block quote of poetry, drama, or song lyrics

For songs and poems, be sure to give line numbers rather than page numbers and to use the original line breaks.

→ The Fresh Prince, an early Will Smith character, sings about parents not understanding:

You know parents are the same, no matter time or place

They don't understand that us kids are going to make some mistakes

So to you, all the kids all across the land, there's no need to argue

Parents just don't understand. (1-4)

37c   Adding or omitting words in a quotation

1. Adding words to a quotation

Use square brackets [ ] to point out words or phrases that you have added to clarify or add context to your quotation but are not part of the original text.

→ Original quotation: "When we entered the People's Republic of China, we noticed that the signage began dropping English translations."

→ Quotation with added word: She said, "When we entered the People's Republic of China, [Dunkirk and I] noticed that the signage began dropping English translations" (Donelson 141).

You can also add your own comments inside a quotation by using square brackets. For example, you can add the word *sic* to a quotation when you know that there is an error in the original to maintain the integrity of the quote's source.

→ Original quotation: "When we entered the People's Repulic of China, we noticed that the signage began dropping English translations."

→ Quotation with added comment: She said, "When we entered the People's Repulic [sic] of China, we noticed that the signage began dropping English translations" (Donelson 141).

2. Omitting words in a quotation

Use an ellipsis (. . .) to represent words, phrases, or sentences that you delete from a quotation. The ellipsis begins with a space, has three periods with a space between each, and then ends with a space.

Original quotation➔ "The Great Wall is something that can be seen from space. When we reach a time when advertisements can be seen from space, we have probably gone too far."

Quotation with words omitted in middle of sentence➔ Frank Donelson, author of *Signs in Space*, remarks, "The Great Wall . . . can be seen from space. When we reach a time when advertisements can be seen from space, we have probably gone too far" (178).

If you omit words at the end of a quotation, and that is also the end of your sentence, use three periods with a space before and between each, and place the sentence-ending period after the parenthetical citation.

Original quotation➔ "The Great Wall is something that can be seen from space. When we reach a time when advertisements can be seen from space, we have probably gone too far with our advertising and signage" (Donelson 178).

Quotation with words omitted at end of sentence➔ Frank Donelson, author of *Signs in Space*, remarks, "The Great Wall is something that can be seen from space. When we reach a time when advertisements can be seen from space, we have probably gone too far. . ." (178).

Helpful hint

MLA guidelines can change with a new edition. Sometimes, class textbooks can use an older MLA documentation style. Our examples use the eighth edition of the *MLA Handbook*, but always check with your instructor if rules seem to be in conflict.

37d Citing online sources

In MLA documentation style, online or electronic sources have their own formatting guidelines for in-text citations because these types of sources rarely give specific page numbers.

For better flow and easier understanding, include the name(s) of the person/people (e.g., author(s), editor(s), director(s), performer(s)) responsible for creating your source in the text, rather than in the in-text citation. For instance, the following is the recommended way to begin an in-text citation for an online source:

→ Roger Ebert says that Shyamalan "plays the audience like a piano" in the film *Signs* (par. 8).

If the author or creator of the website uses paragraph or page numbers, numbered sections (*sec., secs.*), or chapters (*ch., chs.*), use these numbers in the parenthetical citation. If no numbering is used, do not use or add numbers to the paragraphs, pages, or parenthetical citation.

When website does not number paragraphs→ In his review of the film *Signs*, Roger Ebert says that Shyamalan "does what Hitchcock said he wanted to do, and plays the audience like a piano."

When website numbers paragraphs→ In his review of the film *Signs*, Roger Ebert says that Shyamalan "does what Hitchcock said he wanted to do, and plays the audience like a piano" (par. 8).

37e General formatting guidelines for the MLA Works Cited

If you use any material from other sources within a paper, be sure to include a Works Cited list at the end of the paper. Here are some general formatting guidelines to follow when setting up a Works Cited.

1. Put the Works Cited at the end of your paper as a separate page.

2. Use one-inch margins on all sides, and uniform double spacing throughout. Do not add any extra spaces between entries or after the title.

3. Page numbers preceded by your last name should continue into your Works Cited from the body of your paper.

4. Center the title, *Works Cited*, at the top of the page, using no underlining, quotation marks, italics, bolding, or other special type or font.

5. Place the first line of each entry flush with the left margin. Indent any additional lines of the entry one-half inch (or one tab).

6. Alphabetize the Works Cited using the first letter of the last name of the first author listed in each citation. If the cited source does not have an author, alphabetize by using the first word of the source title, not including articles, such as *a, an,* or *the.*

7. Format your individual Works Cited entries using MLA 8's Core Elements. The most recent edition of the MLA style guide no longer distinguishes between citation formats for digital or print sources. Instead, in an effort to streamline the citation process, MLA 8 relies on a set of nine elements common to most source types. Each element is followed by the punctuation mark shown below, and the last element should be followed by a period.

Author. Title of Source. Title of Container, Other Contributors, Version, Number, Publisher, Publication Date, Location.

Though MLA 8 makes no distinction between print and digital source types, it is still quite useful to see how the new core elements work with different types of sources. Therefore, the examples that follow are separated into print and digital sections. Furthermore, in these examples, you'll notice that only the elements available for the sample citation are listed in the example Works Cited entry. To clarify, prior to MLA 8, you would include n. pag. if no page numbers were available for your source and n.d. if you didn't have a publication date. That is no longer the case. If a given element is not relevant to the type of source you're citing (e.g. page numbers on a web page), then simply omit it from your Works Cited entry. If you are working with a source type that contains page numbers and our example of that source type does not include them, you should still include them in your Works Cited, since they are relevant to your particular source. MLA 8 recognizes that not all sources have all of the core elements, and even two of the same type sources may not have all of the same core elements. As noted above, if a source is missing any of the core elements, simply omit them from your Works Cited entry.

The sample Works Cited entries on the following pages begin with a simple single-author book entry, containing the Author, Title of Source, Publisher, and Publication Date elements, and build from there. As the source types listed here require additional elements, those elements, their uses, and their functions will be discussed in more detail.

37f Formats for print sources

1. Book with one author

When including a source on the Works Cited, be sure to note in the citation which pages you are referencing. In print books, add the page number (preceded by *p.*) or range of pages (preceded by *pp.*) following the year of publication.

Author. *Title of Source*. Publisher, Publication Date.

➜ Martin, Anna. *Signs*. Dreamspinner, 2015, pp. 236-45.

Helpful hint

Omit business words like *Company (Co.)*, *Corporation (Corp.)*, and *Limited (Ltd.)* in the *Publisher* element of your Works Cited. For academic publications, replace *University* with *U* and *Press* with *P*. Otherwise, list the full publisher's name. If your source is associated with more than one publisher, separate the publishers' names with a forward slash (/).

2. Books with two authors

If your source has two authors, format the first author listed with the last name first, and the first name last. Follow this with a comma and the word and, then add the second author's first then last name.

Last Name, First Name (first author), and First Name Last Name (second author). *Title of Source*. Publisher, Publication Date.

➜ Childs, Mark, and Ellen D. Babcock. *The Zeon Files: Art and Design of Historic Route 66 Signs*. U of New Mexico P, 2016.

If a book has three or more authors, you should list only the first author followed by a comma and et al. in place of the rest of the authors' names.

Author, et al. *Title of Source*. Publisher, Publication Date.

→ Wysocki, Anne Frances, et al. *Writing New Media: Theory and Applications for Expanding the Teaching of Composition*. Utah State UP, 2004.

3. Two books by the same author(s)

Use the author's or authors' full name(s) in only the first entry, then use three hyphens in place of the name(s) in all consecutive entries. The hyphens stand for exactly the same name(s) in the preceding entry, but remember to add any necessary qualifiers (editor, translator, etc.) by following the hyphens with a comma and the term describing that person's role. If the author name changes in any way (for example, an author might add a middle initial) or is combined with different authors than in the first entry listed, format the entry as you normally would, not using any hyphens. Alphabetize all sources by the same author by their titles.

→ Borroff, Marie. *Language and the Poet: Verbal Artistry in Frost, Stevens, and Moore*. U of Chicago P, 1979.

→ ---, editor. *Wallace Stevens: A Collection of Critical Essays*. Prentice-Hall, 1963.

Both of the above examples include the Version element of MLA 8. If your source indicates that it is one version of a work released in multiple forms, include reference to the version you consulted in your citation. The most common versions you will likely encounter are editions; however, works in other media, especially music and film, often offer different versions of a given album or DVD.

4. Anthology or collection

When citing a complete anthology or collection, which might contain multiple essays, articles, stories, poems, and/or other types of works, the editor(s) fill the author element for your entry. The term *author* spans a range of possibilities in MLA 8. The individual who fits the author role for your Works Cited entry might actually be an editor, translator, performer, creator, adapter, director, illustrator, or narrator. The key question to ask yourself when trying to determine who to list as your author is: "Who or what aspect in this work am I focusing on in my discussion?" You will only list an editor as your author if you are focusing specifically on the content written or chosen by that editor for the source you've referenced. Otherwise, you should list the individual author of the piece within the edited collection, placing the editor(s), instead, in the role of *Other Contributors*. No matter what role the person or people who fill your author element played in the production of your source, you should follow the same formatting guidelines for one, two, and three or more authors.

Author, editor(s). *Title of Source*. Publisher, Publication Date.

→ Iyengar, Sujata, and Allison Kellar Lenhardt, editors. *Health*. Fountainhead P, 2013.

5. Work within an anthology, collection, or reference book

When your source forms only a part of a larger whole, you need to provide both the *Title of Container* and *Location* elements in your Works Cited entry to ensure your readers can easily access the information. Additionally, these types of sources often have *Other Contributors* such as editors, translators, and illustrators to name just a few.

Just like it sounds, the container is what holds the smaller source you're actually citing. In addition to an anthology, collection, or reference book, a container can also be a magazine, newspaper, journal, or even a television series. Anytime your source is part of a larger whole, you should be sure to include the title of that larger whole, usually italicized.

Specifying your source's location is one of the only elements of MLA 8 affected by publication medium. Use *p.* to indicate a single page and *pp.* to indicate a range of pages for print sources. When citing websites, you will include the entire web address in the location element.

Like the *Author* element, *Other Contributors* encompass a wide range of possible roles. This element allows you to note individuals who were instrumental in your source's production, even if they weren't solely responsible for its creation. Other contributors' roles are indicated using a description, such as performance by, translated by, or directed by. If such a description does not fit the type of contributor you need to cite for your source, use a noun or noun phrase followed by a comma. For example: general editor, John Smith.

Author. "Title of Source." *Title of Container*, Other Contributors, Publisher, Publication Date, Location.

→ Chandaria, Kartik. "Weather and Language Lessons." *Health*, edited by Sujata Iyengar and Allison K. Lenhardt, Fountainhead P, 2013, pp. 141-44.

6. Article in a periodical

Sources such as journals, magazines, and newspapers are all periodicals. When citing a selection from one of these sources, you will need to indicate the periodical's volume (*vol.*) and number (*no.*) in the *Number* element. As with all of MLA 8's core elements, if your particular periodical does not contain all of the information for *Number*, simply include what it does offer. Likewise, if your periodical does not indicate a number of any kind, simply leave out that element.

Author. "Title of Source." *Title of Container*, Number, Publication Date, Location.

→ Holbrook, Teri. "An Ability Traitor at Work: A Treasonous Call to Subvert Writing from Within." *Qualitative Inquiry*, vol. 16, no. 3, 2010, pp. 171-83.

7. Review

If your review is titled, list the title in the *Title of Source* element, treating the review as any other selection from within a larger container. If your review is not titled, however, then your title will be the words, *Review of*, followed by the title of the work reviewed, then the word, *by*, and the reviewed work's author.

Author. "Title of Source." *Title of Container*, Publication Date, Location.

> → Ebert, Roger. "A Monosyllabic Superhero Who Wouldn't Pass the Turing Test." *Chicago Sun-Times*, 29 Apr. 2009, p. E4.

> → Stephenson, M.S. Review of *Apocalyptic Sentimentalism: Love and Fear in U.S. Antebellum Literature*, by Kevin Pelletier. *Choice*, May 2015, p. 1500.

8. Religious works

Religious works do not often reference an author; therefore, your Works Cited entry will most likely begin with the title of the work. Be sure to pay close attention to the particular version of the text you're referencing, as this will sometimes be the only means of direction by which your reader can locate your original source material.

Title of Source. Version, Publisher, Publication Date.

> → *The Bible.* Authorized King James Version, Oxford UP, 1998.

Helpful hint

Although MLA 8 recommends including URLs for online sources in the Location element of your Works Cited entries, defer to your instructor's preference about this. When including the URL, copy it fully from your browser, omitting only the *http://* or *https://*. If possible, provide a stable URL (permalink) or Digital Object Identifier (DOI) as a more reliable alternative to the browser address.

37g Formats for online sources

1. Website

Many websites are associated with a company or organization, but the key publisher's name can often be found either at the bottom of the site's home page or, if one is offered, on the site's "About" page. If the website you're citing includes an author or creator, then include it in your Works Cited entry. If not, begin your entry with the site title.

Title of Source. Publisher, Publication Date, Location.

> ➜ *Everyday Health.* Everyday Health Media, 2016, www.everydayhealth.com.

2. Article or item on a website (including blogs, wikis, vlogs, and online audio and video streaming services)

Author. "Title of Source." *Title of Container*, Publisher, Publication Date, Location.

Note: If there is no author given, begin the citation with the article title.

> ➜ George, Nancie. "6 Unusual Signs of Dehydration." *Everyday Health*, Everyday Health Media, 5 May 2016, www.everydayhealth.com/news/unusual-signs-of-dehydration/.

> ➜ Chan, Evans. "Postmodernism and Hong Kong Cinema." *Postmodern Culture*, vol. 10, no. 3, May 2000. *Project Muse*, doi:10.1353/pmc.2000.0021.

Helpful hint

Avoid citing URLs produced by shortening services like TinyURL and bit.ly. These URLs may stop working if the service that produced them disappears.

3. Online journal article

Author. "Title of Source." *Title of Container*, Number, Publication Date, Location.

> ➜ Austen, Veronica. "Writing Spaces: Performances of the Word." *Kairos*, vol. 8, no. 1, 2003, kairos.technorhetoric.net/8.1/binder2.html?coverweb/austen/austen.html.

4. Article from an online database or service, such as General OneFile or LexisNexis

When you access a source through a database or service, such as JSTOR, Google Books, or even Netflix, you are using a source located through "nested" containers. A journal article on a database is held in the smaller container, the journal, and that journal is held by the larger container, the database. In your Works Cited, you should attempt to account for all the containers enclosing your source. To do this, you will simply add the core elements, 3-9 (*Title of Container* through *Location*), omitting irrelevant or unavailable elements, to the end of the entry until all additional containers are accounted for.

Author. "Title of Source." *Title of Container*, Number, Publication Date, Location. *Title of Container*, Location.

→ Pavienko, Sonia, and Christina Bojan. "Exercising Democracy in Universities: The Gap between Words and Actions." *AUDEM: The International Journal of Higher Education and Democracy*, vol. 4, 2015, pp. 26–37. *Project Muse*, muse.jhu.edu/article/557647.

In the above example, the first container is the journal, *AUDEM*, and the second is the journal database, Project Muse. Since the location is the last element in the first container, it is followed by a period. You'll note that, especially in the second container, many of the core elements are missing. Indeed, only the title and location are available for the second container, and this is fine. As noted previously, simply omit those elements that are irrelevant to the container you're working with.

5. Comments on blogs, videos, or social media, etc.

You may occasionally need to cite untitled web sources, such as comments on a blog, images, or Tweets. There are a few ways to approach this. If your source is untitled, provide a description, neither italicized nor in quotation marks, to fill the title element. Use sentence rather than title capitalization.

Title of Source. *Title of Container*, Location.

→ Kitten wearing a sweater. *Google Images*, img.buzzfeed.com/buzzfeed-static/static/2014-11/4/14/enhanced/web-dr06/enhanced-24665-1415129188-3.jpg.

Your description might contain the title of another work if it's commenting on or responding to that work. This will be the case if you wish to cite comments on a blog post or other such interactions as sources. Note also that MLA 8 allows for the inclusion of usernames or "handles" in the *Author* element.

Author. Title of Source. *Title of Container*, Publication Date, Location.

→ Jeane. Comment on "The Reading Brain: Differences between Digital and Print." *So Many Books*, 25 Apr. 2013, 10:30 p.m., somanybooksblog.com/2013/04/25/the-reading-brain-differences-between-digital-and-print#comment-83030.

Short, untitled messages, such as Tweets, are cited by typing the full text of the message, without any changes, in the *Title of Source* element, enclosed in quotation marks.

Author. "Title of Source." *Title of Container*, Publication Date, Location.

→ @persiankiwi. "We have report of large street battles in east & west of Tehran now - #Iranelection." *Twitter*, 23 June 2009, 11:15 a.m., twitter.com/persiankiwi/status/2298106072.

To document an email, use the subject line as the title, and enclose it in quotation marks.

Author. "Title of Source." Other Contributors, Publication Date.

→ Boyle, Anthony T. "Re: Utopia." Received by Daniel J. Cahill, 21 June 1997.

37h Formats for other commonly used sources

1. Television or radio program

Media sources require special consideration when it comes to the *Author* and *Other Contributors* elements. Remember that the deciding factor in this situation is the aspect of the source you're focusing on. If you're discussing Matthew Gray Gubler's performance as Dr. Spencer

Reid in *Criminal Minds*, you would list "Gubler, Matthew Gray, performer." in the *Author* element (as in the first example), but if you're discussing the same show as a part of Jeff Davis's body of creative work, you would cite "Davis, Jeff, creator." as your author (as in the second example). If you're examining the show or an episode with no particular focus on a performer or other contributor, skip the author element and begin your entry with the episode or show title (as in the last example). Note also how location and publication information changes in each example as they move from a show watched on television, to the same show viewed via Netflix, and lastly, that show seen on DVD.

→ Gubler, Matthew Gray, performer. "Mr. Scratch." *Criminal Minds*, directed by Matthew Gray Gubler, season 10, episode 21, FOX, 22 Apr. 2015.

→ Davis, Jeff, creator. "Mr. Scratch." *Criminal Minds*, directed by Matthew Gray Gubler, season 10, episode 21, FOX, 22 Apr. 2015. *Netflix*, www.netflix.com/watch/800668 84?trackId=14170289&tctx=0%2C20%2C952df56e-847a-4278-a591-d2417455114f-109029147.

→ "Mr. Scratch." *Criminal Minds: Season 10*, created by Jeff Davis, directed by Matthew Gray Gubler, episode 21, Paramount, 2015, disc. 6.

2. Sound recording

Artist. "Title of Source." *Title of Container*, Publisher, Publication Date.

→ Five Man Electrical Band. "Signs." *Good-byes and Butterflies*, Lionel Records, 1970.

→ Tesla. "Signs (Live)." *10 Live!*, Sanctuary Records, 3 Jun 2014. Prime Music, Amazon, www.amazon.com/gp/product/B00K9FVUDM?ie=UTF8&keywords=tesla%20signs&qid=1463621153&ref_=sr_1_1&s=dmusic&sr=1-1.

3. Film

Films are handled very similarly to television shows. Your author and other contributors should be chosen based on the aspect of the film you examine in your research. If you do not focus on a particular individual, begin your entry with the film title.

Title of Source. Other Contributors, Publisher, Publication Date.

→ *Signs.* Directed by M. Night Shyamalan, performance by Mel Gibson, Touchstone, 2002.

4. Advertisement

Since advertisements aren't typically titled, follow the guidelines for providing a description in place of a title.

Name of product, company, or institution. Advertisement. Publisher, date of publication. Location or Medium of publication.

→ SunChips advertisement. *Newsweek*, 15 Jan. 2010, p. 33.

→ SunChips advertisement. NBC, 15 Jan. 2010, 10:32 p.m.

Note the difference in how the citations for print and television advertisements are formatted.

5. Painting, sculpture, or photograph

When viewing a physical object, such as a piece of art, in person, the "publisher" of the piece is the museum or gallery, etc. displaying the object. The location in this case is quite literal: Cite the city in which you viewed the piece.

If providing the original date of creation for your source will give your reader more context for your project, place the date(s) immediately following the work's title and follow it with a comma.

Author. *Title of Source.* Date of Original Publication, Publisher, Location.

→ da Vinci, Leonardo. *Mona Lisa.* 1503-6, Louvre, Paris.

If you viewed an object, image, or piece of art online, again, the entity making the piece available to the public fills the *Publisher* element, but you will also include both the physical and online locations of the piece.

→ van Gogh, Vincent. *Cypresses. European Paintings,* The Metropolitan Museum of Art, New York, www.metmuseum.org/art/collection/search/437980.

6. Interview

Author. Title of source. Other contributors, Publication Date.

→ Elbow, Peter. Personal interview, interviewed by John Smith, 1 Jan. 2009.

7. Lecture, speech, address, or reading

In certain circumstances, it may be appropriate to include a descriptive term in your Works Cited entry to indicate for your reader the type of source you're citing. Format your citation as usual, following the final element with a period, and then add the descriptive term followed by a period at the end.

Author. "Title of Source." Publisher, Publication Date, Location. Description.

→ Stephens, Liberty. "The Signs of the Times." MLA Annual Convention, 28 Dec. 2009, Hilton Downtown, New York. Address.

37i   Sample Works Cited using MLA

Following is an example of how a completed Works Cited would look at the end of your paper.

Your Last Name 14

Works Cited

Davis, Jeff, creator. "Mr. Scratch." *Criminal Minds*, directed by

Matthew Gray Gubler, season 10, episode 21, FOX, 22 Apr.

2015. *Netflix*, www.netflix.com/watch/80066884?trackId=

14170289&tctx=0%2C20%2C952d56e-847a-4278-a591-

d2417455114f-109029147.

Five Man Electrical Band. "Signs." *Good-byes and Butterflies*,

Lionel Records, 1970.

Signs. Directed by M. Night Shyamalan, performance by Mel

Gibson, Touchstone, 2002.

Stephens, Liberty. "The Signs of the Times." MLA Annual

Convention, 28 Dec. 2009, Hilton Downtown, New York.

Address.

EXERCISE 1

Directions: Below are four example sources and an in-text citation from each one. Put the correct information in the parentheses for an MLA in-text citation.

From page 89 of the book:

Bazerman, Charles. *Shaping Written Knowledge: The Genre and Activity*

      of the Experimental Article in Science. U of Wisconsin P, 1988.

Yet, it could also be the case that "genre and activity are more closely related than we had previously thought" (   ).

From page 340 of the article:

Bodemer, Brett. "The Importance of Search as Intertextual Practice for

      Undergraduate Research." *College and Research Libraries*, vol.

      73, no. 4, 2012, pp. 336-48.

Bodemer, however, suggests that "increasingly, the ability to search well on the Internet will be as important a literacy skill as reading or writing" (   ).

From a magazine's web-only article:

"Electronic Education: Flipping the Classroom." *The Economist*, 17

      Sept. 2011, www.economist.com/node/21529062.

The Economist has reported that "flipping the classroom is the new teaching technique of the twenty-first century classroom" (   ).

From page 192 of the chapter:

Schwartz, Daniel L., et al. "Toward the Development of Flexibly

Adaptive Instructional Designs." *Instructional Design Theories*

and Models: Volume II, edited by C.M. Reigelut, Erlbaum,

1999, pp. 183–213.

In a study performed by Schwartz et al., students found adaptive
classroom designs more engaging and, finally, more educational
(   ).

EXERCISE 2

Directions: Insert all needed punctuation and formatting into the
following MLA Works Cited entries. The type of source is listed after
each.

Ackerman John M   Reading Writing and Knowing: The Role of

Disciplinary Knowledge in Comprehension and Composing

Research in the Teaching of English vol 25   no 2 1991

133–178   **(article in a journal)**

Baddeley Alan Working Memory Oxford University P 1986 **(book)**

Barlow John Perry   The Economy of Ideas   Wired Mar 1994 www.

wired.com/1994/03/economy-ideas/ **(article in a magazine)**

Flower Linda and John R Hayes   A Cognitive Process Theory of

Writing   College Composition and Communication vol 32

no 4 1981 365–87 **(article in a journal)**

Hacker Douglas J Matt C Keener and John Kircher Writing Is Applied Metacognition Handbook of Metacognition in Education Edited by Douglas J Hacker John Dunlosky and Arthur C Graesser Routledge 2009 **(chapter in a book or anthology)**

Rounsaville Angela Rachel Goldberg and Anis Bawarshi From Incomes to Outcomes: FYW Students' Knowledge Meta-Cognition and the Question of Transfer WPA: Writing Program Administration vol 32 no 1 2008 97–112 **(article in a journal)**

Wilson H 1999 When Collaboration Becomes Plagiarism: The Administrative Perspective *Perspectives on Plagiarism and Intellectual Property in a Postmodern World* Edited by L Buranen & A M Roy SUNY P pp 211-18 **(chapter in a book or anthology)**

37j   Sample Annotated Essay - MLA

Header information should include (in this order): Your name, the professor's name, the course number, and the date. Headers are double spaced and in Times New Roman 12-point font. In MLA, dates are in day, month, year order.

Titles are centered in MLA format, double spaced, and in Times New Roman 12-point font like the rest of the paper. No formatting (bolding, italics, or quotation marks) is needed on the title.

All text should be double-spaced, in Times New Roman 12-point font.

In-text citations are placed after any quotation, summary, or paraphrase of an idea that comes from another source. Make sure the period goes after the parenthetical citation, not inside the closing quotation mark.

John T. Doe

Professor Lorna Lotski

English 301

15 April 2015

Masculinity and Morality in the Modern Era

Before the turn of the twentieth century, "morality" was almost exclusively a religious concept. But religion was, in many ways, severely undercut by secular interests in the modernist period; indeed, the concept of morality slowly evolved to be understood more as a non-religious "set of rules of conduct or obligations towards others" (Collini 63). Without the uniting force of religion for the concept of morality, various secular *moralities* emerged. This paper will investigate these various moralities that bloomed during the modernist period, and illustrate how the various conceptions of morality, both in public discourse and in modernist authors' works, were substantially influenced by contemporary ideas of masculinity.

At the time of Oscar Wilde's 1895 trial for indecency, sexuality was beginning to be

Doe   2

considered scientifically, and previously innocuous

notions of effeminacy and homosexuality were

replaced by medical and psychological claims

that both were instead forms of mental disease.

Underpinned by Spencerian and Darwinian

theories of human and state evolution, popular

philosophies considered diseased individuals a

threat to the health of the nation itself; social critics

such as Max Nordau furthermore argued that non-

conforming, individualistic artists endangered the

state. Singled out as an effeminate artist, Wilde

became the embodiment of the moral threats to

the British Empire. His conviction only served to

further unite a number of key ideas in the public's

mind; Michael Foldy explains that after the 1895

trial, "degeneration," "decadence," "same-sex

passion," and "moral backsliding" were brought

together and conflated in the public discourse,

while the opposites—"manliness," "health," "moral

rectitude," and heterosexual desire—were cemented

as synonymous as well (70).

    A decade or two after Wilde's trial, when

modernist artists began to produce some of the

Your last name and the page number, with two spaces between them, should appear on each page of your essay except the first page.

most influential works of the era, the two discourses underwent

changes in scope, yet were still very much connected in the public

mind. Because of the emerging scientific explanations of gender

and the demonization of effeminacy, definitions of acceptable

and preferred masculinity narrowed, while the secularization of

morality greatly expanded the meanings of that term. In all the

different ways in which morality was conceived, then, masculinity

and heteronormativity were largely still demanded to in order

to avoid possible social "degeneration." Those male authors

and social theorists who showed any concern for the ordering

of society, then, often found themselves arguing in similar ways

about competing and contested moral ideologies.

Considerations of morality in literary works have been

somewhat few and far between, most likely because on the

surface, authors of the modernist period seemingly are united

in their disdain of the concept: because the public's demand

for morality often meant censorship, artists in turn attacked the

concept and those who espoused it. Exceedingly disparate artists

– even ones antagonistic toward each other – seemingly unite in

their objection to moral concerns. In the preface to *The Picture

of Dorian Gray,* for example, Wilde writes, "There is no such

thing as a moral or an immoral book. Books are well written,

Doe   4

or badly written. That is all" (1). Considering

Wilde's well-known belief in the hedonistic

principles championed in Pater's conclusion the

The Renaissance, his pronouncement here sounds

much like Ernest Hemingway in his 1932 treatise on

bullfighting, *Death in the Afternoon*: "So far, about

morals, I know only that what is moral is what you

feel good after and what is immoral is what you

feel bad after and judged by these moral standards,

which I do not defend, the bullfight is very moral to

me" (4). These two pronouncements defend artistic

and experiential freedom by way of relativistic

morality, and are perhaps the singular commonality

between the two authors.

For many post-Wildean male authors,

however, "the radical poetics of modernism mask

a deeply conservative politics" (Schneck 230).

For authors such as Hemingway, Ezra Pound, and

Wyndham Lewis, radical thematic and formal

posturing did indeed hide commonalities with

conservative politics and middle-class dynamics;

although their means differed (uses of the term

"morality," for example), many male authors had the

Notice that the name of the quoted author, Wilde, need not appear in the parenthetical citation because he is named within the same sentence in which his quotation appears.

Doe   5

same ends as the professional classes they otherwise admittedly disdained for their prurient tastes. This idea can be useful in revealing less obvious relationships between authors; for example, while Hemingway's infamous machismo highlights his more hegemonic principles, Pound and Lewis, in the end, were the more conservative.

Far more common a response than stalwart conservatism, however, is one characterized by internal conflict, insecurity, and anxiety. Although this phenomenon exists across nations in the modernist period, Ireland provides particularly fertile ground for this investigation as its revolutionary aspirations and religious backgrounds welcomed a number of fluctuating partnerships and rivalries between the moral ideologies of Catholicism, socialism, and republicanism. The Irish writers Sean O'Casey and W.B. Yeats, for example, specifically illustrate the great concern over national order and chaos, but their responses to the uprisings and wars of the times became increasingly conflicted as the republican ideologies that won the public's attention (colored with strong shades of masculinity) demanded blood sacrifice first.

Still, no matter the country, modernist art reveals incredible anxieties about these two concepts, masculinity and morality. Buy studying some of the great artists and works of the period, a reader can learn a great deal about how people's

Doe 6

ideas of both concepts were conflated while, at the same

time, destabilized. As with many others historical periods

of upheaval, art can show us some of the most important

underlying ideologies in a culture.

Doe   4

Bibliographic information for any and every source that you quote, paraphrase, or summarize in the text belongs here, on the "Works Cited" page. The Works Cited page is always titled "Works Cited" and nothing else. The title "Works Cited" should be centered. The Works Cited page should always begin on a new page.

End-text citations should be double spaced and should use a hanging indent style. That is, the first line should be flush with the left margin, but every other line of a citation should be indented one half inch.

Works Cited

Collini, Stefan. *Public Moralists: Political Thought and Intellectual Life in Britain, 1850–1930.* Oxford UP, 1993.

Foldy, Michael. *The Trials of Oscar Wilde: Deviance, Morality, and Late-Victorian Society.* Yale UP, 1997.

Hemingway, Ernest. *Death in the Afternoon.* Scribner, 1932.

Schneck, Celeste. "Exiled by Genre: Modernism, Canonicity, and the Politics of Exclusion." *Women's Writing in Exile*, edited by Mary Lynn Broe and Angela Ingram, U of North Carolina P, 1989, pp. 225–50.

Wilde, Oscar. *The Picture of Dorian Gray.* Oxford UP, 2006.

Chapter 38

APA DOCUMENTATION

When you do research to find supporting evidence for your ideas or arguments, you need to credit your outside sources. Depending on what type of essay you are writing or which type of course you are writing for, you will need to choose a type of documentation style and continue with that style for the entire essay. Two of the most common styles, especially for freshman and sophomore students, are MLA (Modern Language Association) and APA (American Psychological Association).

If you write an essay in the social sciences, you will usually be asked to use documentation guidelines created by the American Psychological Association. The *Publication Manual of the American Psychological Association*, in its sixth edition, provides a full description of the conventions used by this particular community of writers; updates to the APA manual can be found at <www.apastyle.org>.

Did You Know?

The American Psychological Association was founded in 1892 at Clark University. The APA, now with over 152,000 members, is the primary professional association for social science scholars in the United States.

This chapter provides a general overview of APA documentation style and an explanation of the most commonly used APA documentation formats.

38a   Using APA in-text citations

In-text citations (also called *parenthetical citations*) point readers to where they can find more information about your researched supporting materials. In APA documentation style, the author's last name (or the title of the work, if no author is listed) and the date of publication must appear in the body text of your paper. The author's name can appear either in the sentence itself or in parentheses following the quotation or paraphrase. The date of publication can appear either in the sentence itself, surrounded by parentheses, or in the parentheses that follow the quotation or paraphrase. The page number(s) always appears in the parentheses following a quotation or close paraphrase.

Your parenthetical citation should give enough information to identify the source that was used for the research material as the same source that is listed in your References list. Where this in-text information is placed depends on how you want to phrase the sentence that is summarized, paraphrased, or quoted. Be sure that the in-text citation guides the reader clearly to the source in the References list, where complete information about the source is given.

The following are some of the most common examples of in-text citations.

1. Author's name and date in reference

When using a parenthetical reference to a single source by a single author, use this form: (Author's Last name, Year of publication). Note that the period is placed after the parenthetical element ends.

➔   When a teenager sleeps more than 10 hours per night, it is time to question whether she is having significant problems (Jones, 1999).

2. Author's name and date in text

In APA, you can also give the author's name and date within the sentence, using this form: Author's Full Name (Year of publication)

→ Stephanie Jones (1999) explains what signs to look for and when to be concerned.

3. Using a partial quotation in text

When you cite a specific part of a source, give the page number, using *p.* (for one page) and *pp.* (for two or more pages).

→ Stephanie Jones (1999) describes the signs parents should look for when concerned about their children: "excessive sleeping, refraining from eating, and lying about simple things" (p. 63).

4. No author given

When a work has no credited author, use the first two or three words of the work's title or the name that begins the entry in the References list. The title of an article or chapter should be in quotation marks, and the title of a book or periodical should be in italics. Inside the parenthetical citation, place a comma between the title and year.

→ In a recent *Time* article, a list of 30 common signs of teenage trouble cites lack of sleep as the most common sign ("Thirty," 2010).

5. Two to five authors given

When you use a source that was written by two to five authors, you must use all the names in the citation. For the in-text citation, when a work has two authors, use both names each time the reference occurs in the text. When a work has three to five authors, give all authors the first time the reference occurs in the text, and then, in subsequent citations, use only the surname of the first author followed by *et al.* (Latin for "and others") and the year for the first citation of the reference in a paragraph.

→ The idea that "complexity is a constant in biology" is not an innovative one (Sole & Goodwin, 1997, p. 63).

The last two authors' names in a string of three to five authors are separated by a comma and an ampersand (e.g., Jones, Smith, Black, & White).

→ Most signs in English that the authors encountered on the road had "grammar mistakes, misspellings, or just odd pictures" (Smith, Jones, & Best, 1999, p. 55). The most common mistake was an "incorrect or misplaced apostrophe" (Smith, et al., p. 56).

6. Six or more authors given

When an item to be cited has six or more authors, include only the first author's name followed by *et al.* (Latin for "and others"). Use this form for the first reference to this text and all references to this text after that. Note: be sure to list all six or more of the authors in your References list.

→ In Hong Kong, most signs are in Chinese and English; however, once you are in mainland China, English is rarely found on signs, except in tourist areas (Li, et al., 2007).

7. Authors with the same last names

If your source material includes items by authors who have the same last name, be sure to use each author's initials in all text citations.

→ When a teenager sleeps more than 10 hours per night, it is time to question whether she is having significant problems (S. Jones, 1999, p. 63).

→ Another sign of trouble can be when you do not see your child for meals (B. Jones, 2003, p. 114).

8. Encyclopedia or dictionary unsigned entry

When citing an encyclopedia or dictionary in which you have looked up a word or entry, be sure to include the word or entry title in the parenthetical entry.

→ The word *thing* has more definitions than any other entry in the *Oxford English Dictionary* ("thing," 2001).

9. Indirect quotation

When you use a quotation of a quotation—that is, a quotation that quotes from another source—use "as cited in" to designate the secondary source.

→ Smith has said, "My parents really didn't understand me" (as cited in Jones, 1990, p. 64).

10. Personal communication

Personal communications—private letters, memos, non-archived emails, interviews—are usually considered unrecoverable information and, as such, are not included in the References list. However, you do need to include them in parenthetical form in the text, giving the initials and surname of the communicator and providing as exact a date as possible.

→ A. D. Smith (personal communication, February 2, 2010)

→ J. Elbow (personal interview, January 6, 2009)

38b Using long or block quotations

Long or block quotations have special formatting requirements. A prose quotation that is longer than 40 words is called a *block quotation*. Follow these APA guidelines for block quotations.

1. If introducing the block quotation with a sentence, use a colon at the end of the sentence.
2. Begin the quotation on a new line.
3. Do not use quotation marks to enclose the block quote.
4. Indent the quote five spaces from the left margin, and extend the right margin to the end of the line.
5. Double space the entire quotation.
6. Indent the first line of any additional paragraph.
7. Put a period at the end of the quotation, and then add the parenthetical citation.

➜ However, Lansky (1999) states:

> Despite the statement on
> <www.signspotting.com> that we don't accept signs with
> the intention of being funny, people like sending them in.
> I've opted not to use these as it could encourage people to
> start making them, sticking them up in their driveway, and
> snapping a picture. Plus, funny signs are so much more
> amusing when the humor is accidental. (p. 72)

38c   Adding or omitting words in a quotation

1. Adding words in a quotation

Use square brackets [ ] to point out words or phrases that are not part
of the original text.

➜ Original quotation: "When we entered the People's Republic
of China, we noticed that the signage began dropping English
translations" (Donelson, 2001, p. 141).

➜ Quotation with added words: She said, "When we entered the
People's Republic of China, [Dunkirk and I] noticed that the
signage began dropping English translations" (Donelson, 2001,
p. 141).

You can also add your own comments inside a quotation by using square
brackets. For example, you can add the word *sic* to a quotation when you
know that there is an error.

➜ Original quotation: "When we entered the People's Repulic
of China, we noticed that the signage began dropping English
translations" (Donelson, 2001, p. 141).

➜ Quotation with added comment: She said, "When we entered
the People's Repulic [sic] of China, we noticed that the signage
began dropping English translations" (Donelson, 2001, p. 141).

2. Omitting words in a quotation

Use an ellipsis (. . .) to represent words that you delete from a quotation. The ellipsis begins with a space, then has three periods with spaces
between them, and then ends with a space.

Original quotation➜ "The Great Wall is something that can be seen from space. When we reach a time when advertisements can be seen from space, we have probably gone too far" (Jones, 1993, p. 101).

Quotation with words omitted in middle of sentence➜ Frank Jones, author of *Signs in Space*, remarks, "The Great Wall . . . can be seen from space. When we reach a time when advertisements can be seen from space, we have probably gone too far" (1993, p. 101).

If you omit the words at the end of a quotation that is at the end of your sentence, you should use an ellipsis plus a period with no space before the ellipsis or after the period. Use an ellipsis only if words have been omitted.

Original quotation➜ "The Great Wall is something that can be seen from space. When we reach a time when advertisements can be seen from space, we have probably gone too far with our advertising and signage" (Jones, 1993, p. 45).

Quotation with words omitted at end of sentence➜ Frank Jones, author of *Signs in Space*, remarks, "The Great Wall is something that can be seen from space. When we reach a time when advertisements can be seen from space, we have probably gone too far . . ." (1993, p. 45).

Helpful hint

APA guidelines can change with a new edition. Sometimes, class textbooks can use an older APA documentation style. Always check with your instructor if rules seem to be in conflict.

38d   Citing online sources

In the APA documentation style, online or electronic sources have their own formatting guidelines since these types of sources rarely give specific page numbers.

The APA recommends that you include in the text, rather than in an in-text citation, the name(s) of the person that begins the matching References list entry. If the author or creator of the website uses paragraph or page numbers, use these numbers in the parenthetical citation. If no numbering is used, do not use or add numbers to the paragraphs, pages, or parenthetical citation.

When website does not number paragraphs➔ In his review of the film *Signs*, Roger Ebert says that Shyamalan "does what Hitchcock said he wanted to do, and plays the audience like a piano."

When website numbers paragraphs➔ In his review of the file *Signs*, Roger Ebert says that Shyamalan "does what Hitchcock said he wanted to do, and plays the audience like a piano" (para. 8).

38e   General formatting guidelines for the APA References list

If you cite any sources within a paper, be sure to include a References list at the end of the paper. Here are some general formatting guidelines to follow when setting up a References list.

1. Put the References list at the end of your paper as a separate page.

2. Use one-inch margins on all sides.

3. Include any header used for the paper on the References page.

4. Center the title **References** at the top of the page, using no underlining, quotation marks, or italics.

5. Place the first line of each entry flush with the left margin. Indent any additional lines of the entry one-half inch (or one tab) to form a hanging indent.

6. Double space the entries in the References list, not adding any extra spaces between entries.

7. Alphabetize the References list. Use the first major word in each entry, not including articles *a*, *an*, or *the*, to determine the alphabetical order. If the cited source does not have an author, alphabetize by using the first word of the title of the source.

8. Put the author's name in this order: last name, first initial, and middle initial if given (e.g., Ebert, R.) If a work has more than one author, invert all the authors' names, follow each with a comma, and then continue listing all the authors, putting a comma and ampersand (,&) before the final name (e.g., Ebert, R., & Siskel, G.).

9. Arrange two or more works by the same author(s) in the same name order by year of publication.

10. Capitalize only the first word in a title and a subtitle unless the title or subtitle includes a proper noun, which would also be capitalized.

11. Do not use quotation marks for titles of shorter works, including articles, book chapters, episodes on television or radio, poems, and short stories.

12. Italicize the titles of longer works, including album or CD titles, art pieces, books, films, journals, magazines, newspapers, and television shows.

13. Give the edition number for works with more than one edition [e.g., *Publication manual of the American Psychological Association* (6th ed.)].

14. Include the DOI (digital object identifier), a unique alpha-numeric string assigned by a registration agency that helps identify content and provides a link to the source online. All DOI numbers begin with a *10* and contain a prefix and suffix separated by a slash (for example, 10.11037/0278-6133.27.3.379). The DOI is usually found in the citation detail or on the first page of an electronic journal article near the copyright notice.

38f   Formats for print sources

1. Books (includes brochures, pamphlets, and graphic novels)

Author's last name, Author's first initial. (Year of publication). *Title of book*. Place of publication: Publisher.

→ Lansky, D. (2005). *Signspotting*. Oakland, CA: Lonely Planet.

Helpful hint

Only use the state after the city if the city is not a place that would be commonly known or if there may be more than one commonly known city by that name.

CITATION DETAIL WITH DOI

stet Detail

Title:

An Ability Traitor at Work: A Treasonous Call to Subvert *Writing* From Within.

Authors:

Holbrook, Teri[1] *tholbrook@gsu.edu*

Source:

Qualitative Inquiry; Mar2010, Vol. 16 Issue 3, p171-183, 13p

Document Type:

Article

Subject Terms:

*DISABILITIES

*QUALITATIVE research

*MANAGEMENT science

*SIGN language

*WRITING

Author-Supplied Keywords:

assemblage

disability

multigenre

multimodal writing

NAICS/Industry Codes:

541930 Translation and Interpretation Services

Abstract:

In questioning conventional qualitative research methods, St. Pierre asked, "What else might *writing* do except mean?" The author answers, it oppresses. Co-opting the race traitor figurative, she calls on qualitative researchers to become "ability traitors" who interrogate how a valuable coinage of their trade—the written word—is used to rank and categorize individuals with troubling effects. In this article, she commits three betrayals: (a) multigenre *writing* that undermines the authoritative text; (b) assemblage as a method of analysis that deprivileges the written word; and (c) a gesture toward a dis/comfort text intended to take up Lather's example of challenging the "usual ways of making sense." In committing these betrayals, the author articulates her "traitorous agenda" designed to interrogate assumptions about inquiry, power, equity, and *writing* as practice-as-usual. [ABSTRACT FROM AUTHOR]

Author Affiliations:
[1]Georgia State University
ISSN:
10778004
DOI:
10.1177/1077800409351973
Accession Number:
47934623
Database:
Academic Search Premier
View Links:
Find Fulltext

2. Books with two or more authors

If a work has two or more authors, use a comma between the authors' names.

First Author's Last name, First author's Initial of first name, & Second author's Last name, Second author's Initial of first name. (year of publication). *Title of book.* Place of publication: Publisher.

➔ Maasik, S., & Soloman, J. (2008). *Signs of life in the USA: Readings on popular culture for writers.* Boston, MA: Bedford/St. Martin's.

3. Two books by the same author

Be sure the entries are in sequential time order with earliest date first.

➔ Maasik, S., & Soloman, J. (2004). *California dreams and realities: Readings for critical thinkers and writers* (3ʳᵈ ed.). Boston, MA: Bedford/St. Martin's.

➔ Maasik, S., & Soloman, J. (2008). *Signs of life in the USA: Readings on popular culture for writers.* Boston, MA: Bedford/St. Martin's.

4. Anthology or collection

Editor's Last name, Editor's Initial of first name. (Ed). (Year of publication). *Title of book.* Place of publication: Publisher.

➔ Smith, A. D., Smith, T. G., & Wright, K. (Eds.). (2007). *COMPbiblio: Leaders and influences in composition theory and practice.* Southlake, TX: Fountainhead.

5. Work within an anthology or collection

Author's last name, Author's first initial. (Year of publication). Title of work. In Editor's Name(s) (Ed.) *Title of anthology* (page numbers). Place of publication: Publisher.

➔ Tan, A. (2010). Mother tongue. In R. Bullock, M. D. Goggin, & F. Weinberg (Eds.). *The Norton field guide to writing* (pp. 564-70). New York, NY: Norton.

6. Article in a scholarly journal without DOI (digital object identifier)

Include the issue number if the journal is paginated by issue. If there is not a DOI available and the article was found online, give the URL of the journal home page.

Author's Last name, Author's Initial of first name. (Year of publication). Title of the article. *Journal Title, volume number* (issue number), pages. URL (if retrieved online).

→ Holbrook, T. (2010). An ability traitor at work: A treasonous call to subvert writing from within. *Qualitative Inquiry*, 16 (3), 171-183. Retrieved from E-Journals database.

7. Article in a scholarly journal with DOI (digital object identifier)

Author's Last name, Author's Initial of first name. (Year of publication). Title of the article. *Journal Title, volume number* (issue number), pages. doi:

→ Franks, L. (2006). The play in language. *Child Signs*, 73(1), 3-17. doi:10.1770/69873629

8. Article in a newspaper

Use *p.* or *pp.* before the page numbers in references of newspapers.

Note: if the newspaper article appears on discontinuous pages, be sure to give all the page numbers, separating them with a comma (e.g., pp. A4, A10, A13-14).

Author's Last name, Author's Initial of first name. (Year of publication, Month and Date of publication). Title of article. *Newspaper Title*, pp. page numbers.

→ Genzlinger, N. (2010, April 6). Autism is another thing that families share. *The New York Times*, p. A4.

9. Article in a magazine

Author's Last name, Author's Initial of first name. (Year of publication,
    Month of publication). Title of article. *Magazine Title, volume
    number* (issue number), pages.

Note: include the day only if the magazine is published on a weekly or bi-
weekly basis.

→ Musico, C. (2009, November). Sign 'em up! *CRM Magazine,*
    13(11), 49.

10. Review

Be sure to identify the type of work being reviewed by noting if it is a
book, film, television program, painting, song, or other creative work.
If the work is a book, include the author name(s) after the book title,
separated by a comma. If the work is a film, song, or other media, be
sure to include the year of release after the title of the work, separated
by a comma.

Reviewer's last name, Reviewer's first initial. (Year of publication,
    Month and Date of Publication). Title of review [Review of the
    work *Title of work*, by Author's Name]. *Magazine or Journal Title,*
    volume number (issue number), pp. page numbers. doi number (if
    available).

→ Turken, R. (2008, May 5). Life outside of the box. [Review
    of the film *Signs*, 2002]. *Leisure Times*, pp. A12.

11. Article in a reference book

Author's Last name, Author's Initial of first name. (Year of
    publication). Title of chapter or entry. In A. Editor (Ed). *Title of*
    book (pp. xx-xx). Location: Publisher.

→ Jones, A. (2003). Semiotics. In B. Smith, R. Lore, and T. Rex
    (Eds.). *Encyclopedia of signs* (pp. 199-202). Boston, MA:
    Rutledge.

12. Religious and classical works

In APA, classical religious works, such as the Bible and the Qur'an, and major classical works that originated in Latin or Greek, are not required to have entries in the References list but should include reference to the text within the sentence in the essay. Note: it is always a good idea to check with your instructor on this type of entry since there can be some variety across instructors and schools.

38g   Formats for online sources

1. Website

The documentation form for a website can also be used for online message, blog, or video posts.

Author's Last name, Author's Initial of first name (if author given). (Year, Month Day). *Title of page* [Description of form]. Retrieved from http://www.xxxx

➔ United States Post Office (2010). *United States Post Office Services Locator* [search engine]. Retrieved from http:// usps.whitepages.com/post_office

2. Article from a Website, online newspaper, blog, or wiki (with author given)

Author's Last name, Author's Initial of first name. (Year, Month Day of publication). Title of article. *Name of Webpage/Journal/ Newspaper*. Retrieved from http://www.xxxxxxx

➔ Ebert, R. (2002, August 2). Signs. *Chicago Sun-Times*. Retrieved from http://rogerebert.suntimes.com/

3. Article from a Website, online newspaper, blog, or wiki (with no author given)

Title of article. (Year, Month Day of publication). *Name of Webpage/ Journal/Newspaper*. Retrieved from http://www.xxxxxxx

➔ China's traditional dress: Qipao. (2001, October). *China Today*. Retrieved from http://chinatoday.com

4. Online journal article

The reference for an online journal article is set up the same way as for a print one, including the DOI.

> Author's Last name, Author's Initial of first name. (Year of publication). Title of the article. *Journal Title, volume number* (issue number), pages. doi:xxxxxxxxxxx

> ➜ Franks, L. (2006). The play in language. *Child Signs*, 73(1), 3-17. doi:10.1770/69873629

If a DOI is not assigned to content you have retrieved online, use the home page URL for the journal or magazine in the reference (e.g., Retrieved from http://www.xxxxxx).

> ➜ Austen, V. (2003). Writing spaces: Performance of the word. *Kairos*. Retrieved from http://kairos.com

5. Article from an online service, such as General One-File, LexisNexis, JSTOR, ERIC

When using APA, it is not necessary to include database information as long as you can include the publishing information required in a normal citation. Note: this is quite different from using MLA documentation, which requires full information about the database.

6. Article in an online reference work

> Author's last name, Author's first initial. (Year of publication). Title of chapter or entry. In A. Editor (Ed). *Title of book.* Retrieved from http://xxxxxxxxxx

> ➜ Jones, A. (2003). Semiotics. In B. Smith, R. Lore, and T. Rex (Eds.). *Encyclopedia of signs.* Retrieved from http://brown.edu/signs

38h   Formats for other commonly used sources

1. Television or radio program (single episode)

Writer's last name, Writer's first initial. (Writer), & Director's Last name, Director's Initial of first name. (Director). (Year). Title of episode [Television/Radio series episode]. In Executive Producer's name (Executive Producer), *Title of show*. Place: Network.

→ Bell, J. (Writer), Carter, C. (Creator), & Manners, K. (Director). (2000). Signs and wonders [Television series episode]. In C. Carter (Executive Producer), *The X files*. New York, NY: FOX.

2. Sound recording

Writer's last name, Writer's first initial. (Copyright year). Title of song. [Recorded by Artist's name if different from writer]. On *Title of album* [Medium of recording]. Location: Label. (Date of recording if different from song copyright date).

→ Emmerson, L. (1970). Signs. [Recorded by Five Man Electrical Band]. On *Good-byes and butterflies* [LP]. New York, NY: Lionel Records.

→ Emmerson, L. (1970). Signs. [Recorded by Tesla]. On *Five man acoustical jam* [CD]. New York, NY: Geffen. 1990.

3. Film

Producer's last name, Producer's first initial. (Producer), & Director's last name, Director's first initial. (Director). (Year). *Title of film* [Motion picture]. Country of Origin: Studio.

→ Kennedy, K. (Producer), & Shyamalan, M. N. (Director). (2002). *Signs* [film]. USA: Touchstone.

4. Painting, sculpture, or photograph

Artist's last name, Artist's first initial. (Year, Month Day). *Title of material*. [Description of material]. Name of collection (if available). Name of Repository, Location.

→ Gainsborough, T. (1745). *Conversation in a park*. [Oil painting on canvas]. Louvre, Paris, France.

5. Personal interview

Unlike MLA documentation, personal interviews and other types of personal communication are not included in APA References lists. Be sure to cite personal communications in the text only.

6. Lecture, speech, address, or reading

Speaker's Last name, Speaker's Initial of first name. (Year, Month). Title of speech. *Event name*. Lecture conducted from Sponsor, Location.

→ Stephens, L. (2009, December). The signs of the times. *MLA annual convention*. Lecture conducted from Hilton Hotel Downtown, New York, NY.

Sample References list using APA

Following is an example of how a completed References list would look at the end of your paper.

References

Emmerson, L. (1970). Signs. [Recorded by Five Man Electrical

Band]. On *Good-byes and butterflies* [LP]. New York,

NY: Lionel Records.

Franks, L. (2006). The play in language. *Child Signs*, 73(1), 3-17.

doi:10.1770/69873629

Kennedy, K. (Producer), & Shyamalan, M. N. (Director). (2002).

Signs [film]. USA: Touchstone.

Jones, A. (2003). Semiotics. In B. Smith, R. Lore, & T. Rex

(Eds.). *Encyclopedia of signs*. Retrieved from

http://brown.edu/signs

Lansky, D. (2005). *Signspotting*. Oakland, CA: Lonely Planet.

Stephens, L. (2009, December). The signs of the times. *MLA*

annual convention. Lecture conducted from Hilton Hotel

Downtown, New York, NY.

Tan, A. (2010). Mother tongue. In R. Bullock, M. D. Goggin, &

F. Weinberg (Eds.). *The Norton field guide to writing* (pp.

564-70). New York, NY: Norton.

EXERCISE 1

Directions: Below are three example sources and an in-text citation from each one. Put the correct information in the parentheses for an APA in-text citation.

From page 89 of the book:

Bazerman, C. (1988). *Shaping written knowledge: the genre and activity*

of the experimental article in science. Madison, Wis.: University

of Wisconsin Press.

Yet, it could also be the case that "genre and activity are more closely related than we had previously thought" (   ).

From page 340 of the article:

Bodemer, B. (2012). The Importance of Search as Intertextual Practice

for Undergraduate Research. *College and Research Libraries,*

73(4), 336–348.

Bodemer (   ), however, suggests that "increasingly, the ability to

search well on the Internet will be as important a literacy skill

as reading or writing" (   ).

From a magazine's web-only article:

Electronic education: Flipping the classroom. (2011, September 17).

The Economist. Retrieved from http://www.economist.com/

node/21529062

The Economist has reported that "flipping the classroom is the new teaching technique of the 21st-century classroom" (   ).

From page 192 of the chapter:

Schwartz, D. L., Lin, X., Brophy, S., & Bransford, J. (1999). Toward

the Development of Flexibly Adaptive Instructional Designs.

In C. M. Reigelut (Ed.), *Instructional Design Theories and*

Models: Volume II (pp. 183–213). Hillside, NJ: Erlbaum.

In a study performed by Schwartz et al. (   ), students found adaptive classroom designs more engaging and, finally, more educational.

EXERCISE 2

Directions: Insert all needed punctuation and formatting into the following APA References entries. The type of source is listed after each in in bold to help you out.

Ackerman J M 1991 Reading, Writing, and Knowing: The Role of

Disciplinary Knowledge in Comprehension and Composing *Research*

in the Teaching of English 25(2) 133–178 (**article in a journal**)

Baddeley A 1986 *Working Memory* New York Oxford University

Press (**book**)

Barlow J P 1994 March The Economy of Ideas *Wired* 2(03)

Retrieved from http://www.wired.com/wired/archive/2.03/economy.

ideas.html (**article in a magazine**)

Hacker D J Keener M C & Kircher J 2009 Writing is applied metacognition In D J Hacker J Dunlosky & A C Graesser Eds *Handbook of Metacognition in Education* 1st ed   New York Routledge **(chapter in a book or anthology)**

Rounsaville A Goldberg R & Bawarshi A 2008 From Incomes to Outcomes: FYW Students' Knowledge Meta-Cognition and the Question of Transfer *WPA: Writing Program Administration* 32(1) 97–112 **(article in a journal)**

Wilson H 1999 When Collaboration Becomes Plagiairism: The Administrative Perspective In L Buranen & A M Roy Eds *Perspectives on Plagiarism and Intellectual Property in a Postmodern World* pp 211–218 Albany NY SUNY Press **(chapter in a book or anthology)**

38j   Sample Annotated Essay - APA

Running Head: MASCULINITY AND MORALITY IN   1
THE MODERN ERA

Masculinity and Morality in the Modern Era:

Multiplication, Inflation, Destabilization

John T. Doe

State University

Before the turn of the twentieth century, "morality" was almost exclusively a religious concept. But religion was, in many ways, severely undercut by secular interests in the modernist period; indeed, the concept of morality slowly evolved to be understood more as a non-religious "set of rules of conduct or obligations towards others" (Collini,1993, p. 63). Without the uniting force of religion for the concept of morality, various secular *moralities* emerged. This paper will investigate these various moralities that bloomed during the modernist period, and illustrate how the various conceptions of morality, both in public discourse and in modernist authors' works, were substantially influenced by contemporary ideas of masculinity.

At the time of Oscar Wilde's 1895 trial for indecency, sexuality was beginning to be considered

On the top of each page of your paper, use a shortened version of the paper's title. This is called the running head. On the first page, label it "Running Head," them omit that label from page 2 on.

The title should be centered, 12-point Times New Roman font, and double-spaced. The title should not be bolded, italicized, or underlined.

The author's name and institution should be placed right below the title, and should be centered.

Because the author name was not introduced before the quotation, the author name and year goes in the parentheses. Because it is a direct quote, the citation also needs the page number.

MASCULINITY AND MORALITY IN THE MODERN ERA   2

scientifically, and previously innocuous notions of effeminacy and homosexuality were replaced by medical and psychological claims that both were instead forms of mental disease. Underpinned by Spencerian and Darwinian theories of human and state evolution, popular philosophies considered diseased individuals a threat to the health of the nation itself; social critics such as Max Nordau furthermore argued that non-conforming, individualistic artists endangered the state. Singled out as an effeminate artist, Wilde became the embodiment of the moral threats to the British Empire. His conviction only served to further unite a number of key ideas in the public's mind; Foldy (1997) explains that after the 1895 trial, "degeneration," "decadence," "same-sex passion," and "moral backsliding" were brought together and conflated in the public discourse, while the opposites—"manliness," "health," "moral rectitude," and heterosexual desire—were cemented as synonymous as well (p. 70).

A decade or two after Wilde's trial, when modernist artists began to produce some of the most influential works of the era, the two discourses

For the first part of this citation, the author name is mentioned before the cited information. Always add the year of the source right after the author's last name.

The second part of the citation here is the page number, which always goes *after* the quoted information.

MASCULINITY AND MORALITY IN THE MODERN ERA 3

underwent changes in scope, yet were still very much connected in the public mind. Because of the emerging scientific explanations of gender and the demonization of effeminacy, definitions of acceptable and preferred masculinity narrowed, while the secularization of morality greatly expanded the meanings of that term. In all the different ways in which morality was conceived, then, masculinity and heteronormativity were largely still demanded to in order to avoid possible social "degeneration." Those male authors and social theorists who showed any concern for the ordering of society, then, often found themselves arguing in similar ways about competing and contested moral ideologies.

Considerations of morality in literary works have been somewhat few and far between, most likely because on the surface, authors of the modernist period seemingly are united in their disdain of the concept: because the public's demand for morality often meant censorship, artists in turn attacked the concept and those who espoused it. Exceedingly disparate artists – even ones antagonistic toward each other – seemingly unite in their objection to moral concerns. In the preface to *The Picture of Dorian Gray,* for example, Wilde (2006) writes, "There is no such thing as a moral or an immoral book. Books are well written, or badly written. That is all" (p. 1). Considering Wilde's well-known

MASCULINITY AND MORALITY IN THE MODERN ERA   4

belief in the hedonistic principles championed in Pater's
conclusion the *The Renaissance,* his pronouncement here
sounds much like Ernest Hemingway in his 1932 treatise
on bullfighting, *Death in the Afternoon*: "So far, about
morals, I know only that what is moral is what you feel
good after and what is immoral is what you feel bad after
and judged by these moral standards, which I do not
defend, the bullfight is very moral to me" (p. 4). These
two pronouncements defend artistic and experiential
freedom by way of relativistic morality, and are perhaps
the singular commonality between the two authors.

However, Schneck (1989) argues that for many
post-Wildean male authors their more revolutionary
artistic styles hide their conservative political leanings.
For authors such as Hemingway, Ezra Pound, and
Wyndham Lewis, radical thematic and formal posturing
did indeed hide commonalities with conservative
politics and middle-class dynamics; although their
means differed (uses of the term "morality," for
example), many male authors had the same ends as the
professional classes they otherwise admittedly disdained
for their prurient tastes. This idea can be useful in

More common in
APA citation is
a mention of the
author, the year of the
work in parentheses,
and then a summary
of their ideas, in
which case no page
number is needed.

MASCULINITY AND MORALITY IN THE MODERN ERA   5

revealing less obvious relationships between authors; for example, while Hemingway's infamous machismo highlights his more hegemonic principles, Pound and Lewis, in the end, were the more conservative.

Far more common a response than stalwart conservatism, however, is one characterized by internal conflict, insecurity, and anxiety. Although this phenomena exists across nations in the modernist period, Ireland provides particularly fertile ground for this investigation as its revolutionary aspirations and religious backgrounds welcomed a number of fluctuating partnerships and rivalries between the moral ideologies of Catholicism, socialism, and republicanism. Sean O'Casey and W.B. Yeats specifically illustrate the great concern over national order and chaos, but their responses to the uprisings and wars of the times became increasingly conflicted as the republican ideologies that won the public's attention (colored with strong shades of masculinity) demanded blood sacrifice first.

Still, no matter the country, modernist art reveals incredible anxieties about these two concepts, masculinity and morality. Buy studying some of the great artists and works of the period, a reader can learn a great deal about how people's ideas of both concepts were conflated while, at the same time, destabilized.

MASCULINITY AND MORALITY IN THE MODERN ERA   6

As with many others historical periods of upheaval, art can show us some of the most important underlying ideologies in a culture.

MASCULINITY AND MORALITY IN THE MODERN ERA   7

References

Collini, S. (1993). *Public Moralists: Political Thought and Intellectual Life in Britain, 1850-1930*. Oxford: Clarendon Press.

Foldy, M. S. (1997). *The Trials of Oscar Wilde: Deviance, Morality, and Late-Victorian Society* (Prima edizione). New Haven: Yale University Press.

Hemingway, E. (1932). *Death in the Afternoon.* Charles Scibner Sons.

Schneck, C. (1989). Exiled by Genre: Modernism, Canonicity, and the Politics of Exclusion. In M. L. Broe & A. Ingram (Eds.), *Women's Writing in Exile* (pp. 225-50). Chapel Hill: The University of North Carolina Press.

Wilde, O. (2006). *The Picture of Dorian Gray*. (J. Bristow, Ed.). Oxford ; New York: Oxford University Press.

Bibliographic information is placed in a "References" list in APA format. Being this list on a new page. Center the title "References." Double-space all entries on the page and use hanging indentation. Each source cited in the text of the paper must have an entry here.

Index

A

A, an 3
A while, awhile 87, 89
Abbreviations 131, 136, 162
Abstract nouns 9, 189
Academic degrees 120
Academic writing 47, 75, 78, 82, 211, 228
Accept, except 88, 91
Access date 250, 251
Acronyms 164
APA 114, 279-308
Active verbs 31, 34
Active voice 46
Adapt, adopt 88
Addresses 119, 121, 132, 253
Adjective clauses 190
Adjective phrases 31, 55, 217, 231
Adjectives 53-56
    form 53
    function 56
    type 54
Adopt, adapt 88
Adverb clauses 193, 194, 197
Adverb phrases 58, 233
Adverbs 57-60
    form 57
    function 59
    type 58
Advice, advise 88
Affect, effect 88, 91
African-American, use of 83, 163
Age 82
Agreement of pronoun and antecedent 23-25
Agreement of subject and verb 49-52
Aircraft or airship titles 168
All ready, already 86, 87, 89
All right, alright 89
All together, altogether 87, 89
Allude, elude 89, 91
Allusion, illusion 89, 92
Almost (misplaced modifier) 222-223
A lot, a lot 78, 86, 88
Although 172, 188, 193, 206
Ambiguity 209, 222
American Psychological Association 114, 132, 269-297
Among, between 89, 90
Amongst, among 89, 90
Amoral, immoral 89, 93
Amount, number 89, 94
And 178, 227
Angle brackets 156, 250

Antecedents 13, 23-25

Anybody 21, 87, 89

Anyone 21, 87, 89

Anything 21

APA sample References list 287

Apostrophe 10, 15, 135-140

Appositives 115, 188, 230

Appositive clauses 115, 188, 189

Appropriate language 73, 78, 81-84

Appropriate word choice 69-84

Articles (*a, an, the*) 3

As, like 73

Aspect, verb 31, 34, 42-46

Auxiliary verbs 31, 34, 36, 43-44

Averse, adverse 88

Awhile, a while 87, 89

B

Bad, badly 89

Base form of verb 35, 36

Be 31, 34, 38

Because 65, 72, 187, 188, 193, 206

Beside, besides 65, 90

Between, among 89, 90

Biased language 81-83

Block or long quotations 241, 259

Both . . . and 25

Brackets 155, 156

But 178, 206

C

Can 34, 90, 94

Capital, capitol 90

Capitalization 161-165

Capitol, capital 90

Case 23, 127, 168

Choppy sentences 227

Citation samples, APA 269-298

Citation samples, MLA 237-268

Cite, site 95, 96

Clarity, word 69, 121

Clichés 76, 77

Coarse, course 90

Collective nouns 11

Colloquial words 78

Colons 127-130

Combining sentences 182, 228

Commands 131, 175, 211

Commas 109-121

Comma splices 182, 201

Common nouns 8

Company names 253

Comparative clauses 190

Comparative form of adjectives 190

Comparisons 53, 57, 73, 75, 117, 206

Complement, compliment 90

Complements, object 117, 232

Complements, subject 16, 17, 31, 54, 188, 196, 217, 218, 232

Complete subject 27, 49

Complex sentences 187-198

Compound antecedents 24

Compound-complex sentences 199-201

Compound numbers 148

Compound sentences 111

Compound subjects 51

Compound words 139

Conciseness 69, 72

Concrete nouns 9

Confusing/confused words 85-97

Conjunctions 24, 51, 182

Conjunctive adverbs 59, 60, 117, 123, 179, 182

Conscience, conscious 91

Contractions 135

Coordinate adjectives 116

Coordinating conjunctions 111, 227

Coordination 177, 228

Correlative conjunctions 24, 51

Could of, could have 91

Council, counsel 91

Count nouns 3-5, 7-9

Course, coarse 90

D

Dangling modifiers 224

Dashes 151, 152

Dates 120

Declarative questions 214, 215

Declarative sentences 131, 211

Definite articles. See *the*. 4

Demonstrative pronouns 13, 20, 21

Dependent clauses 173, 187, 188, 191, 195

Descriptive words and phrases 76, 230

Determiners 3, 21

Dialogue 78, 119, 142

Dictionaries 99-101, 240, 259

Digital Object Identifier (DOI) 250-251, 277-279, 281

Direct address 118

Direct objects 14, 16, 188-189, 216-218

Direct questions 153, 225

Direct quotations 142, 225

Documentation of sources
APA 269-297
MLA 237-267

Dots, ellipsis 159-160

Doublespeak 79

E

Each (singular) 21, 23, 49, 51

Effect, affect 88, 91

Either (singular) 21

Either . . . or (singular) 24, 51

Ellipsis mark 159, 160, 242

Email
APA documentation of 273
MLA documentation of 253

Embedded questions 133, 134

Emphasis 128, 133, 152, 175, 206

Empty *it* and *there* 71, 225

Empty phrases and clauses 71, 225

End punctuation 131-134

Even (misplaced modifier) 222-223

Everybody, everyone, everything (singular) 21

Exactness, word 69, 71
Except, accept 88, 91
Exclamation mark 133
Exclamatory sentences 131, 211, 213
Expletives *there, it* 71
Explicit, implicit 91, 93

F

Family (See Collective nouns) 11
Farther, further 92
Fewer, less 92, 93
Figurative languages 73
Focus, sentence 205-210
For 178, 206
Formality 78, 128
Fragments 175, 195, 201
Further, farther 92
Fused (run-on) sentences 183, 201
Future tense 42-46

G

Gender and pronoun agreement 23
Gender-neutral language 81
Generic *he* 81
Generic nouns 24
Geographical names 84, 129
Gerunds 28, 35
Good, well 92, 97

H

Hanged, hung 39, 92
Have (auxiliary verb) 31, 34, 36, 44

Head nouns 48
Helping verbs (auxiliaries) 34, 36
However 60, 117
Hung, hanged 39, 92
Hyphen 147-150

I

Idioms 76
Illicit, elicit 91
Illusion, allusion 89, 92
Imperative sentences 131, 211
Implicit, explicit 91, 93
Imply, infer 93
Inappropriate language 69, 73, 81-84
Incomplete sentence (fragments) 175, 195, 201
Indefinite articles 3
Indefinite pronouns 21, 50, 138
Independent clauses 111, 117, 123, 127, 173, 177, 179, 181, 187, 195
Indirect objects 14, 16, 216-218
Indirect questions 193, 225
Indirect quotations 119, 225, 240, 273
Infer, imply 93
Infinitive phrases 28
Infinitives 35, 223
Informal language 78
-ing ending 7, 35, 43-45, 224
Intensive pronouns 16, 17
Interjections 50, 118
Interrogative pronouns 13, 20
Interrogative sentences 131, 211-213
Intransitive verbs 31, 32, 215

Introductory words, phrases, and clauses 109, 110
Inverted sentence order 120
Irregardless, regardless 93
Irregular verbs 36, 38-42
Italics 167-170
Its, it's 88, 93

J

Jargon 77
Just (misplaced modifiers) 222

L

Language
    appropriate 73, 78, 81-84
    biased 81-83
    clichés 76, 77
    doublespeak 79
    formal 78, 128
    jargon 77
    offensive 69, 73, 81-84
    pretentious 78-80
    sexist 81
    slang 78
    wordy 28, 69-73
Lay, lie 93
Lead, led 93
Legal cases 168
LexisNexis 251, 270
Lie, lay 93
Like, as 73
Limiting modifiers 222
Linking verbs 31, 54, 64, 218
List or series, comma use 113
Long or block quotations 241, 259

Loose, lose 93
–ly ending on adverbs 57

M

Main clauses 111, 117, 123, 127, 173, 177, 179, 181, 187, 195
Main verbs 31, 34, 43, 173
Merely (misplaced modifier) 222-223
Misplaced modifiers 222
Misspelled words 85-87
MLA documentation style 237-267
MLA, sample Works Cited page 257
Modals 34, 42
Modern Language Association. See MLA. 237-267
Modification 187, 229
Modifiers
    adjectives 53-56, 231, 232
    adverbs 57-60
    dangling 224
    limiting 222, 223
    misplaced 222
    squinting 222

N

Naval ships 168
Neither . . . nor 24, 51
Nominal relative clauses 189
Non-count nouns 4, 5, 9
Non-restrictive phrases and clauses 18, 114, 115, 192, 197

Noun clauses 27, 115, 188, 189
Nouns 7-11
Number 41
Numbers 121, 129, 135, 148, 149, 154

O

Object complements 117, 232
Objective case 13, 14
Objects
    direct 188, 216
    indirect 63, 216
Objects of prepositions 188
Offensive language 81
Only (misplaced modifier) 222-223
Or 24, 35, 51, 89, 111, 163, 178
Oral language 135, 228

P

Parallelism 176, 209
Paraphrases 155, 238, 256
Parentheses 153, 154, 161
Parenthetical sentence elements 153-155
Participial phrases 114, 174
Participles 35
Parts of speech 28, 34
Passive voice 46, 47
Past participles 35
Past tense 8, 37-41, 46
Perfect verbs 42, 44-47
Periods 132, 141
Personal pronouns 13, 14, 138

Phrases
    appositive 115, 230
    infinitive 28
Plural nouns 7, 23, 138
Possessive nouns 9
Possessive pronouns 14, 15
Precede, proceed 95
Predicate 31, 175, 187
    adjective 31
    noun 31
Prefixes 147
Prepositions 61 - 65
    form 61
    type 62
    function 63
Present tense 41, 46
Pretentious language 79, 80
Principal, principle 95
Proceed, precede 95
Progressive verbs 43, 46, 47
Pronoun/antecedent agreement 23-25
Pronouns 13-21
Proper nouns 8, 10, 162
Punctuation 108 – 130

Q

Question marks 20, 119, 133, 212
Questions 33, 119, 133, 212
Quotation marks 141-145, 168, 225, 241-243, 259, 271, 273-275

R

Raise, rise 40-95
Ratios 129
Real, really 95
Reciprocal pronouns 21
References, APA 287
Reflexive pronouns 13, 16, 17
Regular verbs 35, 44
Relative clauses 18, 55, 113-115
Relative pronouns 18, 20, 188, 191
Repetition 206, 222
Respectfully, respectively 95
Restrictive phrases and clauses 18, 114, 115, 191, 192
Revising 121, 135, 215, 222
Run-on (fused) sentences 183, 201

S

Salutations 128
Search engines 250, 269
Secondary sources 259
Semicolons 113, 123-125
Sentences
    choppy 227
    fragments 175, 195, 201
    fused (run-on) 183, 201
    inverted 120
    order 206, 207, 215-225
    run-on (fused) 183, 201
    variety in 173-200
    wordy 28, 29, 69, 71-73
Sentence structure 28
Sentence types 173-201

Series or list, comma use 128
Set, sit 95
Sexist language 81
Ships 168
Short stories 141, 168, 246, 263
Sic 155, 243, 260, 261
Simile 73
Simple sentences 111, 123, 173-175
Simple subjects 27. 49-51
Singular nouns 7, 23, 137
Sit, set 40, 95
Site, cite 95, 96
Slang 78
Slash 143, 157, 241, 264
So 96
Somebody, someone, something (singular) 21, 96
Sources, citing
    APA 269-297
    MLA 237-267
Spacecraft 168
Spacing 87, 127, 143, 147, 151, 157
Specific nouns 8, 13, 162
Spell checker 100, 228
Spelling 85-97, 100
Split infinitives 223
Stereotypes 78, 81-84
Subject 13, 14, 16-20, 27, 28, 31, 35, 41, 46, 47, 49-51, 54, 173, 175, 187-189, 195, 196, 211, 212, 215-219, 232
Subject complements 31, 54, 188, 196, 218, 232
Subject-itis 221, 222

Subject-verb agreement 49-51

Subordinate (dependent) clauses 190

Subordinating conjunctions 187, 193

Subordination 187, 229

Subtitles 129, 163

Suffixes 35, 42, 147, 274

Superlative form of adjectives 54

Synonyms 103, 104

T

Tag questions, 119, 212, 213

Tenses, verb 38-42

Than, then 96

That 96, 97

The 4-5

Their 96

Theirselves, themselves 96

There, as expletive 71, 225

Therefore 60, 117, 179, 206

There, their, they're 96

Thesaurus 70, 74, 103-105

Time 117

Titles of persons 120

Titles of works 141

To, too, two 96

Transitions 117, 118, 205, 206

Transitive verbs 33, 216, 217

U

Underlining 245, 263

Understood subjects 175

Unique 96

V

Variety, in sentences 173-200

Verb agreement 49-51

Verb forms 35

Verb(al) phrases 31, 101, 111, 114, 173, 177, 224

Verbs

    active 46

    aspect 42-45

    helping 34, 36

    intransitive 32, 101, 215

    linking 31, 32, 54, 64, 218, 219

    main 31, 34, 43, 44

    passive 46, 47

    perfect 34, 42, 44-47

    progressive 34, 42, 43, 45-47

    regular 35, 36, 44

    transitive 33, 216, 217

Vocabulary 230, 231

Voice 46, 47

W

Weather, whether 97

Web sources, citing

    APA 275

    MLA 250

Well, good 97

Whether, weather 97

Which 97

While 97

Who 97

Who's, whose 97

Wordiness 72

Words

    abstract 70

choice 69-84

colloquial 78

compound 139-147

concrete 9, 69-70

confused 85-97

highlighting 151, 167-169, 205

general vs. specific 69-71

misspelled 85-97

misused 109, 111, 112

Works Cited 257-267

Y

Yet 111, 163, 178, 183, 206, 227

You 14

Your, you're 88, 97